Annals of Life Insurance Medicine 5

Special Edition
Proceedings of the
11th International Congress
of Life Assurance Medicine
Mexico City 1973

Edited by E. Tanner
Swiss Reinsurance Company
Zurich/Switzerland

Springer-Verlag
Berlin · Heidelberg · New York 1974

Professor E. TANNER, M. D., Swiss Reinsurance Company,
CH-8022 Zurich/Switzerland, Mythenquai 60

With 47 Figures

ISBN-13: 978-3-642-65846-4 e-ISBN-13: 978-3-642-65844-0
DOI: 10.1007/978-3-642-65844-0

Softcover reprint of the hardcover 1st edition 1974

Preface

In the preface to Volume 1 of the 'Annals of Life Insurance Medicine' Dr. MAX E. EISENRING described the goal of this publication as follows:

"Any project which aims at contributing substantially to the modern science of medical underwriting can do so only if the many people preoccupied with these problems throughout the world join forces to the ultimate benefit of those most in need of life assurance."

In an endeavour to keep the life insurance medical directors all over the world informed of the developments in the field of life insurance medicine, we have decided to publish the papers which were presented at the 11th International Congress of Life Assurance Medicine in Mexico in 1973 in Volume 5 of the 'Annals'.

We are most grateful to Dr. J. RENDÓN, President of the Organizing Committee of the Congress in Mexico for having consented to our publishing the proceedings of the Congress in a special edition of the 'Annals'. It is a source of great satisfaction to us that in this way a much larger circle of life insurance medical directors can be reached than would have been the case if only the participants themselves were to receive the proceedings of the Congress. Dissemination of the results of medical research on an international basis, in particular those findings that have a bearing on life insurance medicine, is one of our foremost aims.

In our ever-changing world it is important not only to keep pace with the rapid advances being made in medical research but also to give due consideration to external conditions that may shorten life. With this in mind several highly topical subjects were included in the Congress dealing with environmental factors affecting life expectancy.

In many industrialised countries the first signs of this menace have become manifest and if the related environmental conditions are not brought under control it may result in a real threat to mankind. The life insurers must therefore be alert of these new risk factors and preventive medicine must contribute its share to the solution of these newly created problems.

We hope that the broad scope of subjects presented at the Congress in Mexico and covered in Volume 5 of the 'Annals' will bring valuable information to all our readers.

Zurich, Spring 1974 E. TANNER

Contents

Ceremonia de Inauguración. JORGE RENDÓN 1
Presentación de México. RUBÉN MARÍN 3

I Sesión

Water Pollution and its Health Effects in Japan. ITSUZO SHIGEMATSU . . 9
The Epidemiology and Control of Man-Made Diseases. DAVID D. RUTSTEIN 25
Facteurs de haut risque pour le pronostic lointain, provenant des aéro-contaminants et de leurs conséquences sur les voies respiratoires. LAURENT MEEUS-BITH 35
Pollution par les radiations ionisantes. J.-V. MARIQUE 52

II Sesión

Bradicardia y taquicardia sinusales, extrasistoles. OSCAR MEDINA MORA . 69
Taquicardias aspectos fisiopatológicos. M. CÁRDENAS LOAEZA 74
El significado de la taquicardia sinusal, taquicardia auricular, taquicardia de la unión, taquicardia ventricular y el síndrome de Wolff-Parkinson-White. RODOLFO MALO CAMACHO 75
Comunicación preliminar acerca de la incidencia y pronóstico de los hemibloqueos. SALVADOR WAICH T., GUSTAVO ROMERO REVERÓN, JOSÉ E. BARCELÓ, IRVING PEÑA, ALBERTO MÉNDEZ y JAVIER JASSO 77
El electrocardiograma de esfuerzo en el seguro de vida. OSCAR MEDINA MORA, JOSÉ ANTONIO LORENZO, ALEJANDRO FLORES AGUIRRE, CARLOS MUNGUÍA y JAIME ARRIAGA 86

III Sesión

Prognose der chronischen Polyarthritis und der Kollagenosen unter dem Einfluß der Langzeittherapie. FRITZ HARTMANN 93
The Diagnosis of Rheumatoid Arthritis and Allied Disorders. FRANCIS BACH 116
Long-Term Treatment with Corticosteroids in Rheumatoid Arthritis over a Period of 19 to 22 Years. A. DRIVSHOLM, J. BOYE-NIELSEN, and K. BRØCHNER-MORTENSEN 124

IV Sesión

Spätfolgen bei den verschiedenen Malariaformen und Frage der Einschränkung der Lebenserwartung durch das Überstehen einer Malaria. W. MOHR 131

Repercusión económica del absceso hepático amibiano. BERNARDO SEPÚLVEDA 139
Coccidioidomicosis. DÁMASO FERNÁNDEZ LIRA, SERGIO DE LA GARZA y Q. F. B. LILIA L. CORTES 145

V Sesión

Extra Mortality Risk in the Older Insurance Applicant. RICHARD B. SINGER 153
De la influencia de tres enfermedades frecuentes no malignas y a menudo asintomáticas del aparato digestivo, sobre la mortalidad de personas mayores de 60 años. MAX L. HEFTI y AURELIO OLASCOAGA 164
The Influence of Age on Mortality in Diabetics. G. GOODKIN 178

VI Sesión

Social Mechanisms in the Inception of Drug Abuse and Addiction. NILS BEJEROT 199

Author Index 205

Ceremonia de Inauguración

Dr. Jorge Rendón

Presidente del Comité Organizador

Es un honor tener el privilegio de dirigirme a ustedes en esta sesión de Inauguración del XI Congreso Internacional de Medicina del Seguro de Vida, que nos ha tocado en suerte organizar en esta Capital.

Hoy se inicia uno de los acontecimientos de más trascendencia para la industria aseguradora de nuestro país, que polariza la atención de empresas aseguradoras de gran parte del orbe, representadas en este acto por delegados de 32 naciones.

Dos rasgos fundamentales caracterizan esta reunión. Por una parte, la presencia de personalidades relevantes de la Medicina del Seguro de Vida y por otra el hecho de que, por primera vez se celebra una convención de esta categoría en un país del continente americano.

Estas pausas en el camino tienen como finalidad el intercambio fluído de conocimientos y experiencias referentes a los problemas que más afectan la salud y capacidad del hombre. Nos permiten ver el camino recorrido y el lugar y momento en que nos encontramos, los que enfrentamos la asegurabilidad de personas, actividad que involucra el bienestar de familias y que, basada en conocimientos técnicos, tiene repercusión social. Las organizaciones aseguradoras están conscientes, lo mismo que nosotros, de su papel de protección de la familia y de conglomerados, que en su ausencia se verían amenazados por carencias que se antojan agobiantes.

Del reconocimiento de lo que sabemos hasta hoy, se desprenderán interrogantes de lo que sigue. La tendencia filosófica más legítima de todo conocimiento es no detenerse con lo logrado, no darse por satisfecho con lo conseguido, no dejar pasar el tiempo en contentamiento estático de lo que ya se posee, sino al contrario, tratar de avizorar el porvenir, levantar la vista arriba del horizonte para dirigirla al cielo, que en su inmensidad todavía guarda misterios que nos están llamando a su descubrimiento y arcanos que nos incitan a buscar su explicación.

Con manos laboriosas y cerebros prontos al esfuerzo, debemos seguir avanzando, tomando impulso en estos certámenes del saber, en los cuales nos nutrimos de alimento espiritual y nos vigorizamos con la alentadora confianza de que no estamos solos, de que junto con nosotros hombres de variadas nacionalidades, climas, creencias, tendencias y disciplinas siguen el mismo camino; apoyándonos los débiles en los fuertes, los escasos de conocimientos en los que los poseen en abundancia, en una hermandad apretada que conforta el espíritu e infunde esperanza en el destino humano.

Nuestra contribución a esta tarea, no por parca deja de ser importante. Nuestros mejores hombres de ciencia contarán a ustedes sus experiencias en los diferentes temas a ellos asignados. Los comentarios de Vds. pulirán estas gemas y con la aportación de ponentes de países avanzados en técnica y ciencia, tendremos un balance altamente positivo y al final nos regocijará comprobar que nuestros esfuerzos han sido coronados por el éxito.

Este cuadro lucirá en un marco a la altura de su categoría. Nos hemos empeñado en que las actividades sociales muestren de manera diáfana nuestra cultura y aspiraciones y que al mismo tiempo sean descanso y solaz de cuerpo y mente. La imagen rotunda del colorido, el calor de nuestra hospitalidad y afecto hablarán por sí. Es nuestro ferviente deseo que su estancia entre nosotros sea agradable y guarden un recuerdo amable de esta reunión, en la que la gracia y galanura de las damas, contribuye grandemente a su alegría y esplendor.

Deseo testimoniar mi gratitud personal y la del Comité Organizador a las siguientes instituciones que nos han brindado una ayuda inapreciable y a cuyo buen amparo nos hemos acogido, por lo cual les rindo pleitesía con gran satisfacción:

Asociación Mexicana de Instituciones de Seguros y todas las compañías que trabajan el seguro de vida en México, cuyos Directores Generales nos han apoyado constantemente.

Asociación Mexicana de Medicina del Seguro de Vida, cuyos socios nos han ayudado sin escatimar esfuerzo.

Al Comité Internacional de Medicina del Seguro de Vida, que ha encauzado nuestros trabajos con su experiencia valiosísima.

A las Compañías Reaseguradoras del ramo de vida que trabajan en México, que han contribuido en forma generosa.

De manera muy especial a ustedes, señores congresistas, que han robado tiempo precioso a sus ocupaciones para acompañarnos y que nos hacen el honor de venir con sus señoras esposas. Reciban una cordial bienvenida, un afectuoso saludo y, por favor, no vacilen en recurrir a nosotros, que nos proponemos ser anfitriones atentos y solícitos si se les presenta cualquier contratiempo.

Bienvenidos.

Presentación de México

Dr. RUBÉN MARÍN

Vice-Presidente del Comité Organizador

A principios del siglo XVI, surgió en aguas de lo que hoy es México la primera pequeña flota de naves españolas. Ocurrió desde entonces, necesariamente, un choque de culturas milenarias, de una parte la aborigen y de otra la cristiana que venía de Europa. Tal choque fue, al mismo tiempo, una fusión de culturas, la una dentro de la otra conforme a un proceso que ha durado más de cuatrocientos años.

Esta confrontación, muchas veces violenta y trágica, vino fundiendo sangres, espíritus, costumbres y creencias. México es, así, un país mestizo, fruto de una penosa y prolongada labor de mezcla, de una gestación trabajada lentamente en el crisol de los siglos.

El país que abre hoy a ustedes los brazos con la anchura de todas las dimensiones de su tierra, sólo puede ser comprendido si se tiene en cuenta que no es un transplante sino un injerto. Cuando la cultura europea arribó a estas playas encontró establecido un poderoso imperio, el más poderoso y aventajado de América.

Este imperio se había erigido sobre varias culturas misteriosamente desaparecidas, la olmeca, la tolteca, la maya, y heredó de ellas sabiduría, experiencia y espíritu. Pueblos fueron estos de matemáticos que inventaron el símbolo de la abstracción absoluta, el cero, que llegó a Europa por la vía de China muchos siglos después; pueblos de poetas y de pintores; de sabios que conocieron el curso de los astros, el escondido secreto de las yerbas medicinales, la práctica de la craneotomía y de la orificación de los dientes.

Estas culturas, ya acabadas o en plena decadencia en el siglo XVI, se distinguieron sobre todo por su arte y su arquitectura en una época superponible tal vez a la de los asirios y caldeos. Visitarán ustedes algo de lo que resta de estas insólitas y variadas expresiones, algunas que sobrecogen con su bárbara grandeza, y otras cuyos refinados elementos seducen y conmueven.

El imperio azteca heredó estas viejas civilizaciones y las absorbió, las asimiló, y supo hacerlas suyas. El notable pueblo se había establecido, apenas en 1325, en donde hoy estamos, en la ciudad de México, y de aquí, oculto entre los cañaverales y sufriendo de pobreza se lanzó a la conquista y señorío de amplias regiones. Pueblo joven, batallador y profundamente religioso, levantó templos enormes, hizo notables obras de riego, mimó a sus artífices y pintores y llevó sus delegaciones hasta la América del Sur, quizá para atisbar una conquista. En sólo doscientos años realizó el prodigio de convertirse en el pueblo más civilizado, más rico, más fuerte de América.

Cuando a la llegada de los europeos sobrevino el inevitable encuentro y cotejo de culturas, el destino del joven pueblo estaba sellado: no conocía el caballo, ni la pólvora, ni la espada. Y cayó, cayó con honra. España nunca pensó en aniquilar a los vencidos, a quienes supo admirar, sino al contrario, quiso conservarlos y protegerlos. Es más, se mezcló con ellos y transfundió sangre y alma.

La planta europea, así, no vino a esta tierra a sembrarse sino a injertarse en el tronco de la planta indígena. El resultado no es español ni aborigen, sino que a través de mil vicisitudes de crecimiento, es un pueblo nuevo, el mexicano, que tanto se honra en recibir a ustedes, y con el cual convivirán durante unos días. Un pueblo nuevo otra vez, de trazos peculiares tallados en los cimientos de su origen, que no se parece demasiado a otros, ni siquiera a los de América Latina, hermanos suyos por la sangre y el espíritu, cada uno con su perfil, su propio destino, sus caminos muy suyos.

Si visitan ustedes la Plaza de las Tres Culturas, realizada con respetuoso buen gusto por el gobierno de la ciudad, verán los restos de lo que fue un templo importante, el de Tlatelolco, que puede significar la cultura indígena. Junto, y levantados con las mismas piedras del templo, están la iglesia de Santiago, dedicada al Santo patrón de España, y junto el Colegio de Santa Cruz de Tlatelolco, primero de América, fundado apenas en 1536, donde había cátedras de gramática, retórica, lógica, aritmética, geometría y música. Lo sorprendente es que tal Colegio no era para los hijos de los conquistadores sino de los vencidos, a los que la Corona tomaba bajo su protección.

Alrededor de las construcciones anteriores, que pueden representar la época de sedimentación y creación del Virreinato, se alzan grandes edificaciones modernas que caracterizan al México actual.

Desde apenas terminada la conquista, se inició un importante intercambio de toda índole. Un negro de Cortés sembró los primeros granos de trigo; el ilustre soldado cronista Díaz del Castillo, las primeras semillas de naranja, y Hernán Cortés trajo las primeras cepas de caña de azúcar. Pronto llegó el centeno y la cebada, el arroz, la lenteja, al haba, el garbanzo, cierto tipo de frijoles, la lechuga y la col, el nabo, el rábano, la coliflor y el ajo, y se plantaron los primeros árboles de castaño y de moral; se sembró alfalfa, y flores como el rosal o el lirio, y frutales que darían riqueza como la lima y el limón.

Vino el caballo, el ganado bovino, el lanar, el cabrío y el porcino, y como una bendición llegó el asno, resignado y humilde, al alivio de las espaldas indígenas. Junto con ellos la rueda para el carro y para el alfarero, y el perro, fiel compañero de todo indio, y la gallina, complemento de su alimentación.

De México salió para el mundo el maíz, planta de selección artificial lograda, según los entendidos, en algún lugar de los hoy Estados de Veracruz o de Tabasco. Salió también el jitomate, el palo de Campeche, la raíz de Jalapa, la púrpura de la cochinilla, más barata que la de concha mediterránea, la calabaza, el cacahuate, el camote, el cacao y el modo de hacerlo en chocolate. De aquí y del Caribe se exportó el tabaco, y flores para los jardines de otros lugares, como la nochebuena o poinssetia y la dalia.

Es posible que muchos europeos no recuerden, la noche de Navidad, que el indispensable pavo, guajolote mexicano, es oriundo de la altiplanicie de nuestro país. Y salió de México, también, el chicle, el henequén, y sobre todo el hule.

Apenas terminada la conquista, empezó febrilmente la integración de un país nuevo, una España nueva, la Nueva España. Para 1524 se estaba construyendo el primer hospital de América, todavía en servicio hoy después de cuatrocientos cincuenta años, fundado por Hernando Cortés. Se alzaron también, primeros en América, hospitales de especialidad, el de San Lázaro para lazarinos o leprosos, el del Amor de Dios para enfermedades venéreas, el Real de Indios, donde estuvo el primer teatro, y sobre todo el de San Hipólito, para enfermos mentales.

Todos estos hospitales fueron notables en su época por su hermosura y grandeza, pero el de enfermos mentales, primero en América también, merece se recuerde que fue construido por un hombre excepcional, Bernardino Alvarez, aventurero que hizo una vida licenciosa y violenta. Habiendo reunido una gran fortuna en Perú, a donde había huido, al regresar a México la repartió entre los pobres, y mendigando, logró construir el increíble número de ocho hospitales. Cuando en muchas partes se trataba a los locos con la crueldad de castigos corporales, el apostólico hombre los atendía con amor.

Para fines del primer siglo del virreinato existián en la nación más de treinta hospitales. Proliferaron las iglesias, grandes y suntuosas, y casi en cada una, una escuela. La religión pagana, vasta teogonía de númenes crueles y sanguinarios, fue cediendo su lugar, sin gran esfuerzo de los indios, a la doctrina del amor cristiano que les enseñaron frailes descalzos, flacos y pobres.

La primera imprenta de América fue traída por el Obispo Zumárraga, santo varón, y para 1537 salió de sus prensas la Escala Espiritual de San Juan Clímaco, y después una espesa e inacabable serie de libros. Fue también la primera en el Nuevo Continente, la Real y Pontificia Universidad de México, que abrió sus puertas en 1553, almácigo de talentos sapientes y eruditos.

Durante los siglos XVII y XVIII se consolidó en el Virreino la obra básica del XVI. Prolijo y fatigoso resultaría el análisis de los logros alcanzados. Bastará decir que durante ese tiempo se construyeron grandes obras de captación de agua y sorprendentes acueductos; que aquí, en la Escuela de Minas, se descubrió el tungsteno, y en Guanajuato la amalgamación de la plata; que aquí nacieron Ruíz de Alarcón, uno de los más altos dramaturgos del habla castellana, y Sor Juana Inés de la Cruz, poetisa y científica de la más rara elevación.

El ilustre Barón Alejandro de Humboldt, que vivió entre nosotros a fines del siglo XIX, no ocultaba su admiración por un país al que estudió con cariño, un país culto, próspero y rico, el más adelatado, entonces, del Nuevo Continente.

Al iniciarse el siglo XIX, en 1810, sucedió lo que tenía que suceder, el parto de una nueva nación, México, que había llegado a la mayoría de su edad, y ese parto llameante y sangriento fue la guerra de Independencia, de largos diez años de duración. Después vinieron penosísimos tiempos, como ocurre en todo ser sujeto a los dolores del crecimiento, desvalido el país después de su separación de España, ante la concupiscencia de pueblos fuertes que deseaban sustituirla.

La enorme extensión del territorio se encogió a menos de la mitad de su superficie original. Se apartó la América Central en 1824, se apartó también la Provincia de Tejas y perdimos Nuevo México, parte de Arizona y la rica Alta California. En el siglo XIX, débil y agotado por una serie penosa de luchas intestinas en un país que trataba de hallarse a sí mismo, México tuvo dos emperadores y una gran cantidad de gobiernos que se sucedían uno al otro por la violencia y por el encono de las facciones. Después de la guerra de diez años contra España, sufrió nuevo intento de invasión en 1828. En 1836, guerra de Tejas. En 1838, guerra contra Francia. En 1847, guerra contra los Estados Unidos, en 1861 guerra contra Francia.

Las guerras extranjeras y los sangrientos conflictos interiores, iban empobreciendo al país más cada dia y hundiéndolo en problemas que parecían no tener solución nunca. Hacia fines del siglo un hombre inteligente y progresista, Porfirio Díaz, estableció un gobierno dictatorial y autócrata que remedió transitoriamuente el caos y condujo al país por el camino de la prosperidad. Sin embargo ese gobierno incubó durante treinta años tales diferencias económicas, y tan ultrajantes injusticias sociales, que en 1910 explotó la Revolución popular persiguiendo necesarias reivindicaciones. A cien años de la iniciación de la Independencia, cien años convulsos, empezó la guerra intestina que duraría trágicamente los mismos diez años de aquella.

A partir de entonces México ha disfrutado de medio siglo de paz y de tranquilidad durante el cual ha invertido con entusiasmo el empeño de su reconstrucción y de su progreso. Busca su propia mejoría dentro de medidas sociales y económicas justas para todos según fórmula propia y el mismo respeto y comprensión dedica a todos los países de la tierra.

Tal es, señores congresistas, el país que hemos querido presentar a ustedes en acelerado, en vertiginoso resumen. Tal es el país que se honra hoy con su presencia y que les pide rendidamente lo consideren durante su estancia aquí como su propia tierra, y a nuestros hogares como a los suyos propios.

I Sesión

Tema: Contaminación ambiental

Presidente: Dr. A. L. Larson, EE. UU.

Water Pollution and its Health Effects in Japan

ITSUZO SHIGEMATSU, M. D.

22 Figures

Background

Before discussing the effects of water pollution on health, I should like to outline the general situation in Japan as regards environmental pollution as well as the national health in terms of life expectancy. During the last two decades Japan has achieved remarkable growth in industrial production; this has brought not only economic prosperity but also a burden of environmental pollution to the people of this country.

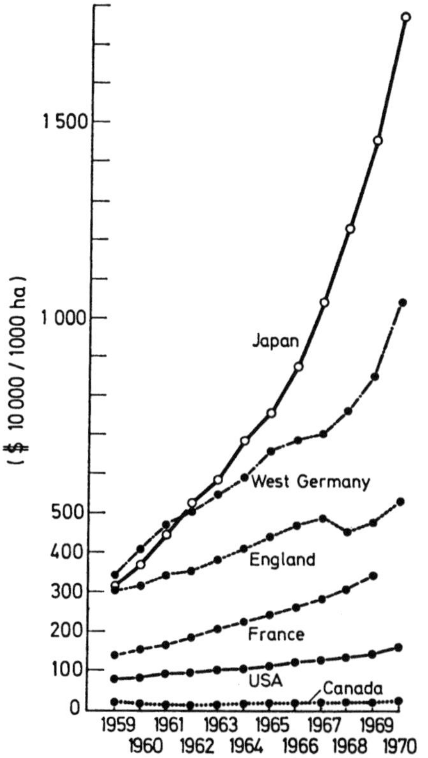

Fig. 1. Changes in GNP per area of flat land (from OECD "National Accounts" and FAO "Production Yearbook". The GNP for 1970 taken from IMF "International Financial Statistics")

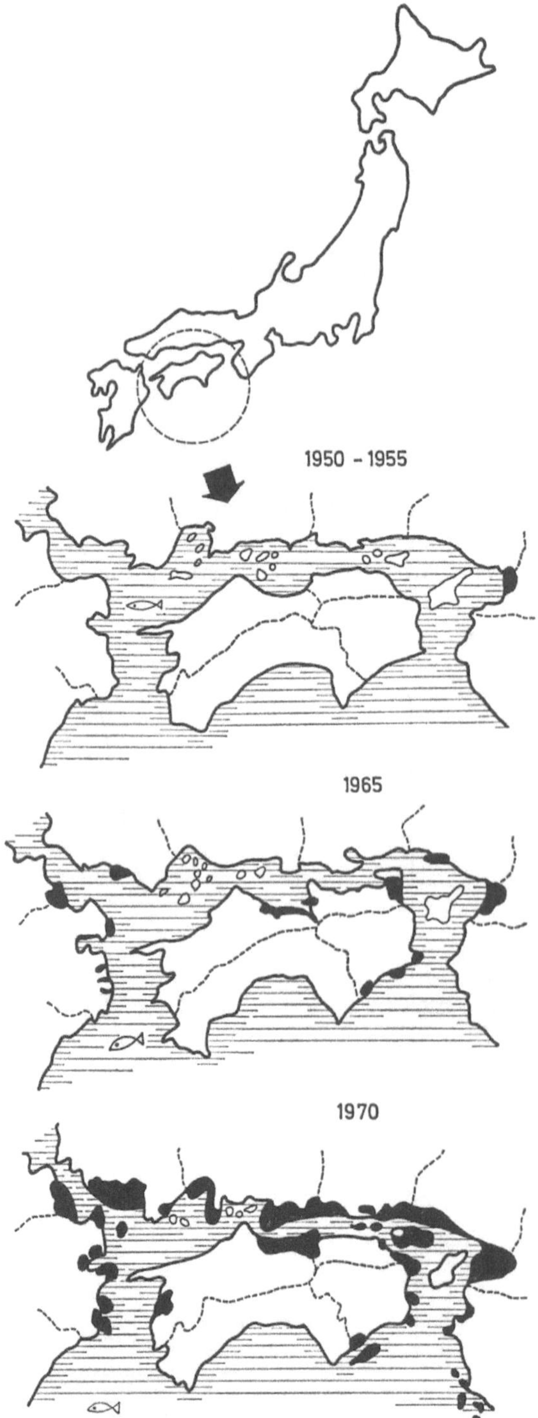

Fig. 2. Outbreaks of the "Red Tide" in the Seto Inland Sea (from Investigation of the Seto Inland Sea Fisheries Development Association)

Japan is a mountainous country with an area of 370,000 square kilometres (less than one fifth of that of Mexico) and only about 20% of the total land is inhabitable. In this limited area there lives a population exceeding 100 million and, as in other industrialized countries, the population is concentrated into large urban areas such as Tokyo, Osaka and Nagoya.

The Japanese economy has made remarkable progress with the rapid development of petrochemicals, steel, and other heavy industries. Accordingly, the large industrial sites together with new highways have been expanded year after year to give a high concentration of industrial plants.

Fig. 1 shows the recent trend in the ratio of GNP (Gross National Product) to the area of flat land in six countries. Japan had the same level of economic density as England in 1959, but in Japan this ratio has increased with remarkable speed and Japan has become very overcrowded. In 1962 Japan overtook West Germany, and in 1970 actually reached a density level 11.3 times that of the United States.

Environmental Pollution

Along with these background factors, environmental pollution problems have grown worse every year until they are now affecting living conditions in the highly industrialized areas, and sometimes even human health itself, in an unfavorable way.

An example of the increasing size of the area affected by pollution can be seen in Fig. 2. The "Red Tide", which is primarily caused by pollution, has steadily expanded each year in the Seto Inland Sea. From 1950 to 1955 the Red Tide did not exceed the limits of its original locality. However, by 1965 there were over 40 outbreaks per year and thereafter they increased rapidly. By 1970 almost all of the Seto Inland Sea was polluted by the Red Tide. This area, designated a national park in 1934, was particularly beloved in the past for its scenic beauty of water; now it is disfigured by the Red Tide.

Another example of pollution is shown in Fig. 3. Once people could enjoy a clear view of Mt. Fuji from Tokyo, but today air pollution has made it much

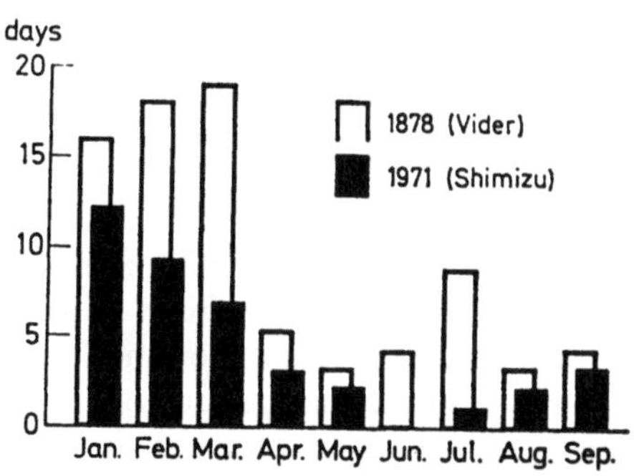

Fig. 3. Number of days Mt. Fuji was visible from Tokyo (from the data by P. V. VIDER who observed Mt. Fuji from Hongo, Tokyo in 1878, and by SHIMIZU who observed the mountain from Shibuya, Tokyo in 1971)

more difficult to see. In 1878 Mt. Fuji was visible from Tokyo one day in three whereas in 1971 it was seen on only one day in seven.

Expectation of Life

Despite this deterioration of environmental conditions, Japan has been favored by a rapid prolongation of life expectancy paralleling economic progress.

Fig. 4 compares the annual change in life expectancy at birth for both sexes in Japan with that in some other countries. The figures for Japan in 1971 are 70.17 years for males and 75.58 years for females, indicating that Japan is now

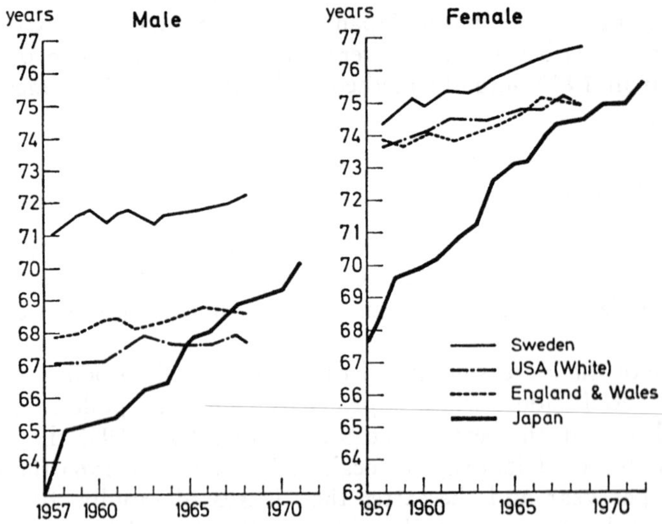

Fig. 4. Annual change of life expectancy at birth (from Demographic Yearbook 1960–1970, U.N. and Ministry of Health and Welfare, Japan)

one of the top countries in the world for longevity. Fig. 5 shows the geographical distribution of life expectancy at birth for Japanese males in 1970 by prefecture. The long-lived prefectures seem to be concentrated in the central part of Japan, which, though polluted, enjoys a higher income per capita (Figs. 6 and 7).

In order to evaluate the influence of environmental pollution upon expectation of life, a multiple regression analysis was attempted on the basis of data from 46 prefectures (excluding Okinawa) in Japan. As shown in Table 1, 19 indices representing the grade of environmental pollution and other socio-economic and demographic factors at prefectural level in 1970 were subjected to analysis as independent variables. Expectations of life at birth and at age 60 for both sexes in each prefecture were calculated on the basis of the 1970 age-specific mortality rates by the abridged life-table method suggested by Prof. C. L. Chiang. Simple correlation coefficients between these variables and partial correlation coefficients of life expectancy were examined and six variables (complaints about pollution, industrial production, medical care, population density, average income, social welfare) were finally selected by stepwise procedure.

As shown in Table 2, the result of the multiple regression analysis thus performed revealed that environmental pollution did not seem to be significantly related to expectation of life for both sexes either at birth or at age 60, and that other socio-economic factors were likely to be more influential. Needless to say,

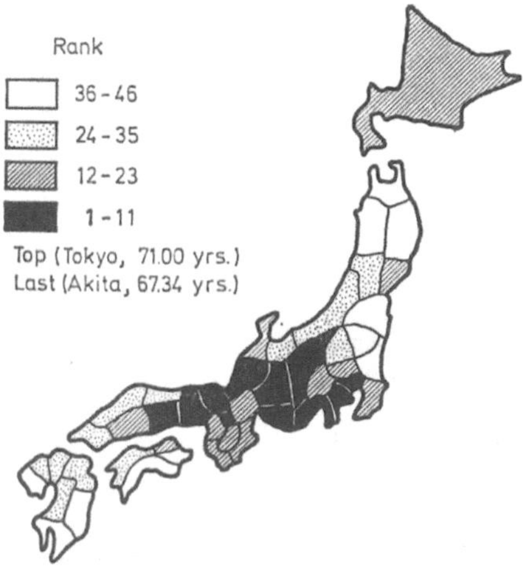

Fig. 5. Rank of life expectancy at birth by prefecture in Japan. Male, 1970

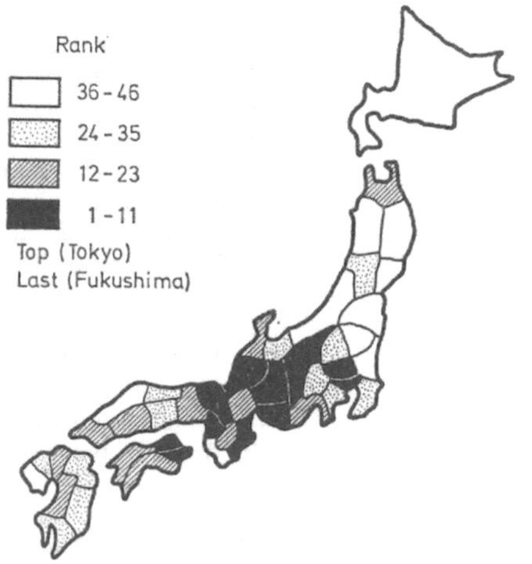

Fig. 6. Rank of pollution by prefecture in Japan. No. of complaints per person, 1970

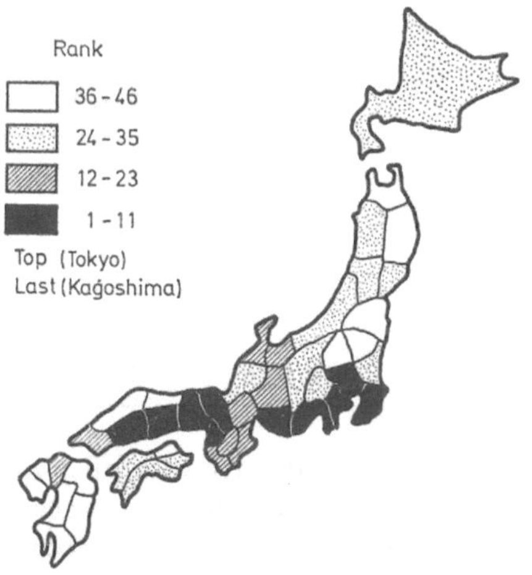

Fig. 7. Rank of income by prefecture in Japan. Average income per capita, 1968

this result does not mean that the influence of environmental pollution upon expectation of life can be neglected. It is suggested, however, that the prolongation of life expectancy in Japan up to the present is mainly attributable to the improvement in socio-economic conditions, which has greatly depended upon industrial development, covering up any unfavorable influence of environmental pollution.

Table 1. 19 indices on prefectural level for multiple regression analysis of life expectancy

1. Citizen's Complaints against Pollution
2. Industrial Production
3. Culture and Welfare
4. Heavy Industry
5. Medical Care
6. Population Density
7. Average Income per Capita
8. Population Increase
9. Social Welfare
10. Consume and Purchase
11. Day/Night Population Ratio
12. Population of 2nd Industry
13. Population of 3rd Industry
14. Coverage of Water Supply Service
15. Population Increase in Densely Inhabited Area
16. Share of Population in Densely Inhabited Area
17. Share of Densely Inhabited Area
18. Population Density in Densely Inhabited Area
19. Average Family Size

Table 2. Partial and multiple correlation coefficients of life expectancy on 6 indices, 46 prefectures, Japan, 1970

		Life expectancy			
		at birth		at 60 yrs.	
		Male	Female	Male	Female
Partial correlation coefficient	1. Pollution	0.179	—0.150	0.005	0.074
	2. Industrial production	0.303	0.409	0.430	0.406
	3. Medical care	0.354	0.551	0.615	0.613
	4. Population density	—0.439	—0.350	—0.387	—0.223
	5. Average income	0.525	0.291	0.032	—0.145
	6. Welfare	0.552	0.532	0.460	0.345
Multiple correlation coefficient		0.851	0.787	0.768	0.694

Multiple regression analyses of age-adjusted mortality rates from all causes and selected causes of death (cerebrovascular disease, cancer of all sites and lung cancer, heart disease, pneumonia and bronchitis, tuberculosis) were also carried out using the same variables as mentioned before on the basis of the 1970 prefectural data for both sexes, as well as for rural and urban areas. The results of these analyses are not given here, but no significant influence of environmental pollution upon various mortality rates mentioned above could be found.

Water Pollution

Pollution in rivers and the sea has increased so fast as to bring about damage to agricultural and fishery products, and contamination of water supplies for domestic and industrial use, thus producing harmful effects on the human body.

As the most serious problem of water pollution, Japan has currently experienced three widely reported episodes of health hazards caused by the accumulation of traces of heavy metals through the complex mechanism of the biological chain and concentration in the environment. The toxicity of any metal, as of any substance, solid, fluid or gaseous, depends upon a great many factors — the nature of the compound, its mode of entry into or contact with the body or skin surface, its concentration and duration of effects, and the susceptibility of the individual exposed to it. All these factors have been examined minutely in the history of industrial health but, where the health effects of traces of heavy metals are concerned, the information so far collected is limited to industrial workers. There is hardly any information available for the general population, who comprise not only healthy adults but also a number of poorly resistant persons such as infants, the aged, and the sick.

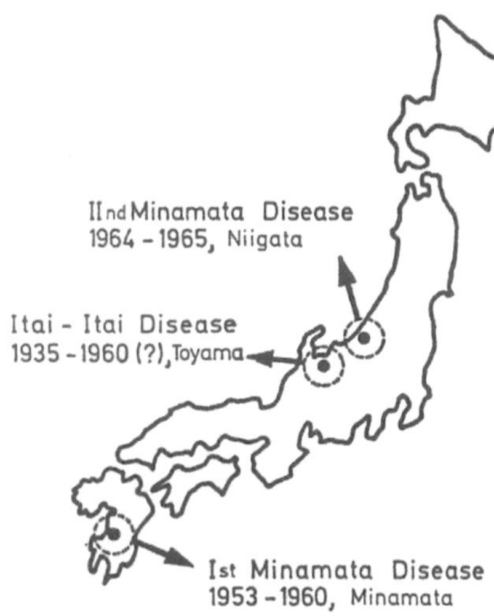

Fig. 8. Location of outbreaks of health hazards due to water pollution

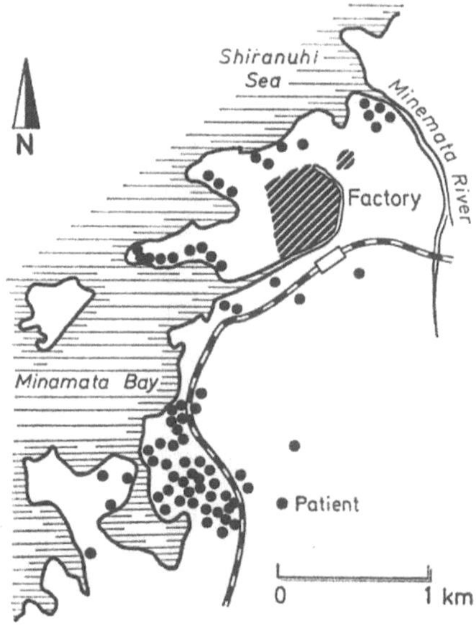

Fig. 9. Minamata district and distribution of patients with 1st Minamata disease

Methylmercury discharged in the waste water from chemical factories producing acetaldehyde was incriminated as the causative agent in two of the above-mentioned episodes. The first episode came to light in 1956 and lasted for several years in the Minamata district; thus the poisoning was called "Minamata disease". The second appeared in 1964 and 1965 in the Niigata district, and was called "Second Minamata disease". During the above-mentioned period both episodes produced a total of more than 160 cases of this disease, including about 50 fatalities. The remaining episode, Itai-Itai disease, which occurred in Toyama Prefecture mainly after World War II, produced 123 patients including 42 fatalities. The disease is now attributed to the pollution of water by cadmium originating from the effluents of mining plants. The location of each episode is depicted in Fig. 8. A brief explanation of these events follows.

First Minamata Disease

Minamata is a town on Kyushu Island, facing Minamata Bay (Fig. 9). Minamata disease was first reported in this area and was concluded to be consistent with methylmercury poisoning after extensive studies conducted mainly by the research group of Kumamoto University School of Medicine. Several years were needed for identification of the disease because of its complicated biological cycle.

Minamata disease is characterized by the "Hunter-Russel syndrome", which involves ataxia, disarthria, deafness, constriction of visual fields, etc. Pathologically, the disease is defined as toxic encephalopathy with degeneration of the

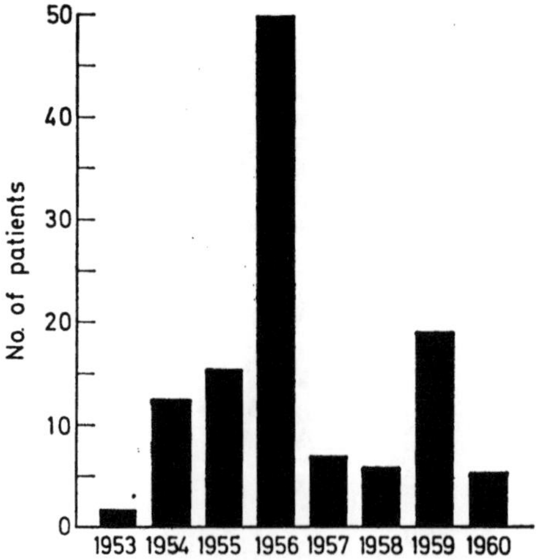

Fig. 10. Number of patients with 1st Minamata disease by year (from Minamata disease, Study Group of Minamata Disease, Kumamoto University, Japan, 1968 (Monograph in English))

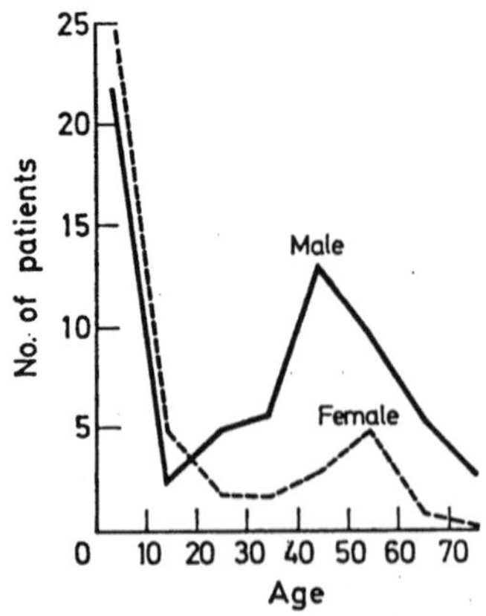

Fig. 11. Number of patients with 1st Minamata disease by sex and age (from Minamata Disease, Study Group of Minamata Disease, Kumamoto University, Japan, 1968 (Monograph in English))

cerebellar cortices. There had been sporadic outbreaks of the disease in Minamata since 1953; the number of patients increased abruptly in 1956 and, thereafter, many new patients were added to a total of 111 cases (0.5% of the population) at the end of 1960 (Fig. 10), of whom 41 (36.9%) had died. It is noteworthy that many cats went mad and died before the outbreak of the disease in this district.

The disease affects people of all ages, though forming two peaks in children and the middle-aged; it is more prevalent in adult males than in adult females (Fig. 11). The patients were more frequent in families of poor fishermen. The majority of those who survived were disabled. In addition, about one year after the outbreak of Minamata disease, 22 infants born in this district were found to be suffering from cerebral palsy, which was named "fetal Minamata disease". This was caused by methylmercury poisoning acquired prenatally from the mother, who did not herself manifest the symptoms of the disease.

It is now established that Minamata disease was caused by ingestion of a large amount of fish und shellfish from Minamata Bay. The methylmercury wastes from the acetaldehyde plant of Minamata Factory had polluted the sea water and were accumulated and concentrated in sea foods (Figs. 12 and 13).

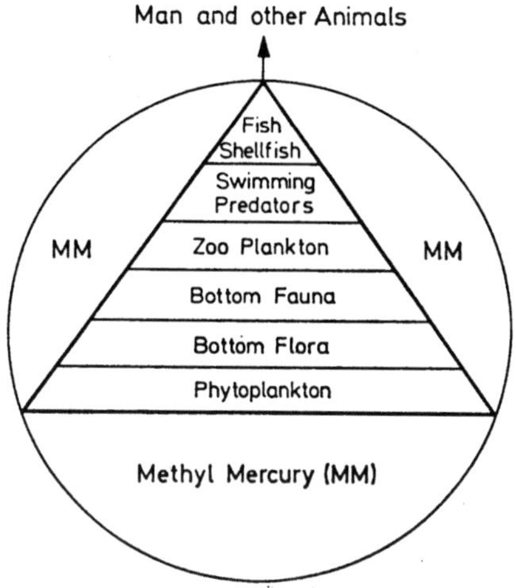

Fig. 12. Process of concentration of methyl mercury by aquatic organisms (from KITAMURA, S.: Working papers of Japanese participants for a Planning Conference United States — Japan Direct Cooperation Program, 1971)

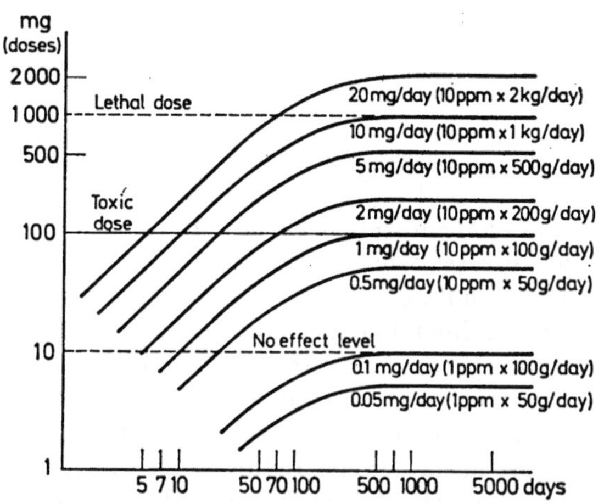

Fig. 13. Estimated accumulation curve of methylmercury in human body (from KITAMURA, S.: Working papers of Japanese participants for a Planning Conference United States — Japan Direct Cooperation Program, 1971)

A large-scale health survey has been going on since 1971 for all the inhabitants (110,000 people) of the coastal areas of Minamata Bay in an attempt to elucidate the total picture of the occurrence of Minamata disease. It is resulting in a tremendous increase in the number of recognized patients. At the end of March 1973, there were 451 patients, including 71 deaths; this figure probably will increase further with the progress of the health survey.

Second Minamata Disease

Minamata disease occurred again in August 1964 in the Niigata district, situated near the coast of the Sea of Japan (Fig. 14). People who ate fish from the Agano River in this district succumbed to the disease: 26 cases including 5 deaths were reported up to the end of 1965, to which must be added 14 cases including 1 fetal

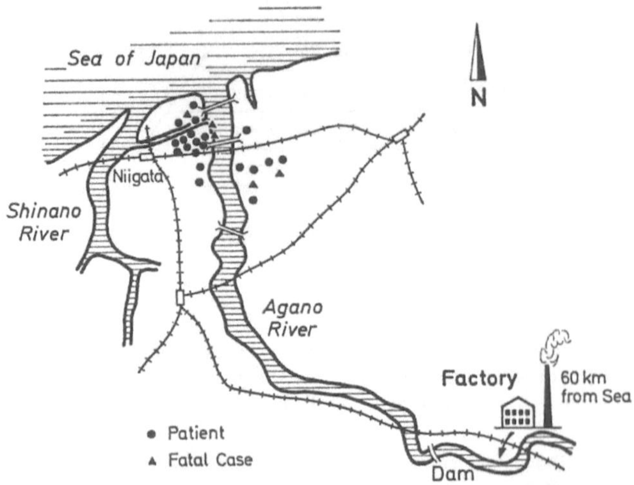

Fig. 14. Niigata district and distribution of patients with 2nd Minimata disease

case up to 1970. Of the 26 cases, 8 occurred in 1964 and 18 in 1965 (Fig. 15) and 23 were males and 3 females. The age distribution of the cases ranged from 18 to 73 years, and most of them were fishermen and their families.

In this episode the disease, which was first recognized as a disorder of the central nervous system of unknown etiology, was promptly identified as Minamata disease due to methylmercury poisoning based on the experience of preceding incident. But, as regards the source of the methylmercury there has been much discussion because there were several ways in which the Agano River might have become contaminated. One possibility was that waste water containing methylmercury from the acetaldehyde factory located 50 kilometres upstream from the endemic area along the Agano River could have polluted the river and ultimately caused the disease by the same mechanism as in the Minamata district. Another was that agricultural chemicals (phenylmercury acetate accompanied by methylmercury) could have spilled from warehouses at Niigata Pier during the great Niigata earthquake in June 1964.

However, epidemiological evidence, such as detection of high concentrations of mercury in the hair of persons living near the factory and chronological changes in the mercury content of hair (Fig. 16) strongly supports the former hypothesis. The same conclusion was reached in the trial of this event, in which the patients sued the factory for compensation for injuries arising from the disease. Although the factory was closed in January 1945, the number of recognized patients is still increasing as a result of a health survey conducted in this district as in the Minamata district. At the end of March 1973, it totaled 317 including 13 deaths.

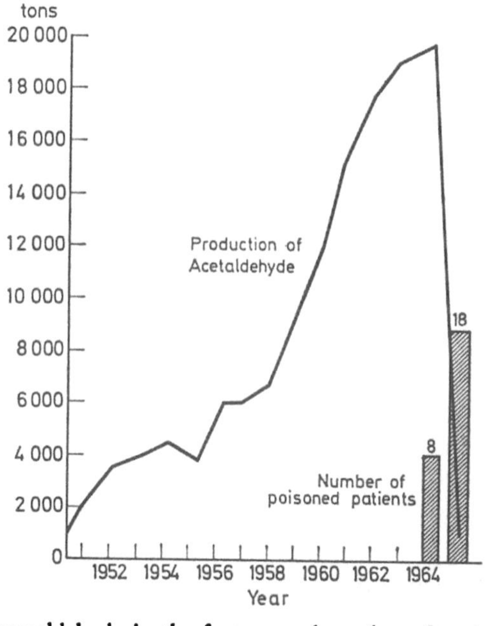

Fig. 15. Production of acetaldehyde in the factory and number of patients with 2nd Minimata disease by year (from TAKIZAWA, Y., *et al.*: Acta Medica et Biologica, 19, 193–206, 1972)

Itai-Itai Disease

A mysterious endemic disease prevailing in the basin of the Jinzu River, which runs through the central part of Toyama Prefecture in north-central Japan (Fig. 17), was first reported at a scientific meeting in 1955. The disease was named "Itai-Itai disease", because one of the most characteristic symptoms of the disease is severe pain in bone and the patients used to scream "Itai-Itai", which means ouch-ouch in Japanese. Another conspicuous symptom is the tendency for bones to fracture easily, resulting in duck gait and shortening of stature.

The roentgenological findings on bone, and the results of urine and blood tests can be summarized as follows:

1. appearance of transformation zone of the bone (Milkman-Looser's pseudo-fracture);
2. fracture and its healing picture, thinning of cortex and decalcification in the shaft of long bone;
3. proteinuria with low-molecular-weight protein and glycosuria;
4. increased alkaline phosphatase and decreased inorganic phosphorus in the serum.

Pathological findings based on autopsy and biopsy studies indicate that the disease is very similar to Fanconi's syndrome in adults, being characterized by tubular changes in the kidney, and may be defined as renal osteomalacia suggesting the existence of toxic nephropathy.

Although no specific treatment for this disease has been available up to the present, most patients responed well to Vitamin D and rapid improvement in the symptoms is observed.

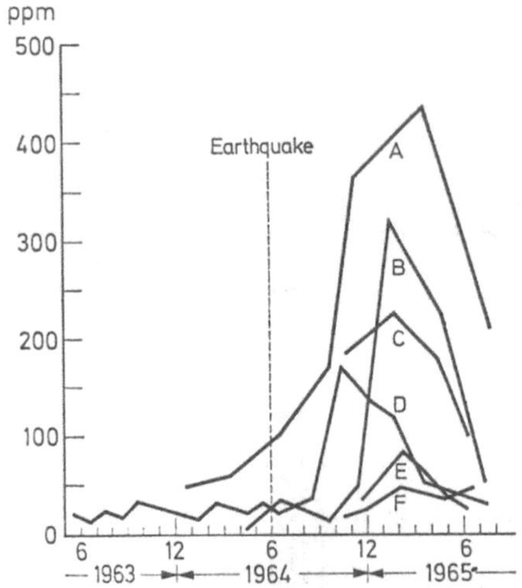

Fig. 16. Estimated chronological change of total mercury in hairs of 6 women from endemic area (from The Study Group supported by the Ministry of Health and Welfare, A Summary Report of Special Study on Niigata Mercury Poisoning, 1967)

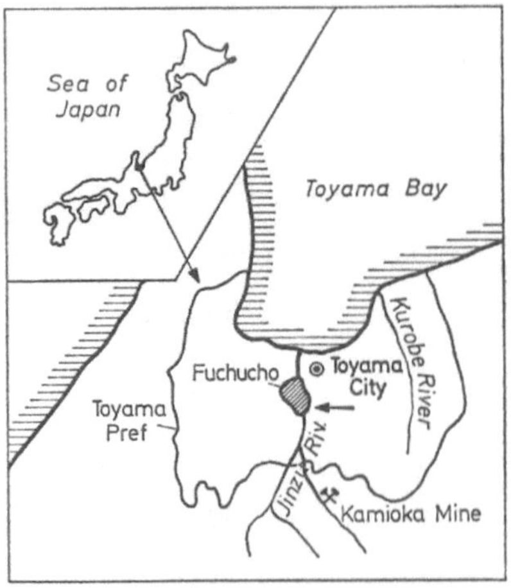

Fig. 17. Endemic area of Itai-Itai disease

Systematic epidemiological investigations, which included extensive mass health examinations as well as case history studies on both patients and controls, have been conducted by the author and his colleagues since 1962. It was thus found that Itai-Itai disease was restricted to a limited area irrigated by the Jinzu River (Fig. 17), the geographical distribution of the patients being consistent with the levels of cadmium concentration in the paddy fields (Figs. 18 and 19).

The age and sex distribution of the patients displayed a very distinct pattern. Clinically apparent cases were limited to women over 40 years of age who were multipara (para 6 on average) and had lived in the area for more than 30 years. Although the age of onset of the disease has not been fully clarified, it is probably between 35 and 65 years. The prevalence of the disease was presumably very high from 1935 to 1960 and at its highest in 1946 and 1947. This implies a strong possibility that many cases existed before World War II.

No correct figures for patients in the past are available, but it is estimated that nearly 100 deaths may be attributed to this disease up to the end of 1965. The most recent patients, the majority of whom had had the disease at least once

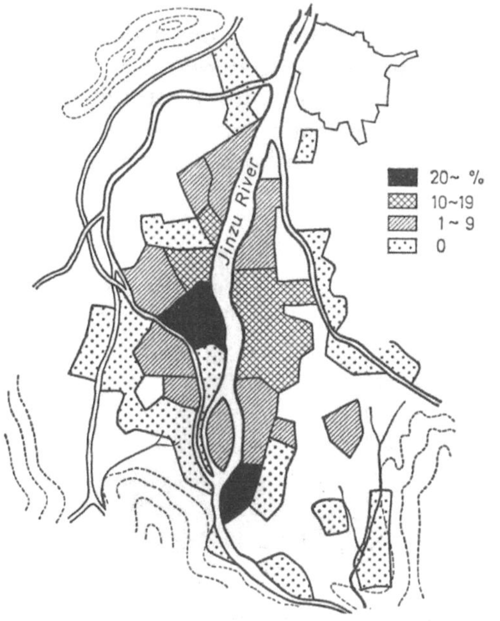

Fig. 18. Prevalence rates of the cases and suspects of Itai-Itai disease by hamlet (per 100 female pop. over 50 yrs.), 1967 (from Research Committee on Itai-Itai Disease (Chairman: SHIGEMATSU, I.), Report on the Etiology of Itai-Itai Disease, Japan Public Health Association, 1968)

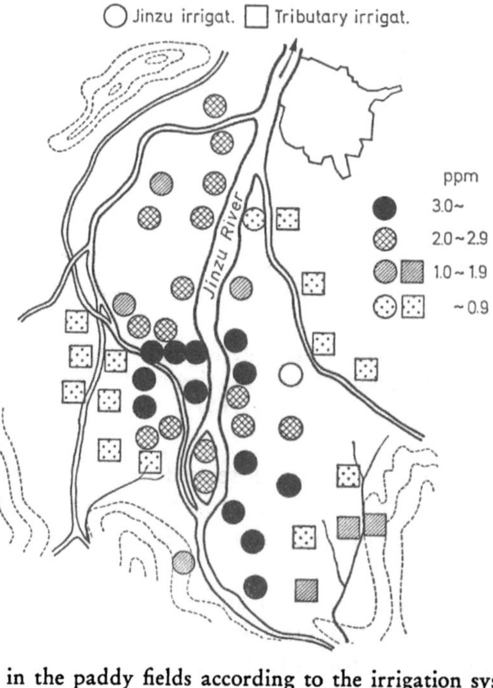

Fig. 19. Cd concentrations in the paddy fields according to the irrigation systems (from Research Committee on Itai-Itai Disease (Chairman: SHIGEMATSU, I.), Report on the Etiology of Itai-Itai Disease, Japan Public Health Association, 1968)

before, numbered 96 (95 females and only one male) at the end of 1970 (Fig. 20); 123 cases including 42 deaths were officially notified of February 1973.

It is worthwhile to note that the positive rates of protein and sugar in urine are markedly elevated in the endemic area as compared with others and the difference becomes greater with age in both males and females (Fig. 21). Further-

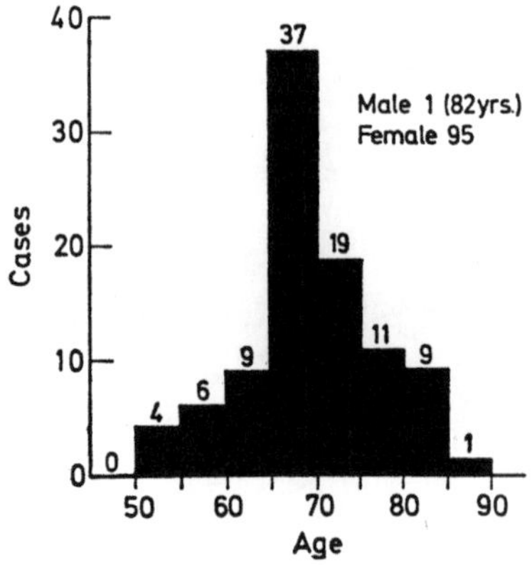

Fig. 20. Age distribution of the cases with Itai-Itai disease Dec. 31, 1970 (from Ministry of Health and Welfare, 1971)

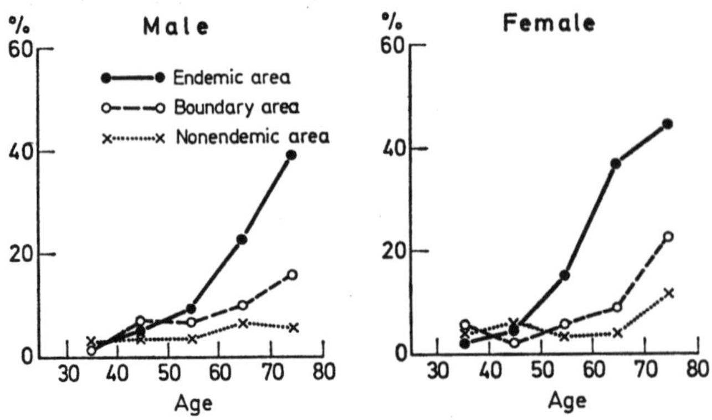

Fig. 21. Percentage of both proteinuria and glycosuria by age and sex, Toyama Pref., 1964–1966 (from ISHIZAKI, A., *et al.*: The 26th Annual Meeting of the Japanese Society of Public Health, 1968)

more, the percentage of proteinuria observed in persons aged 50 years and over from various hamlets in the endemic area and in the controls was closely correlated with the cadmium concentration in rice grown in their own paddy fields (Fig. 22).

An investigation of the nutritional and socio-economic conditions in this area revealed that the patients had been in rather poor living conditions and had drunk the irrigation water from the Jinzu River more frequently than the controls, though there was practically no significant difference in the nutritional conditions for patients and controls.

In addition to the above findings and evidence concerning Itai-Itai disease, laborious work has been carried out to analyze the chemical ingredients, particularly traces of heavy metals such as zinc, lead and cadmium, in various materials obtained from patients with the disease and healthy persons, and in crops, foods, soil, and river and well water in both the endemic and control areas, and from wastes of the mining station. The mine is located 50 km upstream from the endemic area along the Jinzu River and has been mining and smelting sulfide ores containing copper, zinc, lead and cadmium. Animal experiments have also been attempted with cadmium.

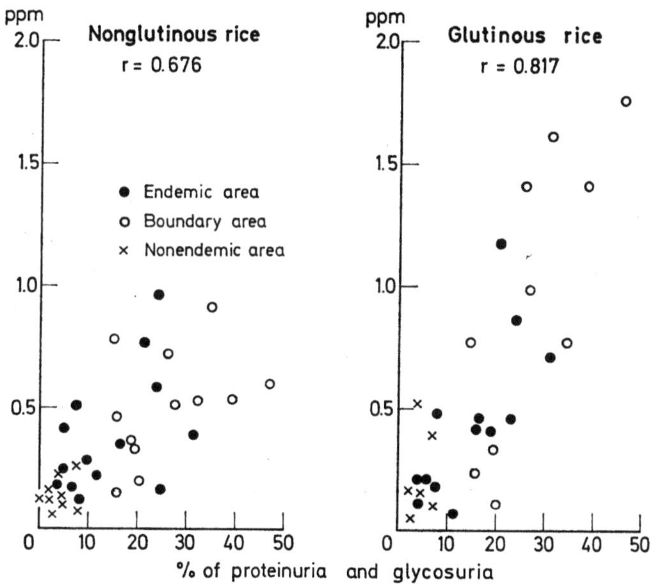

Fig. 22. Correlation between Cd (ppm) in rice and percentage of proteinuria and glycosuria by hamlet, 50 yrs. and over (from Ishizaki, A., *et al.*: The 26th Annual Meeting of the Japanese Society of Public Health, 1968)

It was concluded that Itai-Itai disease is caused by chronic cadmium poisoning, superimposed on such inducing factors as pregnancy, lactation, unbalanced internal secretion, aging, calcium deficiency, etc., the source of the cadmium being the activities of the mine mentioned above.

However, not a few problems remain to be solved concerning the causation of Itai-Itai disease, particularly when it is taken into consideration that there exist several other areas more heavily contaminated with cadmium than the endemic area of the disease, but with no confirmed cases of Itai-Itai disease or even cases of cadmium poisoning.

Comment

These events are typical examples indicating the increasing importance of water pollution due to traces of heavy metals, and they suggest to us that the ecological and biological complex must be studied with more emphasis on the field of environmental sciences. Furthermore, it should not be forgotten that pollution problems like those discussed above have the potential to expand to unexpectedly large areas, as well as to develop in unpredictable directions as regards effects on health.

For instance, methylmercury pollution is now not limited to the above-mentioned areas but is spreading to many other places in Japan, and third or even fourth Minamata disease may well occur in these areas. Furthermore, present studies on the effects of cadmium on health may reveal that cadmium, besides its known toxic action, has some connection with cardiovascular disorders like hypertension, atherosclerosis and myocardial infarction, and even with carcinogenesis and teratogenesis.

The influence of these episodes upon longevity in each district is now under study. According to the results obtained up to the present, there is no significant difference between survival rates in polluted and nonpolluted districts.

With further intensification of the complexity of the industrial structure and the rise in living standards, new products such as polychlorinated biphenyls (PCBs) and others are liable to bring forth even more diversified pollutants. It will thus become necessary to study the effects of these pollutants and act quickly. However, a problem is posed by the fact that treatment of the new pollutants is technically difficult, as experienced in the case of PCBs.

Although a number of studies have been done to achieve the goal of pollution prevention in Japan, much still remains unsolved. What is essential for the efforts to protect the people's health and living environment from pollution is to promote an interdisciplinary approach as well as to strengthen a surveillance activity based on the conviction that pollution should not be regarded as a necessary evil accompanying economic progress.

The Epidemiology and Control of Man-Made Diseases

David D. Rutstein, M. D.

The International Association of Life Assurance Medicine is directly concerned with the increased risk of unnecessary man-made disease, disability, and untimely death resulting from the pollution of our environment. Let us, therefore, examine the epidemiology of the man-made diseases and the effective international application of the epidemiological principles that could lead to the control of these avoidable health problems.

Epidemiology Defined

Epidemiology is the science concerned with the study of all of the factors that affect the occurrence and course of illness. Classically, epidemiologic theory and method that can now be effectively applied to the control of man-made diseases have evolved from the studies of the precise mechanisms of spread of the communicable diseases.

It is useful to review the history of the control of the communicable diseases as a guide to our present efforts to control the man-made diseases. At the turn of the century in the post-Pasteur era, the germ theory of disease was so broadly interpreted that dirt and filth were considered synonymous with the conditions necessary for the transmission of communicable disease. Control was therefore directed toward the elimination of unpleasant conditions offensive to the five senses, particularly of smell. Among others, Charles V. Chapin [1] pointed out that this generalization was too crude since control must be dependent on precise knowledge of the mechanism of transmission of each individual communicable disease. Chapin thus stressed the precise epidemiologic control of the communicable diseases.

History is now being repeated in the control of the man-made diseases. Emphasis tends once again to be placed on those aspects of pollution that are offensive to our senses. To be sure the world around us should be clean and esthetically pleasing. But for the protection of the health of mankind, we must focus sharply down on and control the diseases resulting from the man-made disturbances of our environment. In order to do this effectively we must have precise and sound knowledge of the roles played by each of the environmental agents in the mechanism of the man-made diseases. Control can then be precisely directed on the basis of sound epidemiology. Much epidemiologic knowledge already exists — we know, for example, that the inhalation of rock dust containing free silica particles less than 5 microns in diameter from a grinding wheel, or in a mine, may lead to silicosis while breathing in the silicates in talcum powder will not cause serious illness. But one of our immediate problems is to collate all such knowledge to guide our control programs and to define the gaps which must be filled in by epidemiologic research.

Epidemiological analysis makes it clear that neither in the communicable diseases nor in the man-made diseases can we depend solely on the evidence of our five senses. CHAPIN knew that fecal contamination offensive to the sense of smell might lead to the source of an epidemic of typhoid fever, but he also recognized that the investigator might be misled by the odor of rotting garbage, the latter not being directly involved in the transmission of any communicable disease. Our five senses have to be supplemented by many other kinds of sensors. We need bacteriological cultures to identify the typhoid bacillus that may be responsible for the epidemic spread of typhoid fever by crystal-clear spring water. We must have film badges to protect our laboratory workers against harmful radiation damage. We also need general environmental sensors to monitor as, for example, the mercury concentration of our water supplies. Most important, the data collected by sensors can be most useful if the epidemiology of the relevant diseases are clearly defined.

Man-Made Diseases Defined

For the purposes of this discussion, the man-made diseases are defined as those diseases which would not have occurred if man had not deliberately interfered with his environment[1]. They can be classified into six categories as follows: 1. Toxic substances in the environment such as beryllium in the air in the factory, sulphur dioxide in the smog over a city, insecticide on the farm, or an improperly tested drug regardless of whether they act as a simple toxin or as a carcinogen, mutagen or teratogen. 2. Gamma and other harmful radiation whether made (X-ray), or concentrated (radium) by man; 3. Exposure to strange environments as in a manned satellite in the stratosphere, or in a caisson at the bottom of a river; 4. Accidents in man-made environments; 5. Microorganisms resistant to antibiotics or chemotherapeutic agents and 6. Doctor caused, that is, iatrogenic disease.

In this analysis, a comparison will be made between the epidemiology of communicable disease and the first four categories of man-made disease in this classification. It is clear that item 5, the epidemiology of infections due to resistant microorganisms would already be included within the pattern of the communicable diseases. Iatrogenic disease in item 6 including that due to misdiagnosis, unnecessary surgery, and poor medical judgment follows an entirely different epidemiologic pattern and will not be further analyzed here.

The Nature of Epidemiology

Let us examine the nature of epidemiology. Epidemiology is a science concerned only with abnormalities of health, i. e., with disease, disability and death. In con-

[1] It is recognized that if the concept were extended far enough, all diseases could conceivably be included under the rubric of man-made disease. But this discussion is limited to those diseases in which disturbance of the environment plays a major role and in which the man-made influence is an "essential factor" or a key "sufficient factor" as hereinafter defined.

trast, the term ecology refers to all factors affecting total biological balance in both health and disease. Thus, urban human ecology would comprise all the possible interrelated factors which may influence the status or evolution of a human urban population. Urban epidemiology on the other hand would be limited to those factors leading to disturbances in any aspect of health.

With increasing specialization in medicine there is a growing tendency to approach individual problems in depth in ever more narrowly limited areas. Anatomy, for example, is now being re-examined at the magnification of the electron microscope, and biochemistry at the activity of the specific enzyme. Epidemiology, in sharp contrast, is a generalized science concerned not with individual events but with the constellations created by their interrelationships. Epidemiology thus looks at medicine through the telescope, rather than through the microscope. For example, the virologist might identify a new agent that incites pathologic changes similar to rheumatoid arthritis in the joints of an experimental animal and may suggest that human rheumatoid arthritis may be a virus disease. The epidemiologist might agree, but will demand that the virologist describe a pattern of spread of virus which would not be inconsistent with the epidemiologic observation that the attack rate of rheumatoid arthritis in marital consorts of known cases is the same as that in the general population.

A standard method for epidemiologic investigation has been developed. Observations are made in the parameters of time, place and person. A statement precisely interrelating these three variables is, in fact, a description of an epidemic. The collection of data in a human epidemic cannot be conducted in the form of a controlled experiment because the epidemiologist cannot and should not decide who will or who will not be exposed to and be made sick by an infectious agent or an environmental hazard[2]. In accordance with time tested epidemiological procedure he makes planned, usually retrospective observations related to time, place and person. His observations are made at first hand in a defined population. He avoids, if at all possible, a mere review of records blindly collected without relationship to a previously defined epidemiological hypothesis.

Epidemiological Knowledge Can Prevent Disease

The planned observations of the epidemiologist can often provide leads to the etiology of diseases of unknown cause, even though final definitive answers must await results of laboratory experiments or population studies of the disease. And yet, epidemiological observations have been effective in the control of serious communicable illnesses, long before the exact nature of the external harmful agent had been defined. Smallpox is the classical example. Benjamin Jesty, the Dorchestershire farmer, made the epidemiological observation that milkmaids who had contracted cowpox were not susceptible to smallpox and he vaccinated his wife and his two sons. Jenner provided scientific documentation of these observations by performing a challenge experiment and demonstrated the solid cross immunity conferred by cowpox vaccination. If Jenner's evidence had been gener-

[2] Controlled human experiments can be performed in the general population on the effectivenes of a preventive agent such as a vaccine. Useful epidemiological data are often valuable by-products of such clinical trials.

ally accepted at that time, smallpox could have been eradicated a century before the viruses of smallpox and cowpox were isolated and identified.

In our own day, the established epidemiological relationship between an environmental factor i. e., cigarette smoking and the development of epidermoid carcinoma of the lung, if generally accepted and put into practice by cessation of cigarette smoking, could sharply decrease the attack rate of this fatal disease even though the precise nature of the carcinogen continues to be unknown. It may be expected that as in the case of smallpox, controlled human experiments on the prevention of lung cancer, and animal experiments in the laboratory will identify the carcinogen. But this fatal disease can now for the most part be prevented on the basis of the epidemiologic knowledge alone, although the identification of the carcinogen may sharpen up our methods of control.

The "Cause" of a Disease

Since disease is in fact the result of the interrelationship of multiple epidemiological factors, the concept of a single "cause" of disease has little validity. It is imprecise for example to refer to the tubercle bacillus as the "cause" of tuberculosis, or to consider castor bean dust as the "cause" of epidemics of severe and often fatal cases of bronchial asthma. In the case of tuberculosis, it is not unusual that practically all residents of crowded urban communities where clinical tuberculosis is rife, have positive tuberculin tests by late childhood, i. e., clear evidence that they had been infected with the tubercle bacillus. Yet a relatively small proportion of them will have clinically significant disease. It has been established that such factors as age, sex, genetic susceptibility, rural-urban migration, poverty and crowding affect the attack rate and the clinical manifestations of tuberculosis. But these factors, alone or in combination, in the absence of the tubercle bacillus are incapable of inciting any manifestations of this disease.

Therefore in epidemiologic parlance, the tubercle bacillus may be referred to as an "essential factor" — without which the disease cannot occur, but in the presence of which clinical disease does not necessarily supervene. The other factors listed above are called "sufficient factors" and can convert infection (an essential factor) into overt disease, but cannot singly or in combination, in the absence of that factor induce any single manifestation of the illness. The epidemiologic nature and the development of a disease are dependent upon an essential factor either acting alone or more likely interacting with one or many sufficient factors. These epidemiologic definitions of essential and sufficient factors have mechanistic significance and supersede the now anachronistic terminology of the "cause" of a disease.

These same epidemiologic definitions are applicable to the man-made diseases. In castor bean dust asthma, for example, the dried, highly allergenic dust remaining after the extraction of the oil is the "essential factor" while the allergic susceptibility of the host, the method of handling of the dried residues, and the wind direction from the manufacturing plant are "sufficient factors" in the development of individual cases and of an epidemic of the disease.

Knowledge of the absence of an essential or a key sufficient factor may be useful in reassuring a population against a potential danger. In 1964 when American tourists returned to Chicago with dengue fever contracted on a Caribbean island the rumor that a local epidemic might supervene was quashed by the epidemiological fact that the vector of this disease, the Aedes Egypti mosquito, was not present in that area. Similarly, knowing that silicosis results from the inhalation of free silica of a particle size small enough to permit access to the lung alveoli, and not from the inhalation of relatively large particles of silicon dioxide, we can be sure that children playing in the sand on a beach will not contract this disease.

Epidemiology — a Measure of Reasonableness

Epidemiologic knowledge makes it possible to evaluate the reasonableness of mechanisms whenever a new etiology is proposed. For example, the experimental evidence that caffeine is carcinogenic in animals has been widely publicized. But these findings are not likely to be relevant to human beings. The enormous intake in many population groups of caffeine in coffee and tea should be associated with high cancer rates. Clearly this is not the case. The important generalization here is that all etiologic observations in vitro or in experimental animals should be examined in the light of available epidemiological knowledge before reaching conclusions as to their relevance to human health and disease. When available epidemiological knowledge is inadequate, additional planned observations may have to be collected to determine the significance in man of the proposed etiological mechanism. With such an approach one can always determine whether the new hypothesis "makes sense" in human terms.

The epidemiological characteristics of man-made diseases as in the case of infectious diseases should be included in the medical curriculum so that future physicians may give appropriate consideration to these illnesses in their differential diagnosis. They will also be able to anticipate the natural history of disease and give more precise prognoses to their patients.

Comparison of Epidemiologic Characteristics

Let us now compare the epidemiological characteristics of both infectious and man-made diseases and note the parallelisms and discrepancies between them in the nature of the agents, the reservoir of disease, the channels by which they reach the susceptible host, relevant host factors and mechanisms of prevention.

In both groups of diseases, external agents are essential for the precipitation of illness. In infectious disease, the agent reproduces itself and is therefore self perpetuating. The total number of pathologic external infectious agents however, is relatively fixed except for the slow continuous increase in the number of known infectious agents — including those due to the discovery of new agents; the identification of previously unknown strains of known agents, or the mutation of new strains such as occurs in the influenza viruses. In contrast, the man-made agents tend to be inert, do not reproduce and have to be newly created and/or disseminated. But their number is increasing rapidly due to extensive university and industrial programs of synthesis and discovery of new compounds and the rapid rate of increase in the exposure of humans to these agents in air, water, drugs, foods and household and industrial chemicals. As will be seen, these trends must be taken seriously into account in the control of man-made diseases.

The Reservoirs of Disease

The definition of a reservoir of infectious disease is the natural community of the infection where the agent survives and multiplies. For the man-made diseases, the definition of reservoir has to be modified to the place where and the conditions under which the substance is produced and from which it is disseminated. In contrast with infectious disease, in the man-made diseases there are no human or animal reservoirs and the epidemiological pattern of spread is similar to that from soil reservoirs of infectious disease such as the spore bearing and parasitic agents inciting such diseases as tetanus, gas gangrene, ascariasis, hookworm disease, coccidioidomycosis histoplasmosis and botulism. The nature of the reservoirs of the man-made diseases are really determined by such factors as the state and type of industrial development, the automobile density, climatic conditions and the urban concentration in the area.

Channels of Spread

Since there are no human and animal reservoirs of the man-made diseases, spread from case to case, and from animal to case does not occur, carriers do not exist, and there are no insect or other living vectors. On the other hand, the spread of-man-made diseases via inert vehicles is very common. There are many strong parallelisms between the infectious and man-made diseases in this method of spread. Spores of coccidioidomycosis and insecticides are spread via the air, cholera vibrios and poisons from industrial waste are carried by water, and botulinus toxin and toxic drugs and food additives are conveyed in materials prepared for human ingestion. Spread via direct skin contact is similar for infections such as anthrax and for man-made toxic and allergic substances such as corrosive acids and topically applied therapeutic agents. Man-made diseases however do not have any epidemiological counterpart to respiratory diseases transmitted by contact, including the common cold, measles and diphtheria. It is fortunate that this is the case because contact spread of respiratory disease is difficult to control except by immunization. In this regard, contact transmission of respiratory diseases must be distinguished from air borne spread of illness such as occurs in Q fever.

Host Characteristics

Host characteristics play important roles in exposure to the external agents. In very early life, except in very primitive or in very poor home environments, the host is likely to be sheltered from exposure to both infectious and man-made disease. In childhood, with increasing exposure to both virus infection and toxic substances in the household, both infectious and man-made illness increase in frequency. At the time of puberty in the female, the spread of gonorrheal infection changes from a non-venereal to a venereal pathway. There is also an increasing likelihood beginning at that time, of toxic side effects from contraceptive pills and from such cosmetic agents as hair sprays. In contrast, the young adult male may be infected with tularemia on a hunting trip, and in his occupation he may be exposed to infection from anthrax, tetanus, gas gangrene or schistosomiasis or to the man-made diseases resulting from exposure to unusual physiological environments, toxic substances, radiation and conditions conducive to accidents.

Genetic and familial characteristics influence susceptibility to such reactions as allergic responses to drugs, and to modifications of the natural history of disease as in the case of malaria in individuals with inherited sickle cell anemia. Social-economic and cultural patterns may often determine the qualitative and quantitative exposure to agents of infectious and of the man-made diseases.

There is one major discrepancy between the two groups of illnesses in host characteristics. By repeated exposure to infection or through the use of vaccine, the host may become protected against a specific infectious agent. Human beings do not develop classical immunity against the man-made diseases but do develop tolerance to certain agents. In byssinosis, carders after a weekend of non-exposure to cotton have "Monday morning" expiratory difficulty documented by a decrease in their forced expiratory flow rates. Similarly, workers in the explosives industry exposed to nitroglycerin have post weekend vasodilatation. Tolerance is also said to develop in workers after long exposure to chromic acid and to arsenic.

Prevention of Disease and Methods of Control

The epidemiological characteristics of the man-made diseases dictate the methods of control for their prevention. The absence of human or animal reservoirs, insect vectors, case to case, and animal to case transmission rule out control by quarantine, by treatment of infectious patients, and by insect eradication.

Some prevention of man-made disease can be achieved through direct protection of the susceptible host, even though immunization is not possible. Protected environments can be set up immediately around the worker by shielding with lead against radiation, by the use of masks and filters against airborne toxins, and by creating artificial environments such as a space capsule, a caisson or a specially designed airconditioned building in a high risk industry. But all these alternatives are expensive, relatively awkward, and many seriously interfere with individual mobility.

There is one major method of control of man-made diseases. As in the case of those infectious diseases with a soil reservoir, control against most man-made disease must be directed towards suppression of the source of the harmful agents or to the interruption of the channels by which they are disseminated. This approach has wide applicability and can be used to protect against air and water borne toxins, harmful radiation, drug toxicity, and factors which increase the probability of accidents. Indeed, it is now the standard method of control, and has been more or less effective depending upon local circumstances. Only too often, such control has been limited to the eradication of already existing hazards, although preventive programs are now increasing in number.

This method of control at the source and by prevention of the spread of harmful agents is seriously restricted by economic constraints such as the increased cost of fuel of low sulphur content, the redesign of automobile engines to assure complete combustion, the detoxification of industrial effluents and the development of systematic methods of solid waste disposal. In spite of all these difficulties slow progress is being made, as for example the demonstration in the recent report of the Royal College of Physicians in the United Kingdom that smoke abatement programs have eliminated the excess mortality in London during periods of smog.

Suppression at the source is effective against established varieties of pollution but only when it is clear that the substances in question have been shown to be harmful. Thus, protection at the source presupposes a prior mechanism for determining the potential hazard of existing pollutants and of the large number of new compounds being isolated or synthesized to which humans may be exposed. Actually, there is now no systematic program anywhere for determining the potential toxicity of all newly discovered substances.

Biological Background of Control

To ensure the most effective application of epidemiological principles to protect against the large number of the many kinds of man-made hazards, it is useful to re-examine the course of biological evolution. Man has evolved slowly on the surface of the earth over the millenia through the survival of those mutants best adapted to and most able to compensate for the fixed and changing constraints of the environment. The process is a very slow acting one with the adaptive compensation to new threats to survival taking place over a series of generations.

But, in the 19th century the industrial revolution altered the balance of change. Man suddenly was being increasingly exposed to many new toxic substances and to concentrations of harmful agents far in excess of anything he had known in his evolutionary experience. For example, in the 1890's, man suddenly learned how to create gamma rays and to concentrate their sources so that human exposure in industry, in medicine and later as a result of atomic explosion far exceedeu anything that had been previously observed. Indeed, in medical care alone there has been an exponential increase in the systematic exposure of human beings to gamma radiation.

There is an ever present danger in the constant flow of newly synthesized or isolated chemical compounds coming into close biological contact with man in many ways — in industrial exposure, common household use and in the administration of new drugs. There have been unhappy experiences, including severe toxic reactions to workers from plasticizers in industry, pollution with household detergents of drinking water supplies, and phocomelia from the incompletely tested drug — thalidomide.

In comparison with the number of new substances, the serious effects have been relatively few. But it is obviously only a question of time, as we continue to produce new compounds at an increasing rate, and if we neglect to screen them for health hazards, before a substance appears that is so lethal that it may threaten all life within its range of contact. There is also the fundamental question as to whether the rate of exposure to new toxic agents may become so great as to overwhelm the relatively slow compensatory effects of evolution.

It remains now to indicate how these epidemiological principles may be applied in an international man-made disease control program.

An International Environmental Control Program

The epidemiological characteristics of the man-made diseases are useful guides in the planning of a control program. The many similarities with the epidemiology of infectious disease particularly those with a reservoir in the soil, permit the evolution of existing communicable disease control programs to include the man-made diseases. The control of communicable disease due to man-made resistant microorganisms is already included in local, national and international prevention programs. Existing communicable disease control programs can be expanded to include the control of diseases due to toxins, radiation, abnormal physical environments and accidents. Key personnel with special training in the man-made diseases may have to be added and existing personnel in communicable disease control programs may need additional training. Thus, the existing administrative structure should suffice and it will probably not be necessary to incur the enormous effort and expense of creating new local, national and international administrative units to control the man-made diseases.

An international man-made disease control program is necessary. To accomplish this, the International Association of Life Assurance Medicine should take advantage of and work closely with the World Health Organization which has unusual resources for the world-wide control of the man-made diseases. To begin with, the World Health Organization could develop a guidance program to advise individual countries on the prevention of pollution in the establishment of new industries and industrial centers just as the World Health Organization has in the past advised on malaria control in the building of new dams. Guidance would also be provided on the elimination of existing pollution, just as the World Health Organization has established programs for the eradication of smallpox.

To provide a sound basis for control, as in programs against the communicable diseases, all known epidemiologic information on the man-made diseases must be collated and classified. Once this task is completed, the lexicon could make possible the planning and performance of key epidemiologic studies to fill in the major gaps in knowledge. The World Health Organization would have to establish a research program on pollution control to meet this need. As more specific knowledge on the epidemiology of this group of diseases is thereby yielded, control programs would become more precise just as has occurred in the history of communicable diseases.

In the implementation of a guidance program and in order to meet emergencies, the World Health Organization would have to set up a "flying squad" pollution control service similar to the Epidemic Intelligence Service that has functioned so well in the Center for Disease Control in the United States. Such a service, for example, could have handled incidents such as the sudden poisoning of fish in the Rhine River by diagnosing the mechanism and bringing expert guidance to bear on the control of the emergency. Attention would also be directed to the prevention of similar episodes in the future, and help to avoid the kind of international friction precipitated by such events. As in the case of "flying squad" programs in communicable disease control, routine surveillance data from monitoring programs throughout the world could provide the baseline information needed by the World Health Organization to interpret the significance of acute events.

The World Health Organization could also accept responsibility for the definition of criteria to govern the establishment of standards of permissible exposure to known harmful agents. Guidelines would also have to be laid down for the prevention of disease from agents with potential but not yet established harmfulness. In so doing, advantages must be taken of accomplishments in existing programs in the World Health Organization and in other agencies.

Pollution control does present a problem quantitatively different from that of infectious disease control. The total number of new infectious agents, e. g., Lassa virus, or new strains of known agents, e. g., arborviruses, or mutants such as those of influenza A viruses is small. In contrast, there is a constantly enlarging stream of newly isolated and synthesized chemical compounds, new industrial and household (color television) sources of harmful radiation, accidents harmful to health resulting from man's manipulation of his environment e. g., explosion of a tank of toxic gas, diseases precipitated by placing man in strange environments, e. g., calcium loss from restricted physical activity in astronauts and in carelessly treated chronically ill patients, and new food additives, preservatives and new drugs.

The large number of potential hazards must be screened and the dangerous ones identified and controlled if the man-made disease control program is to be effective. An example of a screening program is the proposed international drug testing program [2]. The World Health Organization would create, and guide or administer the screening program as a necessary adjunct to the control program. In the case of definite or even questionable hazards, particularly when there are competing economic and other interests, it is of vital importance that the World Health Organization assure that the health and welfare of mankind are given the benefit of the doubt.

In summary, precise epidemiology and a screening program for new hazards are essential to the control of man-made diseases. All three could be the responsibility of the World Health Organization. But the World Health Organization cannot act alone. Influential agencies such as the International Association of Life Assurance Medicine must provide support and encouragement to the establishment and maintenance of a program for the international control of the man-made diseases.

References

1. CHAPIN, C. V.: Dirt, disease and the health officer, public health: Papers and Report 28, 296–299 (1902).
2. RUTSTEIN, DAVID D.: A proposed design for the testing of new drugs. In: The ethical design of human experiments, Daedalus 98, No. 2 of the Proceedings of the American Academy of Arts and Sciences, 534–537, Spring 1969.

Facteurs de haut risque pour le pronostic lointain, provenant des aéro-contaminants et de leurs conséquences sur les voies respiratoires

Dr. Laurent Meeus-Bith

1 Figure

La détermination des facteurs de haut risque, susceptibles d'augmenter la mortalité ou la morbidité standard, est un des buts principaux de la médecine d'assurance-vie; le corollaire en est la détermination d'un taux de surmortalité ou l'application de réserves sur la durée ou les garanties du contrat proposé.

Les maladies des voies respiratoires ont longtemps représenté une cause de surmortalité importante, mais le recul de la tuberculose et d'autres maladies infectieuses ont fait méconnaitre le risque persistant constitué par les infections respiratoires communes mais répétées dont l'aboutissement peut être la bronchopneumopathie chronique obstructive (BPO) ou bronchite chronique avec emphysème.

D'autre part, le cancer broncho-pulmonaire connait une augmentation de fréquence que n'expliquent pas seulement les progrès du diagnostic; et si la fréquence augmente, la gravité ne diminue pas, à tel point qu'il représente 2% des causes de décès et 10% des décès par cancer chez l'homme, en France [10].

Ces deux affections sont donc au premier plan des préoccupations des pneumologues et des hygiénistes.

Leur importance relative dans la mortalité et la morbidité a, tout naturellement, fait poser la question de leur relation avec les changements introduits depuis le début et surtout le milieu du siècle, dans les conditions de vie.

Une relation a été entrevue entre la composition de l'air inspiré et l'influence de substances anormales qui polluent l'air [30, 31, 38, 70].

D'autres relations sortent du cadre de cet exposé et concernent des modifications propres à l'individu: facteurs immunologiques ou génétiques, déficits enzymatiques...

C'est à l'occasion de changements massifs et brutaux de la composition de l'air, que l'influence morbide de la pollution s'est imposée à l'évidence.

Le plus proche de ces cataclysmes météorologiques et le premier scientifiquement observé fut le smog de Londres en l'hiver 1952. Il causa près de 4.000 décès excédentaires et permit d'établir une surmortalité par affections respiratoires atteignant jusqu'à 10 fois le taux de mortalité escompté [32, 39, 84] (Tableau 1).

De tels cataclysmes sont néanmoins très rares et n'intéressent le médecin hygiéniste qu'en attirant dès l'abord l'attention sur la vulnérabilité particulière de certains sujets: enfants, vieillards, bronchitiques, fumeurs.

C'est précisement les mêmes sujets qui seront peut être vulnérables à l'action d'une pollution plus insidieuse et plus prolongée.

Tableau 1. Extra mortality from London fog — December, 1952 [Population of the County of London, 3,3 million] (Surmortalité due au fog londonien de décembre 1952)

Cause of death (Cause de décès)	Seasonal rate (Normes saisonnières) Deaths per week (Décès par semaine)	Deaths during week of fog (Décès durant la semaine de brouillard)	Extra deaths (Décès éxcédentaire)	
Bronchitis (Bronchite)	75	704	629	39%
Other pulmonary diseases (Autres maladies pulmonaires)	92	366	268	17%
Coronary diseases (Maladies coronariennes)	206	525	319	20%
Other diseases (Autres maladies)	508	889	381	24%
Total	887	2484	1597	100%

Data from the Royal College of Physicians — London

De nombreux travaux se sont efforcés de mettre en évidence le rôle important de cette aggression chronique et de proposer les moyens pour en assurer la prévention.

Après avoir rappelé la nature et l'origine des principaux polluants de l'air, nous préciserons quels travaux permettent de rapporter à cette pollution une augmentation de la mortalité et/ou de la morbidité par affections respiratoires telles que la BPO et le cancer bronchique.

Nous essayerons enfin de présenter l'incidence de ces données sur la médecine d'assurance-vie, d'une part pour le dépistage des facteurs de haut risque chez les proposants, d'autre part les pénalisations qui découlent de la découverte d'un ou de plusieurs facteurs de surmortalité ou surmorbidité.

Les principaux polluants de l'air et leurs sources

L'air normal est un mélange gazeux qui contient 78% d'Azote, 21% d'Oxygène, 1% d'Argon, 0,03% de CO_2 et quelques gaz rares.

La pollution signifie la présence, dans ce mélange naturel, d'autres gaz, de vapeurs, de gouttelettes, de particules en suspension, minérales ou organiques.

Origine générale des aéro-polluants [80, 82]

Si l'on excepte certaines particules végétales, on peut dire que la pollution est le fait de l'homme et de la civilisation. Elle résulte du rejet volontaire ou accidentel dans l'atmosphère d'un certain nombre de déchets volatils ou en suspension fine.

Les principaux déchets proviennent des combustions et réalisent les fumées quand elles ont une certaine densité particulaire et les brouillards de fumée ou „smog“ quand elles se mêlent aux gouttelettes ou vapeurs.

Il peut s'agir de déchets de combustion industrielle, domestique ou des véhicules à moteur; les trois productions s'additionnent dans les conurbations.

A côté d'une pollution générale de l'air ambiant, il existe des microatmosphères professionnelles, mais aussi domestiques, qui peuvent avoir une densité élevée de pollution.

C'est enfin la pollution individuelle, on peut dire „privée“, qui réalise la source probablement la plus dangereuse de pollution de l'air: moins par le CO_2 expiré que par l'usage du tabac.

Le nombre des polluants dont la présence est possible dans l'air ambiant est considérable. Nous passerons en revue les plus significatifs pour la pollution générale, les moins fréquents intervenant plutôt dans les expositions professionnelles.

1. Il existe des constituants gazeux et particulaires anormaux presque „habituels“ en milieu urbain du fait des éliminations de déchets de combustion (Tableau 2).

Ces constituants ont du reste servi de base à la plupart des „mesures“ de la pollution en raison de leur activité nocive reconnue sur l'animal ou sur l'homme à des concentrations élevées accidentelles.

Le SO_2 est le plus important, le plus communément adopté dans les mesures de niveau de pollution. Il provient des combustions de charbons et fuels industriels ou domestiques, à la concentration de 2 à 5 ppm [1] il a une action bronchoconstrictive et son action est aggravée s'il s'unit aux gouttelettes vaporisées ou s'oxyde en SO_3.

Les concentrations considérées comme tolérables pour les divers combustibles sont passées de 0,7 à 0,5 ppm et devraient atteindre 0,3 en 1978.

Le SO_2 définit pratiquement la nocivité de l'air dans la plupart des stations de mesure [1, 45, 83].

Le CO résulte de la combustion incomplète des composés carbonés. Son effet toxique par combinaison avec l'hémoglobine est bien connu. Ses effets biologiques sont directement proportionnels à la teneur du sang en HbCO et cette combinaison est reversible. Les effets moteurs et généraux sont bien connus; la nocivité cardio-vasculaire et broncho-pulmonaire est mal connue dans l'intoxication chronique; mais ce gaz par son dosage sanguin, a le mérite de donner une idée du degré d'exposition d'un individu [8, 27, 65].

Les oxydes d'Azote, NO, NO_2, N_2O_5, sont produits par les moteurs à combustion interne; ils provoquent des altérations épithéliales et des dilatations alvéolaires (chez l'animal d'expérimentation) évoquant l'emphysème humain.

Ils interviennent dans le smog photochimique et la production d'Ozone [2, 17, 18, 19, 20, 21].

Dans certaines zones urbaines, la combinaison chimique d'hydrocarbures et d'Oxyde d'Azote en présence de fort ensoleillement provoque la formation

---

[1] ppm = partie par million.

Tableau 2. Polluants „habituels" de l'atmosphère urbaine (Pollutants „usually" present in urban atmosphere)

Nature	Origine (Origin)	Toxicité (Toxicity)
SO_2 SO_3-SO_3	Combustion de charbons et fuels [industriels ou domestiques] (Oil and coal combustion [house or industry])	Bronchoconstriction
CO	d° Tabac (Tobacco)	Altération de l'hémoglobine (Change in Hb)
NO $NO_2-N_2O_5$	d° Oxydation photochimique Usine (Factory)	Broncho-alveolite — Oedème (Alveolitis, pulmonary edema)
O_3	Photochemical smog	d° Desquamation muqueuse (Mucosal desquamation)
Plomb (Lead)	Echappement des moteurs	Saturnisme (Neurotoxicity)
Hydrocarbures volatils et goudrons (Oil, gas and tars)	(Automobile engines) (Unburned gases in engine oil)	Cancers?

Tableau 3. Polluants professionnels plus rares (Less usual occupational pollutants)
Particules minérales (Particles of mineral origin)

Plomb (Lead)	Moteurs à explosion Fonderie — raffinage Batteries — accumulateurs — peinture	Automobile engines Smelting — refining Storage batteries — accumulators — painting
Arsenic	Pesticides — insecticides — viticulture	Wine growing
Chlore (Chlorine)	Plastiques — organochlorés Insecticides — D.D.T.	Plastics
Nickel Chrome (Chromium) Beryllium Vanadium	Métaux et alliages	Metallurgic and alloying works
Silice (Silica)	Mines	Mining
Charbon (Coal)	Chaufferies — verreries	Heating — glass making
Amiante (Asbestos)	Fibres de silicates Isolants et ignifuges Freins — construction	Silicate fibers Insulation and fireproof devices (Brakes — building)

d'Ozone et d'autres oxydants; ces composés sont très irritants pour les muqueuses occulaires et respiratoires. C'est à Los Angelès que les effets du „smog" photochimique ont été les mieux observés, la teneur en oxydants pouvant atteindre 0,50 à 0,85 ppm [22].

Enfin l'on retrouve comme polluants urbains habituels, le Plomb issu de la combustion des additifs des carburants, les hydrocarbures volatils ou les goudrons microparticulaires venant des „imbrûlés" des produits pétroliers.

Pour tous ces polluants de l'air urbain, les facteurs météorologiques sont très importants à considérer, particulièrement l'état hygrométrique, la présence des brouillards qui sont des vecteurs de particules ou des solvants de gaz, les vents dominants ou occasionnels qui peuvent chasser ou rabattre les fumées; l'influence de la saison et du froid est considérable dans le développement des affections respiratoires [57].

On peut y ajouter le rôle des infections microbiennes et des particules organiques allergisantes et l'on concevra les difficultés rencontrées dans l'interprétation des conséquences morbides de la composition de l'air et son rôle sur la BPO en particulier [75].

2. Il existe des polluants moins uniformément répandus et surtout professionnels, mais des travaux récents ont montré leur importance; leur diffusion peut dépasser largement le lieu de production.

Ces polluants industriels sont avant tout des particules minérales (Tableau 3).

L'influence néfaste de la silice du charbon est bien connue en région minière [72].

Le plomb qui peut provenir des carburants et de nombreux usages industriels — fonderie — raffinage — laiton — peintures [8].

Des particules de Chrome, Nickel, Béryllium, Vanadium sont souvent retrouvées dans l'air [13].

Mais c'est à l'amiante que revient la vedette en matière d'exposition professionnelle. Ce nom recouvre un ensemble de silicates naturels à structure fibreuse, formés de 40 à 60% de silice en combinaison avec des oxydes de Fer, de Magnésium et autres métaux. On en a dénombré (Hendry 1965) plus d'un millier d'utilisations, en particulier comme isolant thermique ou électrique; on le retrouve dans la construction des appareils domestiques, les freins à disque et incorporé aux matériaux de construction.

Comme l'ont montré Selikoff et Hammond, sa présence est très diffuse en milieu urbain et a justifié une législation stricte de son emploi [49, 61].

Ce rôle de l'amiante a en effet été largement démontré dans les lésions bronchiques chroniques et dans les cancers bronchiques, également dans les tumeurs mésothéliales de la plèvre et du péritoine [42, 43].

Son activité carcinogénétique, mal expliquée, mais pratiquement admise, en fait un des polluants les plus redoutables [26, 58, 85, 86, 87, 88].

Le rôle carcinogène du Fer, du Béryllium, de l'Arsenic, du Vanadium est actuellement étudié, mais la diffusion de ces corps est loin d'atteindre celle de l'amiante et les études sont moins concluantes.

3. Les polluants particulaires organiques (Tableau 4) sont intéressants à citer car ils ne représentent plus le privilège des atmosphères urbaines; ils peuvent se retrouver à des concentrations dangereuses en milieu rural [11, 50].

Ces particules proviennent du coton (byssinose), de la canne à sucre (bagassose), du bois précieux, du foin; ils interviennent soit directement, soit par un mécanisme de sensibilisation et d'allergie [89] soit encore comme vecteurs de mycoses (micropolyspora-polyspora du poumon des fermiers) [25, 36, 40, 56].

Il peut aussi exister des produits chimiques utilisés comme fertilisants ou pesticides: arsenic, organochlorés en particulier le D.D.T.

4. Il serait vain d'étudier la pollution de l'air ambiant sans rappeler que les plus fortes concentrations de produits nocifs, oxyde de carbone, oxydes d'azote, goudrons et hydrocarbures cancérigènes se retrouvent dans la fumée de tabac, les autres drogues volatiles étant plus accessoires dans cette pollution „privée" [3, 4].

Tableau 4. Particules végétales (Particles of vegetable origin)

Foin — poumon du fermier	Hay — farmer's lung	Micropolyspora polyspora Micropolyspora foeni
Maladie des éleveurs d'oiseaux	Bird breeder's disease	Micromonospora vulgaris
Canne à sucre	Sugar cane workers	Bagassose
Cotonniers	Cotton workers	Byssinose
Bois précieux	Fine wood	Canosparium corticale
Fromagers	Cheese makers	Penicillium caséi
Champignoniers	Mushroom farmers	Various moulds
Fourreurs	Furriers	Pneumopathies interstitielles d'hypersensibilité
Malteurs	Malt makers	Pneumopathies interstitielles d'hypersensibilité
Minotiers	Flour millers	Hypersensibility
Grainetiers	Corn chandlers	Pneumonitis

De plus cette pollution individuelle n'est pas exclusivement personnelle, dans la mesure ou elle modifie la composition de l'air, surtout en milieu confiné et les dosages sanguins de HbCO ont montré des augmentations significatives chez des non fumeurs en atmosphère viciée de tabac [59].

Les effets biologiques de ces agents polluants sont discutés et probablement multipleset associés.

Ont été invoqués principalement:

— la bronchoconstriction et la perte du pouvoir de clearance mucocilaire [6, 9, 53, 54, 73].
— les modifications du surfactant.
— la destruction des macrophages et leur remplacement par des fibroblastes favorisant la fibrose [40, 62, 22].
— l'immunodépression locale [12, 24].
— l'hypersensibilité avec phénomènes allergiques et bronchoconstriction retardée (PEPYS-JACQUET) [14, 56].

Nous insisterons simplement sur la valeur pratique des mesures des volumes dynamiques respiratoires, qui servent de base à beaucoup de travaux et que nous retrouverons dans les critères de sélection.

Le pouvoir carcinogénétique de l'air pollué est infiniment plus difficile à établir [60, 63].

Nous avons vu la présence de substances minérales ou organiques dont le rôle oncogène est actuellement reconnu.

Il existe également des composés polycycliques tels le Benzopyrène, la Benzacridine et la di-benzacridine dans tous les types de suies ou de fumées.

Le Benzopyrène, considéré comme la substance cancérigène type peut atteindre la concentration de 100 µg/1.000 m³.

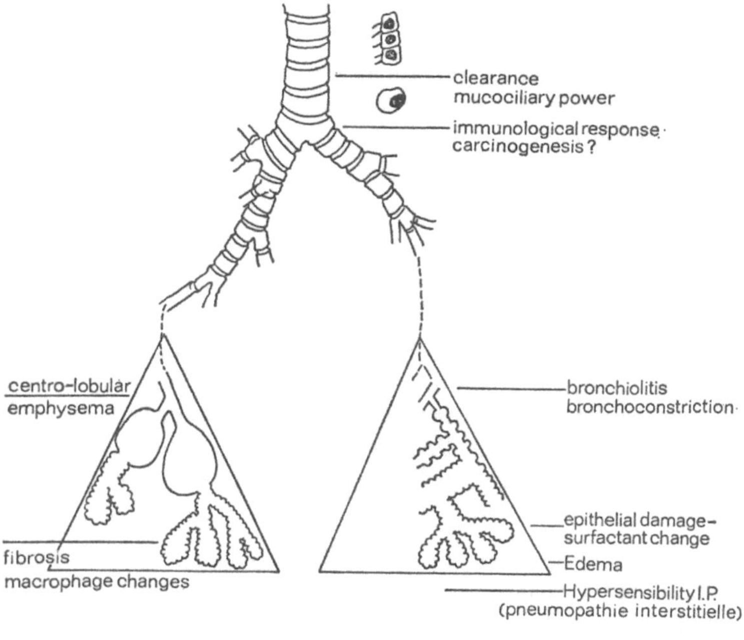

Fig. 1. Pathological effects of pollution (physiopathologie de al pollution)

Les expositions professionnelles et l'expérimentation animale ne permettent toutefois pas une extrapolation et l'on ne peut raisonner par analogie avec les effets d'une pollution aiguë, comme on l'a fait pour la BPO.

Enfin l'évolution lente de la cancérogénèse rend difficiles et décourageantes les enquêtes prospectives.

Ainsi, il existe dans l'air de nombreux polluants générateurs possibles de lésions broncho-pulmonaires, dont le pouvoir pathogène est admis pour des concentrations élevées ou dans des conditions privilégiées d'espace ou de temps: expérimentations, exposition professionnelle, cataclysmes.

Toute la question est de savoir s'il existe à long terme, un risque réel.

Effets de la pollution atmosphérique sur la santé

Ces effets peuvent être appréciés par une double recherche: enquêtes épidémiologiques et enquêtes toxicologiques.

La première méthode étudie les faits observés dans une population humaine considérée comme exposée à un risque, la seconde recourt à des observations sur l'animal d'expérience — voire sur un groupe humain limité.

1. *Les enquêtes épidémiologiques* ont l'intérêt de se consacrer à l'étude globale du milieu, en différenciant des groupes humains en fonction de l'exposition. A ce titre, elles intéressent spécialement le médecin d'assurance-vie, mais elles aboutissent habituellement à une conclusion trop générale et ne permettent que rarement d'incriminer un constituant précis du risque; enfin, elles ne peuvent éliminer le rôle de la pollution privée et particulièrement du tabac.

Différents types de recherches sont à isoler.

a) Les études de surmortalité globale en milieu urbain et plus particulièrement par augmentation des affections respiratoires et cardio-vasculaires sont pratiquement toutes concordantes.

— Une monographie récente éditée par le Conseil de L'Europe analyse la mortalité par cancer bronchique dans les 17 pays membres et retrouve partout une corrélation significative avec la surpopulation urbaine et industrielle [79].

C'est une conclusion identique qui est fournie en France par les études épidémiologiques de la Section Cancer de l'I.N.S.E.R.M. [23, 44].

Parmi les enquêtes américaines, celle faite par Zeidberg à Nashville — Tennessee — met en évidence une surmortalité par affection pulmonaire dans les classes moyennes vivant dans les zones les plus polluées [76, 77, 78].

Il existe dans certaines régions d'Angleterre ou des Pays-Bas une augmentation de mortalité de 20% dans les conurbations par rapport aux petites villes et aux régions rurales.

b) D'autres études se penchent sur la corrélation entre la variation de morbidité et/ou de mortalité et les variations de la pollution de l'air [15, 16, 47, 48].

Dans les principales villes des pays industrialisés existent désormais des stations de „mesure" de la pollution. Parfois réduites à quelques paramètres, ces mesures peuvent être très importantes. Certaines grandes villes des Etats-Unis ayant ainsi en surveillance et en monitoring un véritable quadrillage des zones industrielles et résidentielles et relevant jusqu'à 10 paramètres [33, 34].

C'est toutefois aux Anglais que revient le mérite d'avoir les premiers étudié les effets de la pollution sur la population urbaine.

Utilisant la méthode du „carnet" Lawther a montré la concordance entre les périodes d'aggravation des symptomes fonctionnels, toux, dyspnée, expectoration et l'augmentation de la pollution.

C'est également lui qui a pu montrer les effets bénéfiques des mesures anti-pollution édictées par le „Clean Air Act" de 1956.

A Los Angelès, Mahonny, constate une augmentation de fréquence des affections respiratoires, avec l'éloignement de la mer et l'air vicié ramené par les vents.

Dohan étudiant l'absentéisme dans cinq villes des U.S.A. trouve une corrélation avec la concentration en SO_2 et en particules.

Des résultats analogues sont retrouvés par Ibsen [38, 39] à Philadelphie, Hammond et Selikoff à New-York [32] et en France Marquet et Voisin [75] à Lille; Tacquet à Lille [72], Sadoul à Nancy, Brille et Kourilsky à Paris [41].

Comme il est difficile d'interpréter ces résultats sans faire intervenir le facteur tabac, certains auteurs comme HOLLAND [35] dans les écoles du Kent, font des constations semblables sur des groupes d'enfants.

c) Certaines études portent sur les variations de morbidité dans des groupes limités et se rapprochent des travaux expérimentaux.

Ainsi BRILLE et KOURILSKY étudient les modifications des valeurs spirométriques chez les travailleurs du bois [41].

Des études sont faites en milieu minier. SADOUL (Nancy), TACQUET (Lille) et surtout SELIKOFF chez les travailleurs de l'amiante.

Une étude des valeurs spirométriques et du dosage du Plomb dans les cheveux est faite chez les agents de police de Boston par SPEIZER [64].

2. *L'expérimentation animale* retiendra moins l'attention du médecin hygiéniste. Il est néanmoins intéressant de rappeler les travaux effectués sur l'exposition à moyen terme aux atmosphères riches en oxyde de carbone par STUPFEL, KILLECH et LILIENTHAL sur les rats; LINDENBERG et MUSSELMANN sur les chiens, MALORNY sur les souris [66, 68, 69, 70, 71].

Actuellement, le Dr. STUPFEL, au service de pollution atmosphérique de l'I.N.S.E.R.M. étudie chez le rat, les effets à long terme de l'atmosphère enrichie en gaz d'échappement de moteur [67].

De tous ces travaux et enquêtes, il ne ressort pas actuellement une corrélation évidente entre telle affection respiratoire et telle substance toxique; on ne peut que retenir les notions généralement retrouvées et admises.

Il existe une surmortalité en milieu fortement urbanisé et industrialisé.

Il existe un parallélisme entre les pics de pollution et la morbidité et/ou mortalité par affections respiratoires.

Il existe des expositions „privilégiées" où la corrélation entre pollution de l'air, en général professionnelle, et morbidité est significative.

Il existe des facteurs associés dont le rôle ne peut être négligé:

— fragilité individuelle,
— conditions climatiques,
— infections microbiennes qui vont souvent de pair avec la saison froide,
— enfin et surtout, l'irritation chronique des bronches par la fumée de tabac.

On ne saurait assez insiter sur l'importance du tabac comme facteur associé et aggravant, qu'il s'agisse de la BPO ou du cancer.

Quelques exemples parmi de multiples en illustrent l'importance.

— Chez les ouvriers exposés au risque de l'amiante, les grands fumeurs courent un risque 45 fois plus élevé que les non-fumeurs, et 92 fois plus élevé que les non-fumeurs, non exposés.

Cette potentialisation se retrouve chez tous les travailleurs exposés aux poussières.

Chez les policiers de Boston il n'a pas été démontré de relation entre les variations du volume expiratoire forcé (F.E.V.) et les horaires de présence dans les carrefours très pollués; alors qu'une réduction significative a été constatée chez les fumeurs, qu'ils soient à un poste de bureau ou à la circulation [64].

Plus optimiste est la constatation faite chez les médecins anglais où l'on constate une diminution de la fréquence du cancer bronchique allant de pair avec une réduction de la consommation du tabac; constatation d'autant plus significative que la tendance est inverse pour le reste de la population.

On peut donc s'étonner que la publicité pour le tabac soit tolérée sinon encouragée, quand on considère les sommes engagées dans la lutte contre la pollution de l'air dont les effets nocifs sont loin d'être prouvés.

Les mesures préventives et curatives

Intéressant le médecin et l'hygiéniste parce qu'elles vont probablement modifier l'incidence de la pollution sur la morbidité, elles vont rendre les enquêtes caduques ou d'interprétation difficile, mais on ne peut que se féliciter de l'attitude quasi unanime à ce sujet.

A l'échelle nationale la plupart des pays ont organisé la surveillance de l'air et adapté la législation aux exigences nouvelles. Les mérite revient là encore à la Grande Bretagne qui a montré la voie par le „Clean Air Act“ de 1956 dont l'efficacité a été démontrée: la pollution par les fumées a diminué de 75% à Londres.

Les travaux et projets de législation ne donnent leur pleine efficacité que s'ils sont universellement appliqués, suffisamment diffusés. C'est le rôle dévolu aux organismes tels que le Conseil de l'Europe ou l'Organisation Mondiale de la Santé dont les récentes publications donnent un état détaillé et actuel de la législation de divers pays membres [81, 82].

L'application à la médecine d'assurance-vie des conclusions de ces diverses enquêtes sera nécessairement limitée, modeste et temporaire.

L'expression actuarielle d'une surmortalité liée à la pollution de l'air ne paraît pas possible. Les travaux qui font état d'une surmortalité concernent d'une part des accidents aigus dont on ne peut tenir compte dans le pronostic à long terme, d'autre part, ils font ressortir une surmortalité urbaine et l'urbanisation est une tendance des pays industrialisés telle que l'on peut prévoir que d'ici la fin du siècle 85% de population sera urbaine. On ne peut envisager de surprimer les habitants des villes — peut-être pourra-t'on accorder une bonification aux ruraux.

Mais si l'influence nocive de la pollution ne peut être considérée par l'actuaire, elle intéresse au plus haut point le médecin d'assurance-vie au stade de la sélection des proposants et de l'appréciation du risque.

Dépistage des facteurs de haut risque chez les candidats à l'assurance-vie

Si les effets nocifs de la pollution sont à peu près admissibles pour une population, il est difficile d'établir une corrélation entre leur influence et un individu précis.

De plus, le contact avec l'air pollué, même pour les professionnels les plus exposés, est limité dans le temps et dans l'espace; la plus grande partie de l'existence se passe dans des micro-atmosphères dont la composition est variable pour chaque foyer et ne peut être objectivement appréciée.

C'est en partie, cette différence fondamentale de durée d'exposition, qui explique le faible retentissement global de la pollution générale comparée aux effets indiscutables et importants de la pollution individuelle.

Quoi qu'il en soit, les individus soumis à cette pollution privée, entrent dans les catégories des sujets plus vulnérables aux pollutions professionnelles ou générales.

Ainsi tout proposant chez qui le médecin d'assurance vie peut mettre en évidence des signes d'irritation bronchique ou des habitudes risquant de les provoquer, devra être considéré comme un risque aggravé.

Les résultats de l'interrogatoire du proposant sont particulièrement importants. Ce temps primordial de l'examen médical d'assurance est difficile et surtout trop souvent négligé ou incomplet.

Par comparaison à un simple questionnaire, l'interrogatoire du médecin a la supériorité de pouvoir solliciter les réponses et surtout interpréter certains symptômes et dévoiler les réticences ou les approximations.

Sans insister sur le détail de l'examen, nous pensons qu'il faut souligner l'intérêt des précisions portant:

- sur l'habitat, le quartier, les conditions de logement,
- la profession et l'emploi exact dans une profession,
- les habitudes en ce qui concerne le tabac avec le nombre d'unités quotidiennes et la manière de fumer, l'ancienneté et les variations éventuelles de cette intoxication,
- les symptômes traduisant une bronchite — toux, expectorations, avec leur chronologie — intermittente ou plus ou moins chronique,
- les symptômes traduisant une insuffisance respiratoire — dyspnée à l'effort ou paroxystique.
- les antécédents familiaux plus accessoirement.

L'examen clinique peut recueillir des signes non équivoques:

- d'obstruction bronchiques: râles sifflants expiratoires,
- d'hypersécrétion: toux en fin d'expiration: râles humides,
- d'emphysème — thorax dilaté avec faible variation entre les périmètres mesurés à l'inspiration et à l'expiration.

Les examens complémentaires sont très utiles, dans la mesure où ils confirment un trouble ventilatoire présumé et permettent de l'objectiver par des chiffres qui rendent les conclusions du médecin d'assurance plus crédibles pour le client, le producteur ou le réassureur qui tarifie sur dossier.

Lorsque les capitaux le justifient, lorsque l'examen a fait entrevoir une altération bronchique et surtout si les garanties concernant l'invalidité sont réclamées, il est indispensable de réclamer un enregistrement, au moins succint, de la ventilation, comportant un test de mobilisation expiratoire „Volume expiratoire Maximum Seconde“ (V. E. M. S.) ou „Forced Expiratory Volume“ (F. E. V.) qui puisse objectiver le freinage bronchique.

Cet examen peut et doit se faire lors des bilan de santé systématiques, ou „Check up" et des exemples dont celui de la Compagnie que nous représentons, montrent que la réalisation en est simple et peu coûteuse [2].

L'electrocardiogramme est utile, mais le retentissement cardio-vasculaire, s'il existe, s'apprécie aussi bien à l'examen clinique.

A défaut d'examen fonctionnel respiratoire, ou conjointement, il faut insister sur les renseignements apportés par un examen radiologique bien fait, soit radioscopie, soit radiographie comportant 4 clichés: face et profil, en inspiration et en expiration extrême.

Cette étude radiologique peut mettre en évidence des signes d'emphysème ou du moins une anomalie de la cinétique et du contraste entre inspiration et expiration; elle a de plus l'intérêt de dépister une affection latente, tumorale ou infectieuse.

Au terme d'un examen dont on voit la simplicité et qui correspond à ce que la plupart des compagnies exigent pour des capitaux de moyenne importance, il est possible au médecin d'assurance vie de classer le proposant dans l'une des catégories suivantes:

1. Proposant ayant un ou plusieurs facteurs de haut risque mais ne souffrant pas de maladie actuelle.

Tel nous parait être le cas des fumeurs ou des professionnels exposés.

Il n'a jamais été proposé jusqu'à présent de réclamer une surprime aux grands fumeurs; il est toutefois admis que le risque est significatif au-delà de 10 cigarettes par jour et croît avec la quantité fumée.

Nous pensons qu'une surprime doit être réclamée aux fumeurs de 20 cigarettes quotidiennes ou plus. Chiffre ramené à 10 pour les professions exposées.

2. Proposant ayant des signes de bronchite occasionnels. Cette catégorie ne justifie une surprime que si elle présente en outre un facteur de risque par le tabac ou par la profession.

3. Proposant ayant des bronchites hivernales répétées depuis au moins trois hivers.

4. Proposant ayant des signes de bronchite persistants en dehors des périodes hivernales depuis au moins un an.

5. Patients ayant des signes d'asthme ou d'insuffisance respiratoire chronique.

Ces trois catégories correspondent à des risques tarés de gravité croissante et ne sauraient être acceptés sans augmentation de prime et autres réserves.

6. Patients ayant ou ayant eu des signes d'insuffisance ventriculaire droite ou une poussée d'insuffisance respiratoire nécessitant l'hospitalisation et assistance ventilatoire.

Ce groupe ne peut être assuré, compte-tenu de la gravité du pronostic à ce stade.

Les taux de surmortalité que l'on peut proposer ne sont basés sur aucune étude globale, mais nous avons l'habitude d'attribuer un taux allant de 50% dans les atteintes bronchiques simples, à 100% dans les formes chroniques avec gêne à l'effort.

---

[2] Un service d'examens de santé, traité par ordinateur et portant le nom d'IPC (investigations pré-cliniques) a été suscité par le groupe des Assurances Générales de France.

Mais plus importante peut-être que le taux de surmortalité, nous apparaît la réserve sur la durée d'une part et les garanties d'invalidité d'autre part.

Les affections pulmonaires qui nous concernent, cancer bronchique ou BPO peuvent se rencontrer dès la quarantaine et même avant, mais leur fréquence se manifeste surtout dans les sixièmes et septièmes décennies de l'existence.

Nous pensons donc qu'il est possible de limiter les surprimes et les exclusions pour des contrats dont le terme correspond à l'âge de 50 voire 55 ans.

En revanche, toute durée de contrat dépassant le terme de 65 ans, contrats de plus en plus demandés, devra être accordée avec circonspection et au besoin avec une aggravation de prime plus lourde.

De même, le bénéfice des garanties en cas d'incapacité temporaire ou permanente, ne devrait pas être accordé au delà de la cinquantième année, à moins qu'un nouvel examen médical puisse, à cette date, permettre de prolonger ces garanties.

L'on peut en effet conclure sur l'importance de ce risque et les abus que peut entraîner sa couverture.

La surmortalité par intoxication tabagique a été démontrée, les risques professionnels sont admis, les risques vitaux de la pollution atmosphérique restent à établir par les multiples travaux en cours; mais dans les trois domaines on peut raisonnablement espérer que la prévention permettra de réduire progressivement les risques à long terme.

Autrement dit, en matière d'espérance de vie, il est peu probable que nous assistions à un renversement de la tendance observée depuis les 50 dernières années, à savoir le recul des âges de décès.

En revanche dans les pays industrialisés la législation en matière de retraite et d'invalidité se fait de plus en plus libérale et les compagnies d'assurance devront en tenir compte dans la sélection de leurs proposants et les limites de leurs garanties et se méfier des affections respiratoires chroniques; elles font mourir relativement tard, mais elles rendent invalide tôt et longtemps.

Bibliographie

1. Amdur, M. O.: The respiratory response of guinea pigs to sulfuricacid mist. A.M.A. Arch. indust. Health **18**, 407 (1958).
2. Arner, E. C., Rhoades, R. A.: Long term nitrogen dioxide exposure. Arch. environm. Hlth **26**, 156 (1973).
3. Auerbach, O., Cuylerhammond, E., Garfinkel, H., Carmine, B.: Relation of smoking and age to emphysema. New Engl. J. Med. **280**, 853 (1972).
4. Aviado, D. M., Sadavongvivad, C., Carrillo, L. R.: Cigarette smoke and pulmonary emphysema. Influence of bronchodilators and biogenic amines in experimental induction in rats. Arch. environm. Hlth **20**, 483 (1970).
5. Berson, S. A., Yalow, R. S., Saito, T., Selikoff, I. J.: Antibodies to "alcalase" after industrial exposure. New Engl. J. Med. **284**, 688 (1971).
6. Bouhuys, A.: Airways dynamics. Physiology and Pharmocology. Edit: C. C. Thomas, Springfield (Ill.) 1970.
7. Bouhuys, A., Peters, J. M.: Control of environmental lung disease. New Engl. J. Med. **283**, 573 (1970).
8. Bove, J. L., Siedenberg, S.: Airbone lead and Carbon Monoxide at 45th Street, New York City. Amer. Ass. Advanc. Sci. **167**, 986 (1970).

9. Camner, P., Helstrom, P. A., Philipson, K.: Carbon dust and mucociliary transport. Arch. environm. Hlth **26**, 294 (1973).
10. Chahinian, Ph., Chretien, J.: Fréquence actuelle du cancer bronchitique, données épidémiologiques et facteurs étiologiques. Rev. Prat (Paris) **23**, 1113 (1973).
11. Chretien, J.: Les maladies pulmonaires provoquées par l'inhalation d'antigènes organiques. Journée Méd. Annuelle de Broussais-LaCharité, p. 103 (1969). Edit.: Sandoz, Paris 1969.
12. Desplaces, A., Charreire, J., Izard, C.: Action de la phase gazeuse de fumée de cigarettes sur la transformation lymphoblastique du petit lymphocyte humain. Rev. Eur. d'Etudes Clin. Biol. **16**, 822 (1971).
13. Dilley, R. B. Nadel, J. A.: Powdered tantalum: its use as a roentgenographic contrast material. Ann. oto-rhinol-laryng. **79**, 945 (1970).
14. Easton, R. E., Murphey, S. D.: Experimental ozone preexposure and histamine. Effect on the acute toxicity and respiratory function effects of histamine in guinea pigs. Arch. environm. Hlth **15**, 160 (1967).
15. Ferris, B. G. Jr., Anderson, D. O.: The prevalence of chronic respiratory disease in a New Hampshire town. Ann. Rev. resp. Dis. **86**, 165 (1962).
16. Ferris, B. G. Jr., Anderson, D. O.: Epidemiological studies related to air pollution: comparison of Berlin, N. H. and Chilliwack, British Columbia. Proc. roy. Soc. Med. (suppl.) **57**, 979 (1964).
17. Freemann, G., Crane, S. C., Furiosi, N. J.: Healing in rat lung after subacute exposure to nitrogen dioxide. Amer. Rev. resp. Dis. **100**, 662 (1969).
18. Freeman, G., Furiosi, N. J., Haydon, G. B.: Effects of continuous exposure of 0.8 ppm NO_2 on respiration of rats. Arch. environm. Hlth **13**, 454 (1966).
19. Freeman, G., Crane, S. C., Stephens, R. J., Furiosi, N. J.: Pathogenesis of nitrogen dioxide-induced lesion in the rat lung. A review and presentation of new observations. Amer. Rev. resp. Dis. **98**, 429 (1968).
20. Freeman, G., Crane, S. C., Stephens, R. J., Furiosi, N. J.: The subacute nitrogen dioxide-induced lesion of the rat lung. Arch. environm. Hlth **18**, 609 (1969).
21. Freeman, G., Stephens, R. J., Crane, S. C., Furiosi, N. J.: Lesion of the lung in rats continuously exposed to two parts per million of nitrogen dioxide. Arch. environm. Hlth **17**, 181 (1968).
22. Freeman, G., Stephens, R. J., Coffin, D. L., Stara, J. F.: Changes in dogs' lungs after long-term exposure to ozone. Arch. environm. Hlth **26**, 209 (1973).
23. Garbe, E., Brunet, M.: Cancer et pollution atmosphérique, quelques aspects de pathologie géographique. Bull. l'inserm **25**, 201 (1970).
24. Gell, P. G., Coombs, R. A.: Clinical aspects of immunology. Edit.: Blackwell, Oxford 1968.
25. Gernez-Rieux, C., Voisin, C., Wallarert, C., Roussel, P. A.: Le poumon du fermier. Gaz. Hôp. (Paris) **138**, 877 (1966).
26. Gilson, J. C.: Asbestos Cancer Past and Future Hazards. Proc. roy. Soc. Med. **66**, 395 (1973).
27. Godin, G., Wright, G., Shepard, R.: Urban exposure to carbon monoxide. Arch. environm. Hlth **25**, 305 (1972).
28. Golstein, E., Eagle, M. C., Hoeprich: Effect of nitrogen dioxide on pulmonary bacterial defense mechanisms. Arch. environm. Hlth **26**, 202 (1973).
29. Gross, P., Harvey, R. A., Treville, R. T. P. de: Pulmonary reaction to metallic aluminium powders. Arch. environm. Hlth **26**, 227 (1973).
30. Hammond, E. C.: Epidemiological evidence on the effects of air pollution. 60th Annual Meeting 1967 paper 67–78.
31. Hammond, E. C., Selikoff, I. J.: The effects of air pollution epidemiological evidence. Proc. Internat. Conf. on Pneumoconiosis Johannesburg, South Africa, April 23 – May 2 1969, p. 188. Dept. of Mines Gvt of South Africa édit 1969.
32. Hammond, E. C., Selikoff, I. J.: The effects of air pollution. Epidemiological evidence. Proc. Internat. Conf. on Pneumoconiosis Johannesburg, South Africa, April 23 – May 2 1969, p. 188.
33. Hart, F. C., Ferrand, F., Blade, E.: Data report aerometric network. Calender Year 1971. The city of New York. Environmental protection administration. Department of Air Resourcses 1971.

34. HART, F. C., FERRAND, F., BLADE, E.: Data report aerometric network. Spring season. March to April 1972. The city of New York. Environmental protection administration. Department of Air Resources 1972.
35. HOLLAND, W. W., HALIT, T., BENNETT, A. E.: Indications for measure to be taken in childhood to prevent chronic respiratory disease. Milbank Mem. Fd Quart. **47**, 215 (1969).
36. IMBUS, H. R., SUM, M. W.: Byssinosis. Arch. environm. Hlth **26**, 183 (1973).
37. INOH, T., AVIADO, D. M.: Cardiopulmonary effects of progestational agents in emphysematous rats. Chest Dis. Index **59**, 659 (1971).
38. IPSEN, J., INGENITO, F. E., DEANE, M.: Episodic morbidity and mortality in relation to air pollution. Arch. environm. Hlth **18**, 456 (1969).
39. IPSEN, J., DEANE, M., INGENITO, F. E.: Relationships of acute respiratory disease to atmospheric pollution. Arch. environm. Hlth **18**, 462 (1969).
40. KOCHMAN, S., MARTIN, J. C., BUREAU, G., DUBOIS DE MONTRENAUD, J. M.: Etude infrastructure des lésions pulmonaires après inhalation de micropolyspora faeni chez le lapin sensibilisé. Rev. franç. Allerg. **21**, 220 (1971).
41. KOURILSKY, R., BRILLE, D., HATTE, J., CARTON, J., HINGLAIS, J. C.: Enquête sur l'étiologie et la prophylaxie de la bronchite chronique et de l'emphysème pulmonaire. Paris: Caisse régionale de sécurité sociale de Paris.
42. LANGER, A. M., RUBIN, I. B., SELIKOFF, I. J.: Chemical characterization of asbestos body cores by electron micropores analysis. J. Histochem. Cytochem. 20, 723 (1972).
43. LANGER, A. M., RUBIN, I. B., SELIKOFF, I. J., POOLEY, F. D.: Chemical characterization of uncoated asbestos fibers from the lungs of asbestos workers by electron micropore analysis. J. Histochem. Cytochem. 20, 735, (1972).
44. LASSERRE, O., GARBE, E., FLAMENT, R.: L'enquête française sur la morbidité par cancer en relation avec certains facteurs étiologiques: l'alcoolisme et la pollution atmosphérique. Bull. de l'inserm **23**, 1301 (1968).
45. LEWIS, T. R., MOORMAN, W. J., LUDMANN, M. F., CAMPBELL, K. I.: Toxicity of long term exposure to oxides of sulfur. Arch. environm. Hlth **26**, 16 (1973).
46. LI, C. C.: Theory of path. coefficients. Edit.: University of Chicago Press, Chicago 1955.
47. MCCAROLL, J. R., BRADLEY, H. W.: Excess mortality as an indicator of health effects of air pollution. Ann. J. publ. Hlth **56**, 1933 (1966).
48. MCCAROLL, J.: Measurements of morbidity and mortality related to air pollution. J. Air Pollut. Control Ass. **17**, 203 (1967).
49. MACKLER, A. D., NICHOLSON, W. J., ROHL, A. N., SELIKOFF, I. J.: L'asbeste chrysotile dans l'air ambiant des centres urbains des Etats-Unis. Rev. Tuberc. (Paris) **36**, 1193 (1972).
50. MOLINA, C.: Bronchopneumopathies par inhalation des poussières organiques d'origine végétale ou animale. Encyclopédie médico-chirurgicale Poumon **5**, 6018 (1969).
51. MURPHY, S. D.: A review of effects on animals of exposure to auto exhaust and some of its components. J. Air Pollut. Control Ass. **14**, 303 (1964).
52. MURPHY, S. D., ULRICH, C. E.: Multi-animal test system for measuring effects of irritant gases and vapors on respiratory function of guinea pigs. Amer. industr. Hyg. Ass. J. **25**, 28 (1964).
53. NADEL, J. A., CABEZAS, G. A., AUSTIN, J. H. M.: In vivo Roentgenographic examiantion of parasympathetic innervation of small airways. Use of powdered tantalum and a fine focal spot X-ray tube. Invest. Radiol. **6**, 9 (1971).
54. NADEL, J. A., COMROE, J. H.: Acute effects of inhalation of cigarette smoke on airway conductance. J. appl. Physiol. **16**, 713 (1961).
55. NADEL, J. A., SALEM, H., TAMPLIN, B., TOKIWE, Y.: Mechanism of bronchoconstriction during inhalation of sulfur dioxide. J. appl. Physiol. **20**, 164 (1965).
56. PEPYS, J.: Hypersensitivity diseases of the lungs due to fungi and organic dusts. Edit.: KARGER, Bâle, New York 1969.
57. RIVOLIER, C. et J.: Météoropathologie humaine „Cahiers Sandoz“ N° 22 Avril 1972.
58. ROY-CHONDHURY, A. K., MOONEY, T. F. Jr., REEVES, A. L.: Trace metals in asbestos carcinogenesis. Arch. environm. Hlth **26**, 253 (1973).
59. RUSSEL, M. A., COLE, P. V., BROWN, E.: Absorption by non-smokers of carbon monoxide from room air polluted by tobacco smoke. Lancet **17**, 576 (1973).

60. Scheniderman, M. A., Levin, D. L.: Trends in lung cancer. Mortality, Incidence, Diagnosis, treatment. Smoking and urbanization. Cancer (Philad.) **30**, 1320 (1972).
61. Selikoff, I. J., Nicholson, W. I., Langer, A. M.: Asbestos air pollution. Arch. environm. Hlth **25**, 1 (1972).
62. Sherwin, R. P., Margolick, J. B., Azen, S. P.: Hypertrophy of alveolar wall cells secondary to air pollutant. Arch. environm. Hlth **26**, 297 (1973).
63. Shubik, Ph.: Current status of chemical carcinogenesis. Proc. nat. Acad. Sci. (Wash.) **69**, 1052 (1972).
64. Speizer, F. E., Ferris, B. G. Jr., Burgess, W., Diberardinis, L.: Exposure to automobile Exhaust. I. Prevalence of respiratory symptoms and disease. II. Pulmonary function measurements. III. An environmental Assessment. Arch. environm. Hlth **26**, 313 (1973).
65. Stewart, R. D., Peterson, J. E., Fisher, T. N., Hosko, M. J., Baretta, E. D., Dodd, H. C., Herrmann, A. A.: Experimental human exposure to high concentrations of carbon monoxide. Arch. environm. Hlth **26**, 1 (1973).
66. Stupfel, M., Bouley, G.: Physiological and biochemical affects on rats and mice exposed to smalls concentrations of carbon monoxide for long periods. Ann. N. Y. Acad. Sci. **174**, 342 (1970).
67. Stupfel, M., Magnier, M., Romary, F., Tran, M. H., Moutet, J. P.: Lifelong exposure of S.P.F. rats to automative exhaust gas. Arch. environm. Hlth. **26**, 264 (1973).
68. Stupfel, M.: Bronchites expérimentales par divers polluants atmosphériques. Bull. physio. path. resp. **5**, 485 (1969).
69. Stupfel, M., Romary, F., Magnier, M., Polianski, J.: Toxicité aiguë comparée, chez la souris mâle et femelle de quelques polluants atmosphériques: gaz d'échappement de moteur d'automobile, oxydes d'azote, anhydride sulfureux, ozone, ammoniac et gaz carbonique. Rapport Inserm du 20 mai 1972.
70. Stupfel, M.: Mission d'études aux Etats-Unis et au Canada relative aux relations entre la bronchite et la pollution atmosphérique. Rapport Inserm du 20 mai 1972.
71. Stupfel, M., Roussel, A.: Influence du sexe sur la mortalité par hypoxie, confinement et oxyde de carbone. Comptes rendus de séances de la Société de Biologie **163**, 310 (1969).
72. Tacquet, A., Devulder, B., Martin, J. C., Lebouffan, L.: Appareil respiratoire et nuisances profesionnelles. A — pneumoconiose des mineurs du charbon. Etude expérimentale des interactions de l'empoussiérage pulmonaire et des infections mycobactériennes. Lille méd. **16**, 1231 (1971).
73. Thomson, M. L., Pavia, D.: Long term tobacco smoking and mucociliary clearance. Arch. environm. Hlth **26**, 86 (1973).
74. Vassalo, C., Domm, B. M., Poe, R., Duncombe, M., Gee, J.: NO_2 gas and NO_2 effects on alveolar macrophage phagocytosis and metabolism. Arch. environm. Hlth **26**, 270 (1973).
75. Voisin, C., Macquet, V.: Affections respiratoires aiguës et pollution atmosphérique. Pneumophtisiologie **23**, 343 (1973).
76. Zeidberg, L. D., Prindle, R. A., Landau, E.: The Nashville air pollution study I. Sulfur dioxide and bronchial asthma. A preliminary report. Amer. Rev. resp. Dis. **84**, 489 (1961).
77. Zeidberg, L. D., Prindle, R. A., Landau, E.: The Nashville air pollution study III. Morbidity in relation to air pollution. Amer. J. publ. Hlth **54**, 85 (1964).
78. Zeidberg, L. D., Horton, R. J. M., Landau, E., Hagstrom, R. M., Sprague, H. A.: The Nashville air pollution study V. Mortality form diseases of the respiratory system in relation to air pollution. Arch. environm. Hlth **15**, 214 (1967).
79. Le cancer du poumon en Europe occidentale (Conseil de l'Europe) 2ème édition.
80. La pollution de l'air en Europe. Chronique O.M.S. **26**, 251 (1972).
81. Programme à long terme de lutte contre la pollution du milieu. Evolution de la lutte contre la pollution de l'air en Europe 1971 — Bureau Régional de l'Europe O.M.S. — Copenhague.
82. Risque pour la santé du fait de l'environnement. O.M.S. 1972.
83. La pollution de l'air en France — Résultats de mesure. Environnement XVIIème volume. La Documentation Française — 29–31 quai Voltaire.
84. Royal College of Physicians of London (1970). Air pollution and health: a report for the Royal College of Physicians of London, Londres, Pitman.

85. Bignon, J., Depierre, A., Bonnaud, G., Goni, J., Brouet, G. avec la coll. de Dufour, G., Jaurand, M. G., Leturcq, E., Monchaux, G., Saint-Etienne, L.: Mise en évidence des corps ferrugineux par microfiltration de l'expectoration. Corrélation avec le risque asbestosique. La Nouvelle Presse Médicale, 23 Juni 1973 2. N° 25.
86. Bignon, J., Bonnaud, G., Jaurand, M. C., Goni, J., Dufour, G.: Méthode d'isolement et de concentration des „corps ferrugineux" du poumon humain. Leur fréquence et leur signification. J. franç. Méd. Chir. thor. **24**, 71 (1970).
87. Brouet, G., Bignon, J., Bonnaud, G., Goni, J.: Incidence sur la santé de la pollution atmosphérique par l'asbeste ou autres particules fibreuses. Rev. Tuberc. (Paris) **35**, 461 (1971).
88. Goni, J., Remond, G., Jaurand, M. C., Bignon, J., Bonnaud, G., Brouet, G.: Possibilités actuelles d'identification des corps ferrugineux du poumon humain par la microsonde électronique et le microscope électronique à balayage. Rev. Tuberc. (Paris) **36**, 1223 (1972).
89. Decroix, G., Feldmann, A.: Pneumopathies interstitielles d'hypersensibilité. Le médecin de France **322, 27**.

Pollution par les radiations ionisantes

Dr. J.-V. Marique

Introduction

La pollution radioactive présente un caractère dangereux et complexe. Elle est liée à l'utilisation de substances radioactives et de l'énergie atomique en temps de paix.

L'arme atomique, si elle était encore utilisée, bouleverserait tous les paramètres actuels, livrant l'humanité à un sort peu enviable autant par son action directe que retardée.

La physique nucléaire est une science jeune qui comporte encore beaucoup d'inconnues et n'a pas livré tous les secrets ni tous les dangers que la radioactivité artificielle engendre.

Et cependant, l'industrie atomique s'est entourée de procédés de détection, de contrôle et de prévention jamais égalés dans les autres activités industrielles.

Des accidents se sont produits mais, en général, ils sont mineurs. Il faut se réjouir de la fructueuse collaboration des physiciens, des chimistes, des ingénieurs et des médecins dans le domaine si périlleux que constituent la radiotoxicologie et la radiopathologie.

Nous étudierons successivement:

1. Les unités et doses d'exposition admises.
2. Les sources d'irradiation.
3. Les effets polluants des radiations ionisantes.
4. Les effets sur l'organisme des radiations ionisantes.

1. Unités et doses d'exposition admissibles

1.1. Les radiations ionisantes

Les radiations ionisantes sont
- soit électromagnétiques: photons ou quantité de rayons X ou gamma;
- soit corpusculaires: électrons, positons, rayons bêta, protons, neutrons, particules alpha, particules lourdes, etc.

Elles produisent sur leur passage l'ionisation directe ou indirecte de la matière.

1.2. La dose d'exposition

est la quantité de radiations ionisantes délivrée en un point donné. L'unité de dose d'exposition aux rayons X ou gamma est le Roentgen.

1.3. La dose absorbée

est la quantité d'énergie délivrée par des radiations ionisantes à l'unité de poids de la substance irradiée au point considéré, quelle que soit la nature du rayonnement ionisant utilisé. L'unité de dose absorbée est le Rad.

1.4. Le coefficient d'efficacité biologique relative d'une radiation donnée ou coefficient E.B.R.

est le rapport entre une dose absorbée de rayons X et une dose absorbée de la radiation donnée lorsque ces deux doses ont le même effet biologique.

Ce coefficient E.B.R. est variable selon la radiation ionisante absorbée:

Rayonnement	E.B.R.
Rayons X et gamma, électrons et rayons bêta de toutes énergies	1
Neutrons d'une énergie inférieure ou égale à 5 Kev	2,5
Neutrons d'une énergie supérieure à 5 Kev et inférieure ou égale à 10 Mev	10
Protons d'une énergie égale ou inférieure à 10 Mev	10
Particules alpha et autres particules lourdes	10
Noyaux lourds de recul	20

1.5. Dose biologique efficace ou dose E.B.R.

Produit de la dose absorbée exprimée en rads par le coefficient E.B.R. L'unité de dose biologique efficace est le rem.

1.6. Curie

Quantité de nuclide radioactif dans laquelle le nombre de désintégrations par seconde est de $3,7 \times 10^{10}$; il sert d'unité de radioactivité. Le curie est désigné par le symbole Ci.

1.7. Travailleurs professionnellement exposés:

1.7.1. Catégorie A

Ceux qui travaillent dans un espace où une source de radiations ionisantes est susceptible de délivrer une dose individuelle supérieure à 1,5 rem par an.

1.7.2. Catégorie B

Ceux qui travaillent dans un espace où une source de radiations ionisantes est susceptible de délivrer une dose individuelle inférieure à 1,5 rem par an.

1.8. Doses maxima admissibles

1.8.1. Travailleurs de catégorie A

1.8.1.1. Irradiation totale de l'organisme

a) En ce qui concerne l'irradiation totale de l'organisme, la dose cumulée au niveau des organes hématopoïétiques, des gonades et des cristallins, pour une personne professionnellement exposée de catégorie A ne peut dépasser la valeur D établie par la formule de base suivante: $D = 5\ (N - 18)$ ou D est la dose exprimée en rems et où N est l'âge de cette personne, exprimée en années.

b) Commentaire

1. Un individu peut recevoir 5 rems par an.

2. La dose maximum admissible par trimestre est de 3 rems.

Il s'ensuit que si un individu a reçu 3 rems au 1er trimestre et 2 rems au cours du second trimestre, il ne peut plus recevoir de radiations pendant les deux autres trimestres.

3. Patrimoine d'acceptabilité de dose:

L'on ne peut travailler dans l'industrie nucléaire qu'à partir de l'âge de 18 ans. Supposons le cas d'un homme qui commence son activité dans l'industrie nucléaire à l'âge de 30 ans. $N = 30$, $D = 5\,(30 - 18) = 12 \times 5 = 60$ rems. L'on admet que l'intéressé a un patrimoine d'acceptabilité de dose de 60 rems, ceci veut dire qu'au lieu de recevoir 5 rems par an, il peut recevoir 12 rems par an avec un maximum de 3 rems par trimestre.

Il peut recevoir cette dose de 12 rems jusqu'à épuisement de son patrimoine d'acceptabilité, c'est-à-dire donc pendant 5 ans. A partir de la 6me année, il ne pourra plus recevoir que 5 rems par an, soit 3 rems par trimestre.

4. La dose de 3 rems par trimestre doit être fractionnée. Ce n'est qu'exceptionnellement que l'on peut recevoir 3 rems en une seule fois.

1.8.1.2. Irradiation totale concertée

Lors d'une irradiation concertée, une dose de 12,5 rems peut être admise pour les personnes professionnellement exposées de catégorie A.

Si la dose dépasse alors la valeur maximum admise par la formule de base, l'excédent doit être compensé par une diminution de l'exposition ultérieure de sorte qu'en moins de cinq ans, la dose cumulée soit de nouveau au plus égale à la valeur maximum donnée par cette formule.

Les femmes ne peuvent être soumises à une irradiation concertée avant la fin de leur période de procréation.

1.8.1.3. Irradiation totale accidentelle

Lors d'une irradiation totale accidentelle de personnes professionnellement exposées, une dose comprise entre 3 et 25 rems peut être intégrée dans la dose maximum cumulée.

Si le total dépasse la valeur maximum déterminée par la formule de base, l'excédent doit être compensé par une diminution de l'exposition ultérieure de sorte qu'en moins de 10 ans, la dose cumulée soit de nouveau au plus égale à la valeur maximum donnée par cette formule.

1.8.1.4. Irradiation partielle

Lors d'une irradiation partielle de l'organisme, les doses reçues par les organes hématopoïétiques les gonades et les cristallins, ne peuvent dépasser les limites fixées par la formule de base. En outre, la dose maximum admissible est fixée:

a) pour les irradiations externes intéressant les extrémités (mains, avant-bras, pieds et chevilles) à 15 rems par treize semaines et à 60 rems par an;

b) pour les irradiations externes intéressant la peau dans son ensemble à 8 rems par treize semaines et à 30 rems par an.

c) pour les irradiations intéressant les organes internes, à l'exception des organes hématopoïétiques, des gonades et des cristallins à 4 rems par treize semaines et à 15 rems par an.

1.8.2. Travailleurs de catégorie B

1.8.3. Population avoisinante des centres nucléaires

Pour la population avoisinante, la dose maximum admissible est fixée à 0,5 rems par an, cette dose étant celle effectivement reçue au niveau des organes hémato-poïétiques et des gonades.

1.8.4. Population dans son ensemble

Pour la population dans son ensemble, la dose maximum admissible est de 5 rems per capita cumulée pendant une période de 30 ans. Cette dose doit tenir compte, par pondération, des doses reçues par les personnes professionnellement exposées et par la population avoisinante.

Medecine d'assurance vie

1. Il est *utile* de connaître le patrimoine d'acceptabilité de dose.
2. Il est *nécessaire* de connaître la dose en rem de l'irradiation concertée, accidentelle ou partielle.
   Ces éléments sont renseignés sur la fiche d'irradiation annuelle dont il est aisé de demander une copie.
3. Il faut préciser la fonction et le lieu de travail (centrale nucléaire, laboratoire chaud ou froid, industrie, etc.).
4. Il faut connaître la nature du rayonnement auquel est exposé l'intéressé: α, β, γ, x, noyaux lourds, neutrons.

2. Sources d'irradiation

Les sources d'irradiation sont soit naturelles, soit artificielles.

2.1. Sources naturelles

2.1.1. Rayons cosmiques

Ils proviennent des espaces interstellaires et administrent à l'organisme humain une dose qui a été évaluée à 30 millirems environ par an.

Avec l'altitude, la densité des rayons cosmiques augmente rapidement: à 3.000 mètres d'altitude, la dose est triple.

2.1.2. Le sol et les matériaux de construction

qui nous entourent contiennent des traces d'uranium et de thorium dont certains produits de filiation émettent des rayonnements gamma. La dose qui en résulte varie beaucoup d'une région à l'autre. C'est un gaz qui diffuse dans l'air. Il provoque une irradiation externe par son émission gamma.

Mais il est également inhalé et provoque une contamination interne (alpha, bêta, gamma) de l'organisme. On estime à 50 millirems par an la dose qui résulte de cette irradiation ambiante.

2.1.3. La radioactivité *naturelle* provoque une irradiation qui se situe aux environs de 100 millirems par an.

2.1.4. La richesse du *sol* en uranium peut augmenter l'irradiation naturelle qui atteint dans certaines régions des Indes et du Brésil 1500 millirems par an. Très souvent, cette dose se situe entre 150 et 400 millirems par an pour les populations qui vivent dans des régions granitiques où les habitations sont construites avec des matériaux extraits du sol.

2.2. Irradiation artificielle

2.2.1. L'industrie atomique à tous les stades constitue la source d'irradiation la plus importante.

— *Mines d'uranium*
  L'exposition au rayonnement gamma est faible. Par contre, le risque de contamination de l'air par le radon et par les poussières radioactives est important.
— Dans les *usines de traitement du minerai,* le risque est le même.
— Les *usines métallurgiques* séparent l'uranium ou le thorium métallique de ses descendants contenus dans le minerai. Les risques de contamination existent particulièrement lors des travaux avec des oxydes et des fluors.
— Dans les *usines de séparation isotopique,* il y a des risques de contamination accidentelle par des gaz.
— Les *réacteurs nucléaires* exposent le travailleur à
  — l'irradiation par rayonnement gamma et neutrons provenant directement du réacteur lorsque les canaux sont ouverts;
  — l'irradiation gamma ou bêta provenant des produits d'activation retirés des réacteurs;
  — l'irradiation accidentelle provenant des ruptures de canalisation, de fissures des gaines des barreaux de combustible. Ce fut le cas, par exemple, à Windscale (Royaume Uni) en 1957: les quantités de produits de fission rejetés dans l'atmosphère par la cheminée ont été évalués à 20.000 curies d'Iode 135, 20.000 curies de tellure 132, 60 curies de césium 147, 80 curies de strontium 89 et 9 curies de strontium 90. La consommation du lait a dû être interdite pendant trois semaines dans une zone de 50 km^2 et pendant environ deux mois dans une zone située à 20 km au sud de Windscale, par suite de la contamination des pâturages.
— Les *usines de chimie ou de métallurgie* traitent les produits sortant des réacteurs. Ce sont principalement des émetteurs alpha qui comptent parmi les plus dangereux radionuclides.

2.2.2. Les radio-éléments

sont utilisés en médecine, en agriculture, dans l'industrie. Ce sont en général des émetteurs bêta et gamma. On les utilise sous deux formes:

— Sources scellées (gammagraphie, gamma et bêtathérapie). Les accidents possibles sont l'incendie et la chute qui peuvent endommager les gaines de protection.
— Sources libres: le risque de contamination externe et interne par inhalation de gaz est évidemment considérable ainsi que la pollution atmosphérique.

Les applications industrielles de l'énergie nucléaire sont multiples. Citons:

— le traitement atomique des aliments;
— les racleurs de pipe-line;

— la détermination de l'usure des pierres réfractaires des hauts fourneaux;
— l'examen des pièces de fonderie, des soudures, des cuves à pression dans la construction navale et aéronautique;
— les jauges d'épaisseur, de viscosité;
— les éliminateurs de charges statiques;
— la stérilisation de matériel, d'aliments;
— etc.

2.2.3. Les générateurs de rayonnement

(tubes de rayons X, accélérateurs de particules, bêtatrons, etc.) provoquent une irradiation
— par le faisceau direct;
— par le rayonnement secondaire émis par les cibles.

2.2.4. Le rejet des déchets radioactifs

présente un danger qui est fonction de la qualité et de la quantité des produits rejetés.

— Dans les mines d'uranium, le minerai pauvre en uranium ou en thorium est rejeté. Le seul risque pour la population est celui de la pollution des rivières.
— Les résidus des réacteurs nucléaires sont des produits de fission ou d'activation. Il existe un danger de pollution atmosphérique par les poussières et les gaz radioactifs (argon, xénon, krypton) s'échappant des cheminées. Les poussières sont retenues par des filtres mais l'atmosphère peut être contaminée par des gaz.
— Dans les industries chimiques et métallurgiques, les déchets sont traités pour retenir le maximum de radioactivité. La contamination atmosphérique est faible mais les eaux peuvent être polluées par les produits de fission.

2.2.5. Des appareils ou des objets

d'utilisation courante présentent un risque d'irradiation non négligeable: montres et réveils couverts de peinture fluorescente, appareils de rayons X utilisés par certains marchands de chaussures. Ils ont été responsables d'irradiations externes graves.

2.2.6. L'irradiation d'origine médicale

soit thérapeutique, soit à des fins de diagnostic est négligeable. Il faut cependant être très prudent avec les enfants et les femmes enceintes, qui présentent une sensibilité plus grande aux rayonnements.

Les pionniers du radiodiagnostic ont payé chèrement leur tribut à la science. Il existe à Hambourg un monument aux médecins allemands, électroradiologistes, morts victimes du devoir. Il y a 32 noms inscrits actuellement mais sur les 32, 16 sont morts d'électrocution.

2.2.7. Les explosions atomiques

provenant de bombes à fission, à fusion ou à striction magnétique polluent l'atmosphère. Les retombées immédiates ou retardées contaminent les eaux, la flore et la faune atteignant ainsi toute la chaîne alimentaire.

3. Effets polluants des radiations ionisantes

L'air, le sol, les eaux peuvent être contaminés par des radiations ionisantes.

L'importance de ces différents risques varie selon la forme physicochimique, la nature des radio-éléments, la dispersion des effluents.

3.1. Air

Il existe une différence fondamentale entre les rejets d'effluents en marche normale d'un réacteur et les rejets accidentels.

Dans le premier cas, les rejets sont délibérés et l'opérateur en conserve la maîtrise à tout moment. En cas d'accident, les rejets sont imprévus et échappent à tout contrôle.

Les substances radioactives rejetées dans l'air peuvent entraîner une contamination externe et une contamination interne de l'organisme.

3.1.1. Contamination externe

Les rayonnements bêta et gamma émis par les substances radioactives peuvent irradier les individus qui en sont proches.

3.1.2. Contamination interne

Elle est réalisée par l'inhalation d'air pollué par des radio-éléments.

La voie digestive est indirecte, consécutive à une contamination respiratoire.

La contamination transcutanée est exceptionnelle, à la suite de blessures.

3.2. Sol

Les aéerosols radioactifs peuvent se déposer sur le sol, les eaux, les herbages, les récoltes. De là, les éléments radioactifs passent dans des produits qui sont directement consommés par l'homme comme le lait, les légumes, les oeufs, la viande, etc. et entraînent une irradiation interne de l'organisme humain.

Les radio-éléments peuvent également s'infiltrer à travers le sol jusqu'à la nappe phréatique qui communique avec les eaux de surface utilisées par l'homme.

3.3. Eaux

3.3.1. Contamination externe

Elle est conditionnée par des circonstances particulières: bains dans des eaux contaminées, sports nautiques, séjours sur les rives. Cette irradiation externe n'est pas négligeable.

3.3.2. Contamination interne

Elle est généralement plus importante.

Le captage des eaux de surface pour alimenter les réseaux de distribution peut amener une contamination directe ou par voie digestive.

L'eau peut être utilisée pour l'abreuvage des troupeaux et les radio-éléments se retrouveront dans le lait ou la viande.

L'eau peut servir à l'arrosage et à l'irrigation. Les cultures seront ainsi contaminées

— par l'absorption sur la partie foliaire de la plante;
— par incorporation aux tissus mêmes de la plante.

La contamination de l'eau atteint les poissons, les crustacés, les mollusques, le plancton.

L'utilisation d'algues ou de déchets de poissons pour amender les sols ou nourrir les volailles peut entraîner une contamination de l'homme.

4. Effets sur l'organisme des radiations ionisantes

4.1. Effets médicaux

L'extrapolation à l'homme des résultats de laboratoires obtenus sur l'animal étant peu valable dans l'ensemble, le meilleur enseignement passe par l'irradiation de l'homme lui-même et l'observation systématique de son devenir. Ce sont les accidents aigus d'irradiation totale de l'organisme qui nous en fournissent les moyens.

4.1.1. Doses sublèthales

Déjà pour 10^2 à $2 \cdot 10^2$ r apparaissent les premiers malaises. Ce sont des signes généraux se traduisant par une asthénie parfois fort longue, de l'inappétence et quelques nausées. La composante hématopoïétique est présente mais les troubles sanguins qu'elle engendre sont faibles et récupérables spontanément.

Au fur et à mesure qu'on approche des $5 \cdot 10^2$ r, la symptomatologie se fait plus critique.

On distingue quatre périodes:

a) *Les premières heures qui suivent l'accident* (durée quelques jours)

— asthénie, adynamie,
— anorexie, nausées et vomissements au moindre mouvement,
— sudation,
— paresthésies des membres supérieurs, dépression psychique.

b) *Phase de latence* (durée ± 15 à 20 jours). Nette amélioration toute apparente de l'état général qui contraste avec des
signes cutanés: érythème, radiodermite
signes sanguins: chute des lymphocytes (dès la 6e heure), des granulocytes, thrombocytes et érythrocytes.

Parfois la chute des granulocytes est précédée d'une polynucléose transitoire
signes médullaires: aplasie progressive pouvant être totale après 20 jours
syndromes hémorragiques: épistaxis, gingivoragie, purpura, etc.

c) *Phase critique* (durée de ± 10 jours à ± 21 jours). L'état général s'effondre — sujet stuporeux, fébrile, anorexique. La radiodermite associée à la radioépithélite témoignent des atteintes cutanées et muqueuses. Le contrôle par antibiotiques de la flore intestinale est fort important pour éviter la septicémie sans cependant perdre de vue la possibilité de développement d'une mycose intestinale ou pulmonaire souvent mortelle.

d) *Convalescence* (progression lente). Persistance d'une asthénie pendant longtemps.

4.1.2. Doses léthales

Entre $5 \cdot 10^2$ et 10^3 r, la symptomatologie décrite s'accentue, les manifestations digestives pouvant aller jusqu'à l'apparition d'hémorragies et de perforation intestinale.

La thérapeutique nécessite dans ce cas, en plus de l'antibiothérapie, des greffes de moëlle osseuse.

4.1.3. Doses supraléthales

Dès qu'on dépasse 10^3 r, les possibilités de survie s'amenuisent très rapidement malgré la thérapeutique. Le malade présente une épithélite étendue de la paroi digestive et une nécrose des plaques de Peyer avec possibilité de perforation. Cette phase digestive qui peut s'accompagner d'occlusion intestinale est mortelle.

Enfin, pour des doses de $5 \cdot 10^3$ et plus, la mort survient en quelques heures et semble correspondre à une atteinte du système nerveux central.

La symptomatologie comprend: céphalées, agitation, puis état stuporeux et mort.

4.2. Troubles génitaux

Toute irradiation des organes génitaux entraîne une altération plus ou moins prononcée des cellules germinatives.

Chez l'homme

Les spermatogonies sont très radiosensibles. Leurs mitoses, très nombreuses normalement, sont bloquées en quelques heures et les spermatogonies, elles-mêmes disparaissent en 24 heures environ. Les spermatocytes, spermatides et spermatozoïdes sont plus radiorésistants, donc peu altérés par le rayonnement. Ils fléchissent nettement au bout de 15 jours environ (maturation cellulaire = 3 semaines) et ne réapparaissent, quand l'azoospermie n'est pas définitive, qu'après plusieurs semaines à plusieurs mois.

La glande intersticielle par contre ne subit aucun effet apparent des radiations et le désir sexuel n'est donc pas perturbé.

Chez la femme

A la puberté, tous les ovocytes sont constitués.

Ceux-ci étant radiosensibles, leur destruction par le rayonnement entraîne une stérilisation organique doublée d'une stérilisation hormonale.

C'est ce qu'on appelle la castration radiothérapique ($\pm$ 600 r). La récupération partielle est possible lorsque la dose absorbée n'est pas trop grande.

Mais un danger beaucoup plus insidieux existe aussi pour des doses faibles et répétées au niveau génital: il s'agit de la mutation.

4.3. Effets génétiques

L'action des radiations peut porter:

a) sur le chromosone : lésion chromosomique;
b) sur le gène : mutation.

Le matériel chromosomique humain comporte 46 chromosones. Les gènes se disposent en un ordre précis le long des chromosones. Ils sont environ 500.

4.3.1. Lésions des chromosomes

Elles peuvent atteindre soit une chromatide soit le chromosome entier (constitué de deux chromatides) et ceci en un ou en plusieurs endroits.

La restitution ad integrum est possible. Dans le cas contraire, il y a recombinaison selon des types divers ou création d'un morceau de chromosome qui va évoluer pour son propre compte.

Les conséquences pour la vie cellulaire sont importantes et entraînent souvent la mort de la cellule lors des divisions suivantes.

4.3.2. Lésions des gènes ou mutations

Sans atteinte apparente du chromosome, les radiations peuvent entraîner des modifications de structure des gènes qu'ils supportent et créer ainsi des modifications qui répondent au rôle joué par le ou les gènes touchés.

Ces modifications irréversibles mais compatibles avec la vie cellulaire, se retrouvent donc dans les cellules filles.

Ceci implique d'une part que des irradiations ultérieures auront un effet cumulatif, d'autre part que le caractère d'irréversibilité du phénomène prend une importance toute particulière dans l'atteinte des cellules reproductrices. Nous pouvons donc définir la mutation génique comme une modification soudaine, fortuite, stable d'une caractéristique héréditaire.

4.4. Effets cancérigènes

Rappelons que les cancers représentent environ 13% de la mortalité générale dans les pays européens.

4.4.1. Cancers radio-induits

— Les cancers sur radiodermites peuvent survenir après un temps de latence très long, de l'ordre de 15 à 20 ans.

— Le cancer des radiologues obéit aux mêmes lois: l'irradiation chronique répétée des mains mal protégées fait apparaître des troubles trophiques de la peau qui se transforment progressivement et deviennent des épithéliomas. Ce fut principalement le sort de la première génération de radiologues.

— Rappelons le premier accident spectaculaire survenu pendant la guerre de 1914, dans l'usine de montres lumineuses de New-Jersey: on utilisait une pâte phosphorescente renfermant des traces de radium et les ouvrières humidifiaient les pinceaux avec leur salive; il en résulta rapidement une épidémie de fractures spontanées; mais un certain nombre des survivantes firent des sarcomes osseux et des carcinomes des sinus après 8 à 10 ans. Le radium et ses dérivés comportent des émetteurs alpha qui se fixent dans les os; ils renferment le Ra D dont la période est de 22 ans; c'est un émetteur bêta, mais il engendre le Ra F, émetteur alpha. Si la période physique du radium et de ses descendants est de 1600 ans, leur période biologique se situe entre 21 et 44 ans et la période effective est voisine de 44 années. Il en résulte que, si la quantité fixée est insuffisante pour entraîner des troubles sanguins rapidement mortels, le sujet sera soumis pendant toute son existence à une irradiation extrêmement caustique de son squelette.

— Une autre variété de cancer professionnel radio-induit se rencontre dans les mines d'uranium. Dès 1926, Rostodki signalait que, dans les mines de pechblende de Schneeberg en Saxe, 50% des travailleurs décédés entre 1921 et 1926 avaient un carcinome pulmonaire.

Peu après, une hécatombe analogue était signalée dans les mines de Tchécoslovaquie. L'étiologie en est complexe car l'atmosphère de ces mines renferme d'autres poussières peut-être cancérigènes (arsenic, cobalt, nickel, silice, etc.); mais on est d'accord pour estimer que le principal coupable est le radon. Des mesures faites en 1945 par Mitchell ont montré que la concentration moyenne de radon à laquelle ces mineurs avaient été exposés était d'environ $1{,}5 \times 10^8$ Ci/l et que les cellules épithéliales des grosses bronches avaient reçu 0,13 rads de rayonnement alpha par journée de huit heures, alors que la dose admissible doit être inférieure à 5×10^{11} Ci/l.

— Etant donné l'énorme importance économique qu'a pris l'uranium, on a étudié, dans de nombreux pays, les conditions de travail dans les mines et on est arrivé à des conclusions très analogues. Dans les mines de fluorine de Terre-Neuve, 45% des décès enregistrés entre 1952 et 1961 sont dus au cancer pulmonaire. Les mines d'uranium du Colorado dégageaient, en 1948, des doses de radon comprises entre 20 et 230 fois les valeurs maxima admissibles. En 1960, on a estimé qu'environ 10.000 travailleurs avaient été exposés à un risque qui devra se traduire par 60% de cancers pulmonaires avec un temps de latence de 7 à 27 ans. Depuis lors, des mesures draconiennes ont été prises pour assurer une ventilation convenable des mines et une protection individuelle par masques, mais les travailleurs ayant inhalé antérieurement ces poussières restent très menacés et doivent être soumis à un contrôle pulmonaire très strict.

— Un troisième exemple est donné par le thorothrast, suspension colloïdale de bioxyde de thorium qui a été utilisée très couramment entre 1928 et 1945 comme opacifiant en radio-diagnostic. Introduit dans une cavité ou dans un tissu, le thorothrast ne se résorbe pas et demeure en grande partie au lieu d'injection.
Utilisé par voie intra-veineuse, il se concentre progressivement dans le tissu réticulo-endothélial du foie et de la rate. En 1962, une enquête faite par Dahlgen relevait 68 cas de sarcomes ou de carcinomes survenus soit au lieu d'injection (35 cas), soit dans le foie (33 cas), avec des périodes de latence variant entre 13 et 24 ans. Depuis cette époque, les recherches se multiplient, mais il est très difficile de retrouver les malades radiographiés avec ce produit, et surtout de connaître les doses administrées. Lorsque l'on a pu faire des autopsies, on a toujours trouvé du thorium présent dans la zone cancéreuse. Dans certains cas, on a pu estimer que les doses cumulées par le foie étaient de l'ordre de 1000 à 1500 rads.

— Il est abusif d'accuser la radio-iode et les scintigrammes de provoquer des cancers de la thyroïde. Les doses sont très faibles; la période effective est très brève; d'autre part, les carcinomes thyroïdiens ne sont pas fréquents.

4.4.2. Leucémies

— La leucémie peut être un effet pathologique tardif de l'irradiation.

— On distingue:
  a) Leucémie aiguë: délai d'apparition de 3 mois à 15 ans;
  b) Leucémie myéloïde chronique: délai d'apparition de 10 ans maximum;
  c) Leucémie lymphoïde chronique: délai d'apparition de 18 à 35 ans.

— La fréquence des leucémies chez l'adulte est de 1,5/10 000, chez l'enfant de 4,6/10 000, soit moins de 1% du nombre total de cancers.
— Les médecins japonais de l'hôpital d'Hiroshima ont dressé la statistique suivante, concernant les cas de leucémies observés de 1945 à 1955:

Distance de l'épicentre	Survivants	Leucémies	Pourcentage
moins de 1000 mètres	1.250	16 cas	128/10.000
de 1000 à 1500 mètres	10.350	28 cas	28/10.000
de 1500 à 2000 mètres	18.450	6 cas	3,8/10.000
de 2000 à 3000 mètres	30.350	7 cas	2,3/10.000
plus de 3000 mètres	37.700	4 cas	1,6/10.000

— Une enquête importante américaine a recherché l'influence carcinogénétique des examens radiologiques de pelvimétrie pratiqués au cours de la grossesse et impliquant une irradiation totale de l'embryon.
Cette étude porte sur 734.243 enfants américains nés entre 1947 et 1954 et suivis jusqu'en 1960. Elle démontre que le taux de leucémie pendant la première décennie double, passant de 4,6/10.000 à 9,2/10.000. C'est pourquoi on a conseillé aux radiologues de ne pratiquer des radiographies abdominales aux femmes en âge de procréer que pendant les deux semaines qui suivent la menstruation.

Assurance vie et Assurance cancer

1. Il faut prendre en considération:
— une irradiation accidentelle dans les antécédents d'un candidat;
— une irradiation professionnelle ou médicale qui pourrait provoquer un cancer radio-induit.

2. En valeur absolue, le nombre total des cas de leucémie n'est pas très élevé (1,5/10.000) mais en valeur relative, l'influence des radiations est indubitable.

Annexe

Critères médicaux pour la manipulation de radiations ionisantes

Il existe plusieurs degrés d'inaptitude:

1. Inaptitude complete

1.1. Anamnèse

— Irradiation antérieure pour néoplasie, Hodgkin, etc.
— Cure de désintoxication antérieure (alcool, drogues)

1.2. Peau

— Acné rebelle
— Ichtyose généralisée (décontamination difficile)
— Psoriasis
— Eczéma chronique

1.3. Système pulmonaire

— Sinusite chronique
— Amygdalite chronique
— Bronchite chronique
— Pneumoconiose
— Stase par décompensation
— T.P. évolutive

1.4. Système rénal

— Urée supérieure à 0,45 gr ‰
— Albuminurie
— Affection rénale chronique
— Fonction rénale déficiente (créatinine)

1.5. Système cardio-vasculaire

— Hypertension
— Crises d'hypotension
— Infarctus antérieur
— Bloc de branche
— Affection cardiaque décompensée ou mal compensée
— Fibrillation ou flutter antérieur
— Tachycardie paroxystique
— Arythmie cardiaque

1.6. Système nerveux

— Toxicomanie même antérieure
— Epilepsie
— Troubles caractériels (dépression nerveuse)
— Affection mentale même antérieure

1.7. Système osseux

— Affection chronique des os (émetteurs α)
— Ostéomyélite
— Ostéite

1.8. Système endocrinien

— Hyperthyroïdie

1.9. Sang

— Anémie
— Leucopénie en-dessous de 3.500 G.B.

1.10. Yeux

— Opacité du cristallin
— Daltonisme (signaux visuels)

1.11. Oreille

— Surdité (signaux acoustiques de sécurité)

2. Inaptitude provisoire différée

2.1. Yeux

— Acuité visuelle insuffisante mais améliorable

2.2. Denture

— Caries dentaires
— Pyorrhée alvéole dentaire

2.3. Irradiation

concertée ou accidentelle importante

2.4. Os

— Fracture en voie de guérison

2.5. Irradiation

concertée ou accidentelle importante

3. Inaptitude incompléte

Certaines tares médicales peuvent provoquer l'écartement du travail dans une centrale nucléaire, un laboratoire chaud, mais peuvent être compatibles avec une activité dans un autre milieu.

Bibliographie

CORK: Radioactivité et physique nucléaire. Michigan.
DENOUX: Carcinologie. 1967.
I.C.R.P. Publications Vienne.
JAMMET, RODIER: Les maladies causées par les radiations.
MARIQUE, J. V.: Etat de nos connaissances actuelles en cancérologie. Brussels: Assubel 1969.
MARIQUE, J. V.: Les unités et doses admissibles. Brussels: Assubel 1966.
MARIQUE, J. V.: Radioactivité industrielle. Brussels: Assubel 1966.
MARIQUE, J. V., VANDERBECKEN: Pollution par radiations ionisantes. Brussels: Assubel 1972.
DE MEYER, MARIQUE, J. V.: Radioactivité naturelle. Brussels: Assubel 1966.
SIMON, S.: Problèmes causés par les cancers radio-induits. Bruxelles.

II Sesión

Tema: Pronóstico a largo plazo de las taquicardias

Presidente: Dr. Harry Ungerleider, EE. UU.

Bradicardia y taquicardia sinusales, extrasistoles

Dr. Oscar Medina Mora

Una pauta de salud o de enfermedad es la sensación de enfermedad o salud que las personas mismas refieren; al lado de los datos subjetivos, existen los objetivos. Al médico no le cuesta trabajo admitir como patológico o como anomalía todo aquello que se aparta mucho de una figura ideal que viene a ser la suma promedio de una imagen considerada como normal o saludable. Pero cuando los signos objetivos no se alejan sino en grado leve o mínimo surge el conflicto diagnóstico.

Por otra parte existen situaciones que aun no siendo normales, no constituyen todavía una enfermedad a que permiten actividad plena, sensación subjetiva de salud y tal vez larga vida.

Con estas premisas puedo decir que las alternaciones del ritmo cardíaco que me corresponde exponer pueden pertenecer tanto a situaciones no normales pero que aún no constituyen enfermedad, como también a manifestaciones reales de alteraciones orgánicas subyacentes.

Muchos de los trastornos del ritmo y alguno de la conducción se dan en personas por todo lo demás sanas y con corazón saludable.

Tanto la Bradicardia sinusal como la taquicardia del mismo origen, las extrasístoles auriculares y las ventriculares pertenecen a estos grupos. Constituyen éstas además las alteraciones que se ven corrientemente en la población asegurable puesto que por una parte son las más frecuentes y por otra son las que pueden coincidir con un estado de salud o apenas modificado, como el de muchos de los prospectos a negociar seguros de vida.

Llamamos bradicardia, a la condición en la cual el corazón late menos de 60 veces por minuto y cuyo marcapaso está en el nódulo sinusal. Su pronóstico dependerá no de ella misma sino de la causa que la engendre.

En clínica las frecuencias de 50 y 40 no son raras, pero han sido descritos casos de hasta 30 por minuto. Debe ser medida su frecuencia con la auscultación precordial, para eliminar bradiesfigmias por déficit de pulso. Los latidos deberán ser rítmicos, las pequeñas variaciones no son significantes ya que frecuentemente se acompaña de arritmia sinusal. La etiqueta de sinusal sólo se logra con seguridad, mediante el trazado electrocardiográfico donde se compruebe que la onda P es sinusal y que cada estímulo del seno va seguido de excitación ventricular.

En esta bradicardia no es infrecuente la arritmia sinusal, tampoco lo es un bloqueo A-V de primer grado, ya que frecuentemente esta bradicardia es por vagotonía, la que puede también actuar retardando la conducción A-V. En este caso el ejercicio hace desaparecer tanto la bradicardia como la prolongación del P.R. Conviene no olvidar que la bradicardia, con el aumento del volumen de expulsión que determina puede producir un aumento radiológico del tamaño del corazón, hecho no infrecuente en los atletas.

Decíamos que el pronóstico está en relación con la causa. Desde el punto de vista de su etiología, la bradicardia la observamos de modo fisiológico durante el sueño, están descritos casos de bradicardia como respuesta a emociones. Se les ha encontrado en personas sanas como en muchos atletas y hay casos que la presentan varias personas de una familia. Todos estos casos de bradicardia no alteran el pronóstico de la vida general del promedio de mortalidad.

Las bradicardias sinusales debidas a enfermedades sistémicas las vemos poco frecuentemente en medicina del seguro de vida, pueden deberse al uso de los digitálicos, al empleo de vagotónicos, se le observa por maniobras vagales, también en la hipotermia, en la ictericia obstructiva, en el mixedema, hipotituitarismo y recientemente por el empleo de Betabloqueadores, y también en el síndrome cráneo-hipertensivo, cualquiera que pueda ser la causa.

Excepto en el caso del uso de los Betabloqueadores, en general puede encontrarse la condición de fondo y entonces el pronóstico será el de ese padecimiento.

Se debe realizar el diagnóstico diferencial con el bloqueo sino auricular 2 : 1. Este es raro y en general de poca duración. El electrocardiograma es idéntico al de la bradicardia sinusal y sólo se diagnostica retrospectivamente pues cuando al quitarse este bloqueo la frecuencia ventricular pasa súbitamente al doble, ya que en la bradicardia sinusal verdadera las maniobras vagolíticas aceleran gradualmente al corazón.

Otro diagnóstico diferencial sería con las extrasístoles auriculares bigeminadas pero bloqueadas donde la P no se vea fácilmente por estar enmascarada con la T precedente, el análisis de esta onda puede dar la pauta.

Otro diagnóstico diferencial sería con el ritmo de escape auricular, éste por definición es un ritmo lento o relativamente lento y si el ritmo de escape nace cerca del seno entonces la P es casi normal, se puede diferenciar sólo si con las maniobras vagolíticas el seno toma el mando y entonces cambia la morfología de la P.

Llamamos taquicardia sinusal aquella cuya frecuencia es mayor de 100 por minuto (habitualmente no es mayor de 130), y cuyo estímulo inicial nazca en el seno. Su pronóstico dependerá sobre todo de la causa que la determine.

Fisiológicamente se le ve en el ejercicio físico e inmediatamente después de él, por esfuerzos mayores puede llegar a 180 y 190 por minuto, es más frecuente en personas no entrenadas.

Otras causas de taquicardia, serán la fiebre de cualquier origen, la ansiedad y en general los estados de angustia, la tirotoxicosis, la anemia, la insuficiencia cardíaca, las carditis, algunos medicamentos la determinan como la atropina, la tiroidina, la adrenalina, etc., así como cualquier causa de hipoxemia. En general se debe la taquicardia sinusal al aumento del tono simpático y/o a la disminución del vagal.

La taquicardia sinusal se identifica por su frecuencia y por la relación adecuada de la P con el QRS; en estos casos habitualmente desaparece la arritmia sinusal, no es raro que el AP y el AQRS viren un tanto a la derecha.

Las causas más frecuentes en la población asegurable serán los estados de hiperemotividad. Es difícil por la diversidad de causas llegar a un pronóstico confiable a largo plazo.

Debe hacerse diagnóstico diferencial con la taquicardia auricular paroxística, tema que desarrollará el doctor Rodolfo Malo Camacho.

Otros trastornos del ritmo de la más alta frecuencia en la población general y en la asegurable, son las extrasístoles, su interés radica justo en esto, en la frecuencia cotidiana con que la encontramos y puesto que suceden tanto en personas con corazones normales, como en cardiópatas es útil conocerlas, identificarlas y si es posible darles su justo valor. Aunque en general no tienen significado ominoso pueden ser el aviso de arritmias más grave y de la existencia de una cardiopatía subyacente.

Por su origen se reconocen las extrasístoles sinusales, las auriculares, las de la unión A-V y las ventriculares, una quinta variedad serían los latidos recíprocos.

Tres hechos caracterizan en común a las cuatro variedades: son prematuras, tienen un punto de partida ectópico y un tiempo de acoplamiento virtualmente constante en un caso dado.

Las *auriculares* son frecuentes, las segundas en frecuencia; las *sinusales* son relativamente raras ambas con un pronóstico o significado semejante.

Las extrasístoles auriculares se caracterizan por:

1. Ser prematuras.
2. Por tener una P no normal ya que tienen origen ectópico y no sinusal.
3. Por su tendencia a acoplarse.
4. Por tener pausa compensadora que suele ser incompleta.
5. Habitualmente por tener una PR de 0.12″ o mayor.
6. Usualmente con un contorno normal del QRS que le sigue, aunque si es muy prematura puede haber aberrancia en él.

El pronóstico depende en general de si esta extrasistolia que tenemos enfrente se da en un corazón sano o en uno patológico; recordemos los hechos que frecuentemente indican que en el fondo hay alguna cardiopatía:

1. Extrasístoles frecuentes y persistentes.
2. Extr. en sucesivas observaciones.
3. Extr. auriculares multifocales.
4. Que éstas sean bi o trigeminadas.
5. Que aumenten por el ejercicio.
6. Que se presenten por el uso de digital.
7. Que existan cambios en la onda T en el latido postextrasistólico.
8. Por supuesto que coincidan con otros datos de cardiopatía.

Las extrasístoles persistentes sobre todo si son multifocales y bigeminadas frecuentemente son precursoras de fibrilación o taquicardias auriculares.

Electrocardiográficamente debe hacerse diagnóstico diferencial con la arritmia sinusal y con la extrasistolia del tejido de la unión.

En cuanto al pronóstico podemos decir que el hallazgo de extrasístoles auriculares ocasionables en un corazón por toda otra parte normal se da en situaciones completamente benignas y sin importancia y su pronóstico será benigno también;

pero los otros tipos como los que señalamos como sospechosos sugieren cardiopatía.

Las extrasístoles del tejido de la unión son relativamente raras, representan según Marriot tan sólo un 3.5% de las supraventriculares.

Los datos electrocardiográficos serán:

1. Ser prematuras.
2. Tener acoplamiento fijo.
3. Con onda P enmascarada en el QRS o sucediéndolo (actualmente no se aceptan como extrasístoles de la uníon las que tienen P negativa antepuesta, se les consideran como auriculares bajas), la P posterior al latido prematuro de la unión puede ser negativa si la aurícula se activa desde el nodo, o bien positiva si el estímulo nodal se bloqueó hacia las aurículas y en cambio se inscribió una P sinusal que cayó en el ST de la extrasístole.
4. QRS en general de contorno normal, alguna vez aberrado.
5. Pueden tener pauta completamente compensadora.

Son raras y más raro aún que las presenten personas sanas con corazón sano. Inclina a pensar aún más en cardiopatía:

1. El que sean reiteradas en observaciones distintas.
2. Frecuentes en un mismo trazado.
3. Que aparezcan por el uso de digital.
4. Que aumenten con el ejercicio.
5. Que la T postextrasistólica sea anormal.

Su significado pronóstico y calificación será el de la cardiopatía de base, muy rara vez podrán darse en corazones sanos como en algunos casos de Cealocitopenia.

Extrasistoles *ventriculares,* éstas son los ritmos ectópicos activos más frecuentes. Así Hiss y colaboradores las encontraron en 419 pilotos aviadores de un total de 67,375 lo que equivale a un 0.62% de una población saludable y en edad asegurable. Gray los encontró en el 0.8% de un grupo de 1,000 jóvenes sanos. En general las estadísticas en sanos dan un porcentaje de frecuencia del 0.6 al 0.8%, estos grupos siguen el patrón de pronóstico de vida de las personas calificadas como clínicamente sanas.

Se les reconoce al electrocardiograma:

1. Por ser prematuras.
2. Por tener tendencia al acoplamiento fijo.
3. Por tener morfología anómala.
4. Por tener anchura de QRS amplia a menudo considerable.
5. Por presentar ST y T secundarias.

Otra vez como en las extrasístoles no ventriculares éstas pueden darse en individuos sanos, pero también pueden ser ya manifestación de cardiopatía; las siguientes características sugerirán esta última probabilidad, naturalmente no me referiré especialmente a aquellos casos en los que el corazón está dañado y ello es reconocible clínica o electrocardiográficamente o con ambos métodos.

Serán sospechosos de cardiopatía los trazados cuyas extrasístoles ventriculares tengan:

1. Origen multifocal y por ello sean multiformes.
2. En series de tres o más sucesivas.
3. Que aparezcan por primera vez después de los 40 ó mejor de los 50 años.
4. Que sean más de 10 por minuto.
5. Que aparezcan por primera vez después del ejercicio.
6. Que aumenten en frecuencia después del ejercicio.
7. Cuando sean bi o trigeminadas.
8. Que aparezcan pese a existir taquicardia sinusal.
9. Que la anchura del QRS sea de 0.18″ o mayor.
10. Que el latido prematuro aparezca en la onda T precedente.
11. Cuando el complejo postextrasistólico tenga anomalías en el ST o en la T.
12. Cuando el QRS de la extrasístole comience con onda Q en derivaciones distintas a AVR y AVL ya que serían sospechosas de zona de necrosis subyacente.

El diagnóstico diferencial debe establecerse con las extrasístoles supraventriculares pero con conducción aberrante.

Ungerleider ha afirmado que la mortalidad de las personas con extrasístoles como hallazgo único, en la época del examen para el seguro fue relativamente normal; pero que asociadas a alguna otra subnormalidad, la mortalidad fue algo superior y en ellos la muerte por padecimiento cardiocirculatorio se elevó en $^{2}/_{3}$ de la esperada.

Parasistolia. El reconocimiento de una parasistolia ventricular es interesante en medicina del seguro pues casi siempre está presente una enfermedad cardíaca orgánica, esto es especialmente cierto en la parasistolia ventricular.

Se reconoce en los trazados si se cumplen las tres reglas que la identifican: 1. variaciones en los tiempos de acoplamiento, es decir no hay realmente acoplamiento, 2. los intervalos interectópicos guardan siempre una relación numérica. 3. La aparición de vez en cuando de latidos de fusión.

Lo más frecuente es que la parasistolia se presente en las cardiopatías reumáticas y en las coronarias, los primeros son en general fácilmente reconocibles y tendrán el pronóstico y la calificación de ellas; las segundas si no son manifiestas deberán sospecharse cuando no se descubra otra cardiopatía, sobre todo si aparece esta arritmia después de los 40 ó mejor de los 50 años.

Taquicardias aspectos fisiopatológicos

Dr. M. Cárdenas Loaeza

Al músculo cardíaco se le describen desde el punto de vista fisiológico cuatro propiedades fundamentales: contractilidad, automatismo, excitabilidad y conducción. Las taquicardias se deben a alteraciones en las tres últimas propiedades.

La causa de las taquicardias es generalmente transitoria y posteriormente el trastorno se autosostiene por un mecanismo que puede ser el mismo que le dio origen o totalmente diferente.

La causa desencadenante de la arritmia casi siempre es una extrasístole debida a una alteración del automatismo o a un fenómeno de re-entrada. Los mecanismos capaces de sostener un arritmia son cambios en el automatismo, re-entrada, o movimientos circulares.

Desde el punto de vista hemodinámico la taquicardia disminuye el gasto cardíaco; el aumento de frecuencia se hace a expensas de la diástole, al disminuir el período diastólico disminuye el llenado ventricular y por consiguiente el volumen látido, con la consiguiente disminución del retorno venoso cerrándose un círculo vicioso con mayor disminución del volumen minuto.

El consumo de oxígeno por el miocardio aumenta; la taquicardia consume más energía para lograr un mismo gasto. A este aumento en las demandas se agrega una disminución del flujo coronario por la caída del gasto y el acortamiento de la diastole. El resultado es insuficiencia coronaria.

Si a la taquicardia se agrega la pérdida de la relación cíclica de contracción de aurícula y ventrículo la caída del gasto será mayor por: diferente duración de los ciclos cardíacos; pérdida de la contracción auricular; y disminución de la presión de llenado ventricular. Cuando hay una activación ventricular anormal se disipa energía en fricción y se pierde en tensión por lo que hay menos energía utilizable para trabajo externo con pérdida de eficiencia miocárdica.

Todos estos trastornos serán más graves en tanto la frecuencia sea mayor, la arritmia dure más tiempo o el miocardio esté más dañado.

El significado de la taquicardia sinusal, taquicardia auricular, taquicardia de la unión, taquicardia ventricular y el síndrome de Wolff-Parkinson-White

Dr. Rodolfo Malo Camacho

El Seno Auricular es el marcapaso normal del organismo y tiene mecanismos de adaptabilidad que le permiten aumentar o disminuir la frecuencia cardíaca dependiende de multiples situaciones. Cuando la frecuencia de descarga de estos estímulos eléctricos sobrepasa a 100 por minuto, decimos que nos encontramos en presencia de una Taquicardia Sinusal. La reconocemos en el electrocardiograma porque siempre es posible identificar ondas „P" de morfología normal y con PR también dentro de límites normales.

En algunas ocasiones aparecen focos ectópicos de automatismo aumentado, localizados en cualquier parte del tejido auricular, que transitoriamente toman el mando del corazón, con frecuencia cardíaca que oscila entre 150 y 220 por minuto, cuyo inicio y fin es súbito y de una duración variable de segundos a horas. Pueden aparecer en corazones sanos o en cardiopatías de cualquier etiología. Se caracterizan en el electrocardiograma por ser absolutamente regulares con ondas P generalmente superpuestas en la onda T o ST precedente, lo que oscurece su reconocimiento. Auriculas y ventrículos laten a la misma frecuencia y la aplicación de una maniobra vagal hace que desaparezca en forma súbita. Se denomina Taquicardia Auricular.

Recibe el nombre de Taquicardia de la Unión aquella que se origina por la aparición de un foco ectópico en el sistema de conducción A-V, así como tejidos circunvecinos. Se reconocen dos tipos, las llamadas „taquicardias nodales no paroxísticas" que representan una forma acelerada de ritmo de la Unión A-V, que es similar a la taquicardia sinusal, pero de menor frecuencia y que en el ECG se identifican por un PR menor del normal. La segunda que es la forma paroxística tiene una mayor frecuencia de descarga, que varía de 140 a 220 por minuto; generalmente se encuentran en presencia de cardiopatías, algunas intoxicaciones medicamentosas o trastornos electrolíticos.

La inmensa mayoría de los casos con Taquicardia Ventricular traducen la existencia de una cardiopatía de fondo. Cuando un foco ectópico de localización ventricular, por la mayor frecuencia en la descarga de estímulos eléctricos, toma el mando de la actividad ventricular decimos que estamos ante una Taquicardia Ventricular. Se acepta como tal la existencia de 5 ó más extrasístoles ventriculares, una tras otra. La frecuencia cardíaca varía de 140 a 240 por minuto, pero en ocasiones puede ser un poco más rápida. ECG se reconocen complejos ventriculares aberrados del alta frecuencia y que no guardan relación con un ritmo auricular independiente, generalmente de menor frecuencia de descarga y por la existencia de capturas o fusiones.

El Síndrome de WPW representa una anomalía en la activación ventricular, que tradicionalmente se reconoce por un PR corto, un complejo QRS aberrado, que semeja un bloqueo de rama, en individuos que en otras ocasiones tienen un electrocardiograma normal. Aparece con gran frecuencia en sujetos portadores de un corazón sano, así como en cardiopatías adquiridas y algunas congénitas. Su identificación es de gran interés pues por un lado presentan una alta incidencia de taquicardias paroxísticas y además pueden exhibir morfologías ventriculares que conducen a diagnósticos y establecimiento de patologías no existentes.

Comunicación preliminar acerca de la incidencia y pronóstico de los hemibloqueos

Dr. SALVADOR WAICH T. *, Dr. GUSTAVO ROMERO REVERÓN **, Dr. JOSÉ E. BARCELÓ ***, Dr. IRVING PEÑA, Dr. ALBERTO MÉNDEZ y Dr. JAVIER JASSO

10 Figuras

El bloqueo de una de las divisiones principales de la rama izquierda del Haz de His, se conoce con el nombre de hemibloqueo [1, 2].

La Fig. 1 tomada de los estudios de ROSENBAUM muestra el concepto moderno y esquemático del sistema de conducción intraventricular en el ser humano.

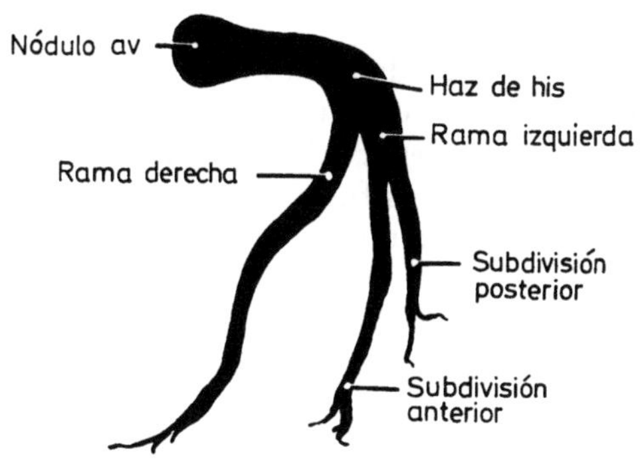

Fig. 1. Sistema de conducción intraventricular

El nodo aurículo ventricular se continúa con el Haz de His, el cual se divide en dos ramas: la derecha y la izquierda, a su vez la rama izquierda se divide en dos fascículos denominados posterior y anterior; la interrupción o el bloqueo de uno de estos fascículos por separado recibe la denominación de hemibloqueo, y cuando coexiste un hemibloqueo y un bloqueo de la rama derecha del Haz de His se denomina bloqueo bifascicular [3].

Establecer la importancia y el pronóstico de los hemibloqueos y bloqueos bifasciculares es extremadamente difícil, ya que no es posible en la mayoría de

* Compañía Suiza de Reaseguros (Ofatec Venezuela C.A.).
** Seguros Caracas.
*** General de Seguros S.A.
Servicio de Cardiología. Hospital Central de las Fuerzas Armadas. Caracas, Venezuela.

los pacientes obtener con exactitud la fecha del inicio de este disturbio de la conducción del ritmo cardíaco.

Los hemibloqueos tienen diferentes causas etiológicas como factores predisponentes, pero también pueden ocurrir en ausencia de otras anormalidades clínicas [1].

Material y método

Se revisaron 10.100 electrocardiogramas del Servicio de Cardiología del Hospital Central de las Fuerzas Armadas de Caracas, Venezuela, correspondientes a 8.500 pacientes, examinados durante los últimos 10 años.

Todos los electrocardiogramas fueron analizados al menos por tres observadores diferentes.

Se diagnosticaron 293 hemibloqueos y bloqueos bifasciculares, siguiendo los criterios de ROSENBAUM y MEDRANO para hemibloqueos anteriores (HBA) y bifasciculares (1-2-3-4-) y los de MEDRANO solo para hemibloqueos posteriores (HBP) [5], lo cual nos da una incidencia de un 3,4%. De éstos, 197 casos correspondieron a HBA, 43 casos a HBP y 53 a bloqueos bifasciculares.

Se estudió posteriormente la historia clínica de cada caso, tratando de relacionar el diagnóstico de los mismos con los hemibloqueos encontrados; se dividieron los pacientes de acuerdo a las diferentes décadas de la vida, a partir de la tercera década en adelante.

Se trató de establecer la sobrevida de los casos desde el momento del diagnóstico hasta la fecha de su última consulta o hasta la muerte en número de años, asimismo, si la causa de muerte tenía relación con el hemibloqueo. El promedio general de control de todos los casos fue de 5,3 años, desde el momento en que se diagnosticó el hemibloqueo hasta la última consulta.

Del total de hemibloqueos, 200 correspondieron al sexo masculino, o sea el 68,2% con una edad promedio de 52,3 años y 93 al sexo femenino, lo cual equivale al 31,8% con edad promedio de 56,1 años, siendo la edad promedio general en todos los grupos de 53,6 años.

Resultados

De los 197 HBA, (Tabla 1), se apreció que 62 casos correspondían a cardiopatía isquémica, 63 a hipertensión arterial, 7 miocardiopatía Chagásica, 1 cardiopatía congénita y en 64 no había relación entre ninguna afección cardiovascular con el diagnóstico de HBA, los cuales se consideraron como corazón sano con presencia del hemibloqueo.

La mayor incidencia corresponde a las décadas 5 a. a 8 a. de la vida, asimismo la mortalidad es mayor en estos años.

De los 20 casos de muerte ocurridas en este tipo de hemibloqueo, 14 correspondían a causas cardiovasculares como arritmias, insuficiencia cardíaca e infartos y en 6 la causa de muerte no tenía relación con el corazón, como eran: muertes por cáncer, neumonía, etc.

La mayoría de las muertes correspondían a los casos con diagnóstico clínico de cardiopatía isquémica e hipertensión arterial.

El período de sobrevida desde el diagnóstico hasta la fecha de la muerte fue de 4,5 años: 6 casos evolucionaron a bloqueos bifasciculares, 3 casos a bloqueo avanzado de rama izquierda del Haz de His, en todos ellos estaba como causa predisponente la cardiopatía isquémica.

Tabla 1. Hemibloqueos anteriores

	Diagnóstico clínico					
Edad	Card. isq.	H.A.	Miocard.	C. cong.	Cor. sano	Muertos
<30	1	0	1	1	8	0
31 a 40	0	0	1	—	12	0
41 a 50	9	10	2	—	15	3
51 a 60	18	25	1	—	13	2
61 a 70	16	15	0	—	7	8
71 a 80	13	10	2	—	8	5
>80	5	2	0	—	1	2
Total	62	63	7	1	64	20

La Fig. 2 muestra las características electrocardiográficas de los HBA (1–4) que se señalan a continuación:

1. Un AQRS alrededor de —60°.
2. Una configuración tipo q1 S3.
3. El intervalo QRS normal o ligeramente prolongado.
4. R terminal o empastada en AVR.
5. Ondas S hasta V5 y V6 en ausencia de bloqueo de rama derecha.
6. Complejos tipo R o qR en D1 y AVL con empastamiento de la rama descendente de R.

Se diagnosticaron 43 HBP (Tabla 2) siguiendo los criterios de Medrano, ya que los de Rosenbaum exigen un examen clínico de descarte de otras afecciones, lo cual no era posible en este estudio, 7 casos correspondían a cardiopatía isquémica, 3 casos a hipertensión arterial, 1 miocardiopatía, 2 cardiopatías congénitas y 30 a corazón aparentemente sano.

De acuerdo con el estudio de los pacientes se encontró una incidencia prácticamente similar en cuanto al número de HBP, aparecidos durante las diferentes décadas de la vida; lo que varió fue la etiología relacionada con la década de aparición del hemibloqueo.

En pacientes jóvenes la mayoría corresponden a corazones aparentemente normales, y en nuestra serie no hubo mortalidad.

Después de la década del 40 la cardiopatía isquémica es uno de los factores predisponentes significativos para los HBP, los otros diagnósticos clínicos cardiovasculares, no fueron de importancia.

La mortalidad en los pacientes con HBP, se relacionó en tres casos con el diagnóstico de cardiopatía isquémica, los tres decesos tuvieron lugar en el grupo correspondiente a la 5 a. década de la vida. El otro caso que falleció con HBP, tenía el diagnóstico de corazón aparentemente sano y la causa de muerte no se pudo determinar. Correspondía a la 6 a. década de la vida.

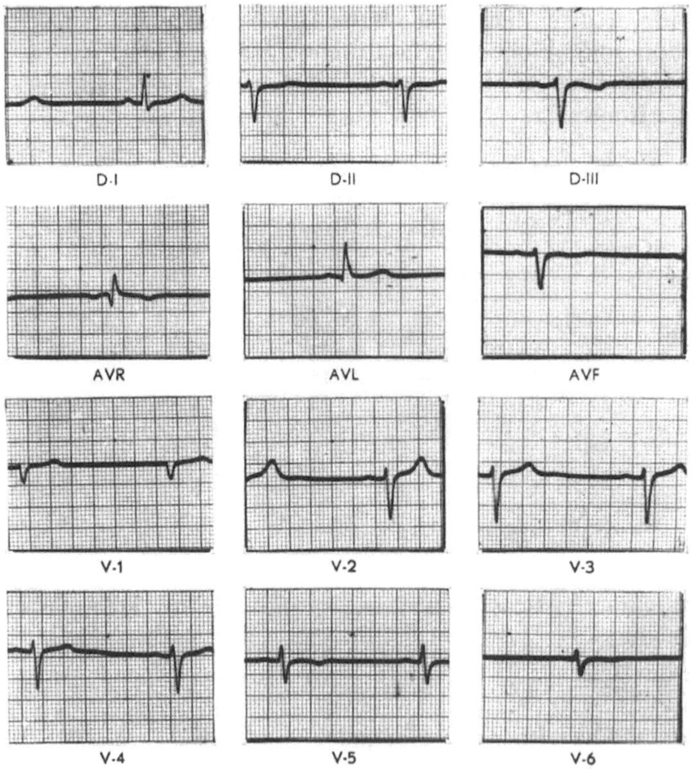

Fig. 2. Electrocardiograma de un caso hemibloqueo anterior

Tabla 2. Hemibloqueos posteriores

	Diagnóstico clínico					
Edad	Card. isq.	H. A.	Miocard.	C. cong.	Cor. sano	Muertos
<30	—	1	—	1	14	—
31 a 40	—	—	—	1	6	—
41 a 50	3	—	1	—	5	3
51 a 60	2	1	—	—	3	1
61 a 70	1	1	—	—	2	—
71 a 80	1	—	—	—	—	—
>80	—	—	—	—	—	—
Total	7	3	1	2	30	4

La sobrevida desde el diagnóstico hasta la muerte fue de 3,8 años.

La Fig. 3 muestra un electrocardiograma típico con HBP (5):

1. Un AQRS alrededor de +100°.
2. Una configuración S1 q3.
3. Complejos tipo qR en D2, D3 y AVF con onda R de voltaje aumentado y onda q normal.
4. Empastamiento de la rama descendente de R en D3, AVF, V5 y V6.

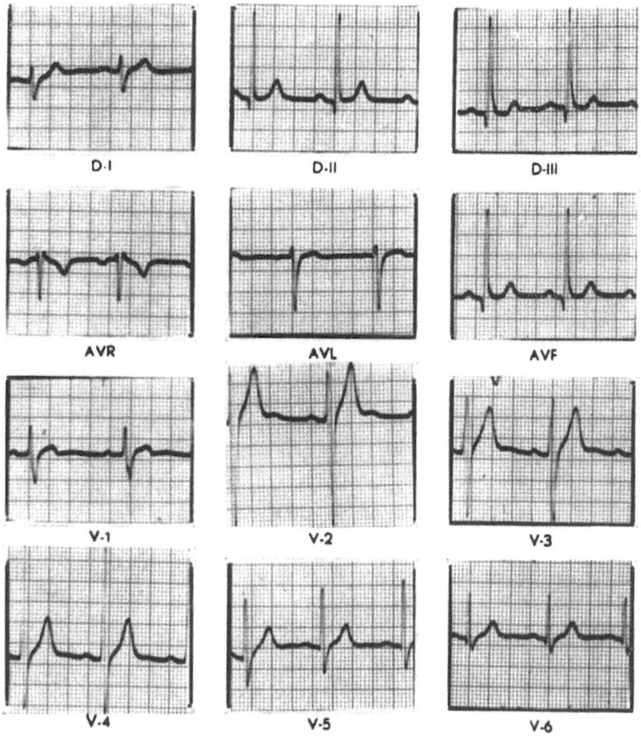

Fig. 3. Electrocardiograma de un caso hemibloqueo posterior

Tabla 3. Bloqueos bifasciculares

	Diagnóstico clínico					
Edad	Card. isq.	H.A.	Miocard.	C. cong.	Cor. sano	Muertos
<30	—	—	2	1	2	2
31 a 40	—	—	1	—	2	1
41 a 50	2	1	1	—	2	1
51 a 60	7	3	—	—	2	3
61 a 70	8	8	—	—	2	2
71 a 80	5	2	—	—	—	4
>80	1	1	—	—	—	1
Total	23	15	4	1	10	14

5. Deflexión intrinsecoide retardada en D3 y AVF (0,05″) y normal o retardada en V5 y V6.
6. QRS ligeramente aumentado (0,10″).

Se encontraron 53 bloqueos bifasciculares (Tabla 3), siendo su mayor incidencia las décadas 6 a., 7 a. y 8 a. de la vida. 23 correspondían a cardiopatía isquémica, 15 a hipertensión arterial, 4 miocardiopatías, 1 cardiopatía congénita y 10 a corazón aparentemente sano.

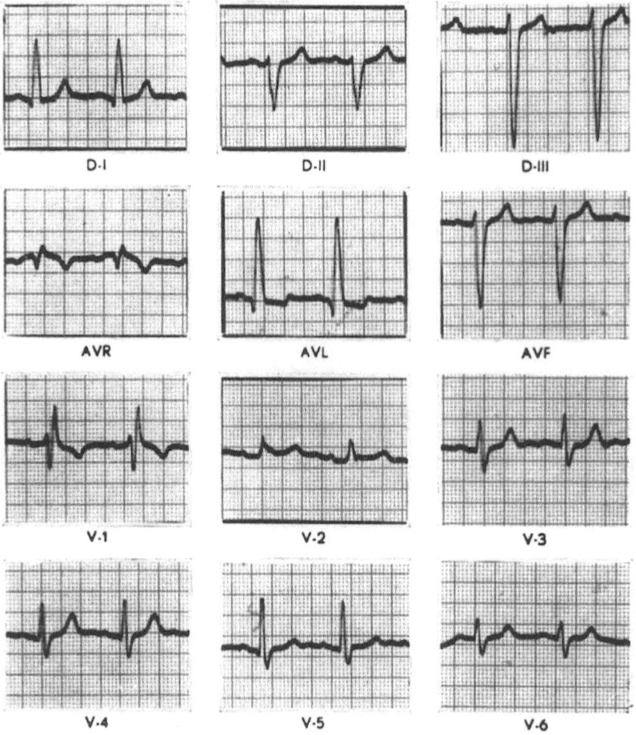

Fig. 4. Electrocardiograma de un caso bloqueo bifascicular

Tabla 4. Hemibloqueos

	Diagnóstico clínico					
Edad	Card. isq.	H. A.	Miocard.	C. cong.	Cor. sano	Muertos
<30	1	1	3	3	24	2
31 a 40	0	0	2	1	20	1
41 a 50	14	11	4	0	22	7
51 a 60	27	29	1	0	18	6
61 a 70	25	24	0	0	11	10
71 a 80	19	12	2	0	8	9
>80	6	4	0	0	1	3
Total	92	81	12	4	104	38

En este grupo el número de casos con diagnóstico de corazón aparentemente sano fue significativamente menor y correspondió solo a un 20%.

Lo más resaltante fue la mortalidad de los bloqueos bifasciculares, ya que el 26,4% de los casos mueren en un período promedio de 2,8 años, casi todos ellos debido a cardiopatía isquémica e hipertensión arterial o combinación de ambas.

Los casos con diagnóstico de miocardiopatía chagásica tienen peor pronóstico ya que de 3 casos, 2 de ellos murieron a consecuencia de arritmias cardíacas estando hospitalizados y correspondieron a pacientes menores de 30 años. 4 casos evolucionaron a bloqueo AV completo, a uno de ellos se le implantó un marcapaso cardíaco.

La combinación del bloqueo de rama derecha con HBA usualmente significa una enfermedad miocárdica avanzada, y esto se refleja por una mortalidad mucho mayor que cuando sólo existe un hemibloqueo aislado [6].

La Fig. 4 muestra un electrocardiograma con bloqueo de rama derecha y HBA.

Del total de hemibloqueos, 293 casos (Tabla 4), 92 correspondieron a cardiopatía isquémica, 81 a hipertensión arterial, 12 a miocardiopatías, 4 a cardiopatía congénita, 104 a corazones aparentemente sanos, con una mortalidad total de 38 casos.

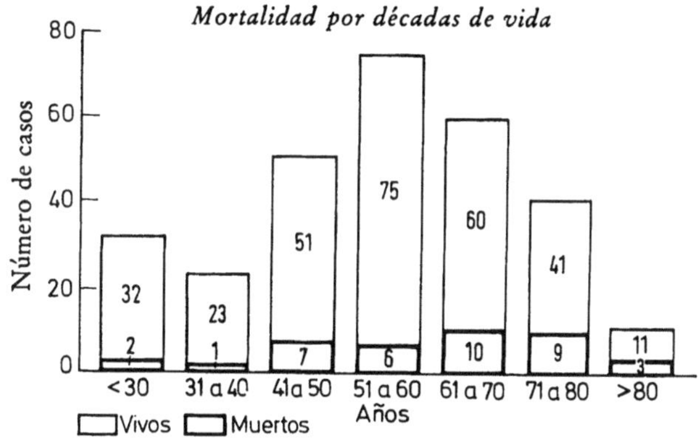

Fig. 5

Se estudió la mortalidad correspondiente a las diferentes décadas de la vida (Fig. 5), y se pudo observar que en pacientes menores de 30 años sólo fallecieron 2 casos que correspondían a bloqueos bifasciculares de un total de 32 pacientes.

La mayor mortalidad corresponde a las décadas 5 a. a 8 a. de la vida, en donde es también mayor la incidencia de los hemibloqueos.

Se trató de relacionar la mortalidad con el diagnóstico clínico que tenían los pacientes (Fig. 6). De los 92 casos con diagnóstico de cardiopatía isquémica fallecieron 21 o sea el 23%. De 81 pacientes con hipertensión arterial fallecieron 12 o sea; un 15%. De los 12 casos con miocardiopatía 4 murieron o sea un 33%.

No hubo mortalidad en los 4 casos de cardiopatía congénita y un solo caso murió del grupo de 104 con diagnóstico de corazón aparentemente sano.

La mortalidad general de los hemibloqueos fue la siguiente:

HBA: 197 casos: 20 murieron o sea el 10,6%
HBP: 43 casos: 4 murieron o sea el 9,3%

Bloqueos bifasciculares: 53 casos, murieron 14 pacientes o sea el 26,4%.

La mortalidad para la edad promedio de este grupo de pacientes, es mucho mayor que la esperada y, en los casos con bloqueos bifasciculares prácticamente es el triple que en los otros grupos.

Nuestro estudio aunque no fue hecho en personas aspirantes a seguros de vida, sugiere que los hemibloqueos tienen una sobremortalidad significativa, y deberán ser tomados muy en consideración al efectuar la tarificación correspondiente en un examen médico de seguro de vida.

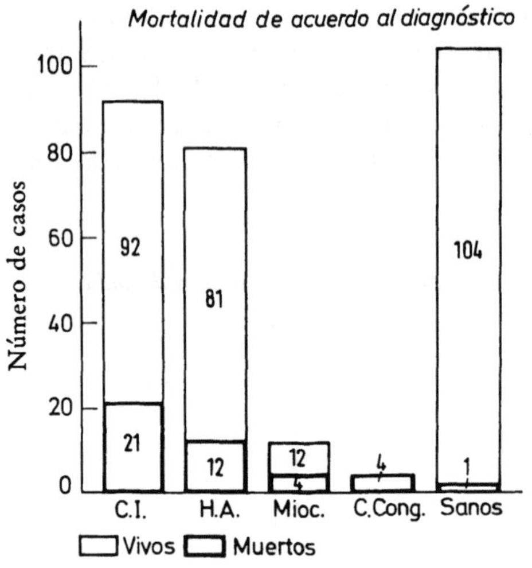

Fig. 6

Resumen

Los hemibloqueos son un trastorno de la conducción del ritmo cardíaco producidos por el bloqueo de una de las divisiones principales de la rama izquierda del Haz de His.

Fueron estudiados 10.100 electrocardiogramas correspondientes a 8.500 pacientes del Servicio de Cardiología del Hospital Central de las Fuerzas Armadas, de Caracas, Venezuela, diagnosticándose 193 hemibloqueos. De éstos, 197 eran hemibloqueos anteriores, 43 hemibloqueos posteriores y 53 bloqueos bifasciculares. La evolución de estos pacientes fue seguida por un período de tiempo promedio de 5,3 años. Todos los electrocardiogramas fueron analizados al menos por tres observadores diferentes.

Se dividieron los casos de acuerdo a las diferentes décadas de la vida y se trató de relacionar el diagnóstico cardiovascular principal de la historia clínica como causa predisponente en la etiología del hemibloqueo.

De los 197 hemibloqueos anteriores fallecieron 20 casos o sea el 10,6%. De estos sólo 14 murieron por causas cardiovasculares exclusivamente y 6 por otras causas.

De los 43 hemibloqueos posteriores 4 murieron o sea el 9,3%, tres como consecuencia de insuficiencia coronaria y en el otro caso no se pudo establecer la causa de la muerte.

De los 53 bloqueos bifasciculares murieron 14 pacientes o sea el 26,4% todos por causas cardiovasculares, algunos de ellos en edades menores de 40 años.

Se trató de relacionar la mortalidad con el diagnóstico clínico y con las diferentes décadas de la vida, apreciándose que la misma era mayor porcentualmente en los casos con diagnóstico de miocardiopatía chagásica, cardiopatía isquémica e hipertensión arterial, y en las décadas 5 a. a 8 a. de la vida.

Se concluye que los pacientes con diagnóstico de hemibloqueo, tienen una mortalidad mayor que la esperada y que estos casos deberán ser tomados en consideración al efectuar la tarificación correspondiente en un examen médico de aspirantes a seguro de vida.

Bibliografía

1. Rosenbaum, M. B.: The Hemiblocks: Diagnostic criteria and clinical significance. Modern Concept Cardiovascular Disease **39**, 141 (1970).
2. Rosenbaum, M. B., Elizari, M. V., Lazzari, I.: Los hemibloqueos. Ed.: Paidos, Buenos Aires 1970.
3. Rosenbaum, M. B., Lepeschkin, E.: Bilateral bundle branch block. Amer. Heart J. **50**, 38 (1955).
4. Medrano, G. A., Brenes, P. C., de Michelli, A., Sodi Pallares, D.: El Bloqueo de la subdivisión anterior de la rama izquierda solo o asociado al bloqueo de la rama derecha. Arch. Inst. Cardiol. México. **39**, 672 (1969).
5. Medrano, G. A. et al.: El Bloqueo de la subdivisión posterior de la rama izquierda del Haz de His aislado y asociado al bloqueo de la rama derecha. Arch. Inst. Cardiol. México. **40**, 423 (1970).
6. De Pascuale, N. P., Bruno, M. S.: Natural history of combined right bundle branch block and left anterior Hemiblock (bilateral bundle branch block). Amer. J. Med. **54**, 297 (1973).

El electrocardiograma de esfuerzo en el seguro de vida

Dr. Oscar Medina Mora, Dr. José Antonio Lorenzo,
Dr. Alejandro Flores Aguirre, Dr. Carlos Munguía y Dr. Jaime Arriaga

Desde siempre el hombre médico se ha preocupado por conocer desde el exterior, lo que sucede en el interior del hombre enfermo.

Con el tiempo la piel ha debido de ser perforada para fines diagnósticos ya con agujas de biopsia ya con catéteres exploradores y cuando la necesidad así lo ha exigido, el médico ha practicado la cirugía diagnóstica.

En la medicina del seguro de vida, sólo es realizable la venopuntura como recurso explorador cruento.

La electrocardiografía que nació como procedimiento para gabinetes de alta investigación, pronto fue utilizada por las compañías de seguros para la mejor clasificación de sus riesgos.

La alta frecuencia en morbilidad y mortalidad de los padecimientos cardíacos, entre la población asegurable, requiere cada vez más, de un método electrocardiográfico confiable, tanto para aceptar al que goce de salud, como para rechazar o gravar al que no la tenga cabal.

El electrocardiograma de esfuerzo efectuado e interpretado correctamente, es el mejor procedimiento accesible a las compañías aseguradoras para el enjuiciamiento del problema de la „Insuficiencia Coronaria".

I. Objetivo

El objetivo es descubrir si existe o no, insuficiencia coronaria mediante la realización de un esfuerzo submáximo confiable.

Llamamos confiable a todo esfuerzo que provoquemos al corazón y en el que no nos quede duda de que fue puesto a buena prueba y por tanto podamos tomar como negativa o como positiva la respuesta en los trazados correspondientes.

Este esfuerzo está acondicionado a diversos factores y debe traducirse por aumento de la frecuencia cardíaca.

Los diversos factores que deben tomarse en cuenta para efectuar esta prueba, son principalmente: Edad, sexo, talla, peso y sobre todo actividad física a la que está acostumbrado, ya que, es lógico suponer que necesitará mayor esfuerzo físico en un paciente joven y atleta que un sujeto de edad y vida sedentaria para obtener ese „esfuerzo confiable".

Para esto se toma la frecuencia cardíaca del sujeto en reposo y se trata de que aumente entre 75 y 90%, ejemplo:

Sujeto en reposo	75%	90%
80 × minuto	140 ×′	152 ×′

De esta forma se consigue someter al corazón a un esfuerzo suficiente para que en caso de existir daño coronario, aparezcan las alteraciones electrocardiográficas que permitan hacer el diagnóstico.

De acuerdo con el promedio de diferentes estudios y escuelas y tomando en cuenta que conviene darle sencillez a la prueba, pedimos que el esfuerzo realizado, produzca una taquicardia no menor de 120 ×′. Sin embargo deben hacerse estas dos excepciones: a) En gente joven, atleta con vagotonía acentuada y bradicardia alrededor de 50 ×′; ya que frecuentemente no es posible aumentar le frecuencia cardíaca por arriba de la cifra mencionada (120 ×′); sin embargo, en ellos cifras alrededor de 100 ×′ significan un aumento de más del 90%, lo que es suficiente; b) Por otro lado los sujetos „hiperreactores" en los que, el solo hecho de colocarlos ante el médico y el electrocardiógrafo, determinan que su frecuencia cardíaca de reposo sea mayor de 100 ×′. En ellos se deberá tratar de obtener una frecuencia muy superior a la de 120 ×′.

II. Indicaciones

Estará indicada la realización de un electrocardiograma de esfuerzo, en las siguientes situaciones:

A. Por sospecha de insuficiencia coronaria.

a) Por sospecha médica de insuficiencia coronaria, (a condición de que el electrocardiograma que se tome previo al esfuerzo, no demuestre alteraciones francas de padecimiento coronario — isquemia, lesión y/o necrosis —).

b) Electrocardiograma previo o actual „sospechoso" de insuficiencia coronaria.

c) Por aviso de la O.I.I. en este sentido.

B. Por suma de factores médicos predisponentes (la existencia de 2 ó más de los siguientes factores, invitará al electrocardiograma de esfuerzo a juicio del director médico):

a) Antecedentes familiares de enfermedad coronaria, (sobre todo en gente joven es decir, familiares que hayan padecido o padezcan insuficiencia coronaria por debajo de los 50 años de edad).

b) Existencia en el solicitante de: Hipertensión arterial, diabetes mellitus, obesidad, hiperlipidemia.

C. Por la combinación de edad y suma asegurada. A reserva de los criterios de cada compañía, sugerimos la prueba de esfuerzo en los siguientes casos:

Hasta los 45 años y $ 750 000 o más,
De los 46 a los 59 años y $ 600 000 pesos o más y
de los 60 en adelante y $ 300 000 pesos o más.

III. Contraindicaciones

a) Ausencia de supervisión directa por médico cardiólogo con suficiente entrenamiento en la interpretación de electrocardiogramas y en maniobras de reanimación.

b) En presencia de un infarto del miocardio reciente; esta posibilidad debe ser precisada cuidadosamente mediante el estudio minucioso del electrocardiograma tomado inmediatamente antes del esfuerzo. (La mayoría de las muertes ocurren en pacientes que son sometidos a este esfuerzo y en quienes no se ha reconocido en el electrocardiograma de reposo, la presencia de un infarto del miocardio agudo o reciente).

IV. Procedimiento y técnica

El estudio deberá ser practicado por el cardiólogo o bajo la supervisión de él. (Ver contraindicaciones, letra (a). El paciente deberá estar preferentemente en ayuno de cuando menos 3 horas y habrá suspendido cualquier tratamiento (en especial digital), cuando menos 3 días antes de la prueba.

1. Se tomará un electrocardiograma en reposo con la técnica habitual.

2. Deberá ordenarse el esfuerzo, siempre y cuando el electrocardiograma de reposo no lo contraindique (ver contraindicaciones). El tipo de esfuerzo deberá escogerse de acuerdo con las circunstancias del local y de la persona en estudio. Ténganse en cuenta el grado de entrenamiento e integridad física, para la realización de tal o cual ejercicio. Sugerimos: Abdominales o sentadillas o subir y bajar cualquier escalera, deberá realizarse rápidamente y por unos 3 minutos o al criterio del médico.

3. Se tomará un trazo inmediato al esfuerzo comenzando con las derivaciones que hayan resultado sospechosas en el electrocardiograma de reposo. Cuando en el electrocardiograma de reposo no exista ninguna derivación sospechosa, se seguirá el siguiente orden: V6, V4, V2, D1, D2, VL y VF.

4. Se registrarán dos trazados más, a los 2 y 6 minutos después del esfuerzo. En ellos se usará la técnica habitual; es decir, de D1 hasta V6; ya que, en estos momentos el factor tiempo no es tan importante como en el electrocardiograma inmediato al esfuerzo.

Cada derivación después del ejercicio, deberá contar con 5 complejos cuando menos. Es deseable que 2 ó más complejos sucesivos tengan línea isoeléctrica horizontal.

5. Se deberá registrar la firma del solicitante y anotar edad, talla, peso y tensión arterial.

En caso de aparecer dolor durante la prueba, sospechoso de insuficiencia coronaria, se deberá suspender la prueba y se tomarán electrocardiogramas immediatamente y a los 2 y a los 6 minutos subsiguientes.

V. Criterios de interpretación

El dato electrocardiográfico que nos permite hacer el diagnóstico de insuficiencia coronaria y considerar la prueba de esfuerzo como positiva es la presencia de una depresión „isquémica“ del segmento ST, posteriormente al esfuerzo.

Es característico el que este desnivel negativo del segmento ST sea mayor de un milímetro, de tipo horizontal o con declive distal o con morfología cóncava hacia arriba pero con duración mayor a 0.08 segundos. Es importante señalar estos atributos ya que, frecuentemente personas sanas presentan desnivel del segmento ST mayor de un milímetro en el trazo inmediato al esfuerzo; sin embargo, sin presentar las características antes señaladas.

Otros datos menos específicos, pero que nos pueden ayudar a diagnosticar insuficiencia coronaria son:

1. Cambio de dirección de la onda T con morfología de „tipo primario".
2. Ensanchamiento del QRS.
3. Punto J mayor de 2 milímetros de desnivel.
4. QX-QT por arriba del 50% (QT prolongado).
5. Onda U negativa.
6. Extrasístoles ventriculares; sobre todo si no las presenta en el electrocardiograma de reposo y aparecen *durante* el esfuerzo. (Es de desearse monitoreo continuo.)
7. Las extrasístoles supraventriculares, la fibrilación auricular, el flutter auricular o la taquicardia paroxística supraventricular, pueden ocurrir; sin embargo si no existen las alteraciones del segmento ST (con depresión „isquémica") no deben interpretarse como signos positivos; aunque debe sospecharse la presencia de una cardiopatía.

III Sesión

Tema: Artritis reumatoide y otras enfermedades de la colagena

Presidente: Dr. K. A. Latter, Inglaterra

Prognose der chronischen Polyarthritis und der Kollagenosen unter dem Einfluß der Langzeittherapie

Dr. Fritz Hartmann

1 Abbildung

Die Erwartungen der Kranken und das volkswirtschaftliche Interesse richten sich bei chronischer Polyarthritis nicht auf den vorzeitigen Tod, sondern auf die vorzeitige Invalidität.

Die Prognose der chronischen Polyarthritis ist deswegen so schwer zu beschreiben, weil diese Allgemeinkrankheit der Bindegewebe sehr unterschiedliche Spontanverläufe und Schweregrade hat. Sie kennt viele Varianten des klinischen Beginns und Bildes. Heute wird fast jeder Fall behandelt. Der Wechsel der Therapie, der nicht immer ein Fortschritt war, macht den Vergleich von Kollektiven von Patienten sehr schwer. Das gleiche gilt für Längsschnittuntersuchungen an Individuen. Hinzu kommt, daß die Beurteiler sich an quantitativ schwer zu erfassende Kriterien halten müssen, die international vereinbart werden.

Man kann prognostische Aussagen deswegen heute nur zu der Frage machen: Hat sich die Prognose der behandlungsbedürftigen und tatsächlich behandelten chronischen Polyarthritis in den vergangenen 30 Jahren, in denen Längsschnittstudien mit vergleichbaren Kriterien gemacht wurden, unter dem Einfluß der Therapie überhaupt und allgemein, sowie unter besonderen Therapieformen und -programmen in bestimmten Situationen geändert?

Für Kranken und Arzt konzentriert sich das Problem auf die Verhinderung des Fortschreitens des Gelenkverfalls oder auf Heilung. Heilung kann aber immer nur Freiheit von klinischen Symptomen, d. h. Abwesenheit von Schmerzen und von Behinderung der Gelenkbeweglichkeit auf Dauer sein. Die pathogenetischen Elementarprozesse bestehen auch dann fort — wie bei der Tuberkulose — wenn die Blutkörperchensenkungsgeschwindigkeit und die γ-Globuline zur Ruhe gekommen sind und wenn das histologische Bild der Gelenkkapsel von Narben beherrscht wird. Man spricht vom ausgebrannten Fall.

Noch unbekannt ist, wie sich der *Typ der Entzündung* — ähnlich wie bei der Tuberkulose — auf Verlauf und Prognose auswirkt: es gibt exsudative, proliferative und vernarbend-schrumpfende Formen. Die Synovitis kann reich an Lymphocyten und gefäßreich sein, mit und ohne Nekrosen; sie kann auch aus einem autonom tumorartig-proliferierenden, mesenchymoiden Gewebe aufgebaut sein. Es fehlen Längsschnittstudien, die auch mit Gelenkbiopsien und Zytologie der Gelenkergüsse kontrolliert sind.

Die juvenile chronische Polyarthritis (Still-Syndrom)

Die jugendliche Form der chronischen Polyarthritis hat Besonderheiten, die die Prognose bestimmen. Zu ihr gehören die chronischen Polyarthritiden vor dem 16. Lebensjahr. Jedoch zeigen auch seronegative Fälle, die später beginnen, etwa bis zur Mitte des 3. Lebensjahrzehnts, — und besonders bei Männern — häufiger einen Verlauf wie bei der jugendlichen Form und seltener ein Bild wie bei der typischen klassischen seropositiven Form des Erwachsenen. Man gruppiert diese, auch versicherungsmedizinisch wichtige Gruppe von Kranken auch als atypische chronische Polyarthritis.

Die juvenile Form ist gekennzeichnet durch den meist akuten Beginn mit Fieber, hoher Senkung und Leukozytose. Sie ähnelt dem rheumatischen Fieber. Es fehlen ihr aber die Endokarditis — obgleich eine solche vorkommen kann — und der ansteigende Antistreptolysintiter. Gegen die chronische Polyarthritis des Erwachsenen ist sie abgegrenzt durch das Fehlen von klassischen Ig-M Rheumafaktoren, die Bevorzugung der großen Gelenke, des Sakroiliakalgelenks und der Spondylitis sowie durch Schwellung von Milz und Lymphknoten.

Das Epiphysenwachstum wird gestört; denn die Krankheit fällt in das Wachstumsalter, und die Ernährung von Knorpel und subchondralen Knochen hängt auch von der Ernährung aus der Synovialis ab. Die Folgen sind: Kurze Beine, kurze Finger, kleiner Unterkiefer. Die Wachstumsstörung wird akzentuiert durch die Bewegungsarmut und den fehlenden Belastungsreiz der Knochen. Werden die Kinder lange Zeit mit Steroiden behandelt, so verursacht der eiweißkatabole Effekt dieser Hormone eine therapiebedingte Störung des Knochenwachstums. Die schwersten Fälle mit Befall vieler Gelenke und der Wirbelsäule verkrüppeln trotz sorgsamer Behandlung mit Steroiden, Azathioprin oder Cyclophosphamid und physikalisch-orthopädischer Therapie. Es sind etwa 25%.

Trotzdem ist die Prognose der jugendlichen chronischen Polyarthritis in der Regel gut, zumindest besser als bei Erwachsenen mit seropositiver chronischer Polyarthritis. Die Prognose ist umso besser, je früher die Krankheit begann, am besten vor dem 10. Lebensjahr. Späterer Beginn, Befall auch kleiner Gelenke und verlängerte akute Phase verschlechtern die Prognose. Bywaters beobachtete 140 Kinder 15 Jahre lang: 80% befanden sich nach dieser Zeit so gut, daß sie ein selbständiges unabhängiges Leben führen konnten, also nicht invalide waren. Aber bei 1/3 war eine Dauerbehandlung mit anti-entzündlichen Mitteln notwendig (Tab. 1).

Schlechte Verläufe sind erkennbar an Ähnlichkeiten mit der chronischen Polyarthritis des Erwachsenen: Positive Rheumafaktoren, Erosionen an den Gelenken und subkutane Rheumaknoten. Es wirkt sich der gewebezerstörende Effekt der Rheumafaktoren aus; diese sind autoaggressive Antikörper.

Auf die Größe der Gruppe von Kranken, die verkrüppelt, scheint die Therapie keinen Einfluß zu haben. Jedenfalls hat sie sich nicht überzeugend verkleinert, wenn man die Ergebnisse vor Einführung der Steroid- und Zytostatika-Therapie vergleicht mit denen der 60er Jahre.

Die Todeshäufigkeit der jugendlichen Polyarthritis liegt bei 4–5%. Sie ist bedingt durch Infekte, Beteiligung des Herzens und Amyloid der Nieren. Amyloidniere ist bei kindlicher chronischer Polyarthritis dreimal häufiger als bei Erwachsenen. BYWATERS sah als Todesursache bei 400 in 20 Jahren von ihm beobachteten Fällen 21mal Infektionen und 11mal Nierenversagen — wohl durch Amyloid.

Nimmt man die Aktivität der Krankheit als prognostischen Maßstab, so wird die Hälfte der Fälle — 95 von 216 in der Beobachtungsgruppe von ANSELL und BYWATERS — in einer mittleren Zeit von 3,1 Jahren (1–12 Jahre) inaktiv. Davon waren 1/3 schon nach einem Jahr ausgeheilt. Das prognostische Schicksal entscheidet

Tabelle 1. Prognose der juvenilen chronischen Polyarthritis (nach BYWATERS)

Zahl	Beobachtungszeit	Verstorben	Normales Leben	Arthritis
140	15 Jahre	12	88% ♂ 76% ♀	30%

sich also im Beginn der Krankheit. Ein günstiger Einfluß der Frühbehandlung ist möglich. Fraglich bleibt, ob die Behandlung den Verlauf grundsätzlich verändert, oder ob der anfängliche Behandlungserfolg nur eine Tendenz zur spontanen Besserung fördert und beschleunigt.

Chronische Polyarthritis des Erwachsenen
Epidemiologie

Die Epidemiologie der chronischen Polyarthritis könnte auch prognostische Hinweise geben, wenn sie Faktoren aufdeckte, die die Krankheit auslösen und ihren Verlauf beeinflussen.

An sicherer chronischer Polyarthritis, die nach internationalen Standards 5 von 10 Kriterien der amerikanischen Rheumagesellschaft erfüllen muß, leiden 0,5% der Männer und 1,6% der Frauen über 15 Jahre. Nimmt man wahrscheinliche chronische Polyarthritis hinzu, die 3–4 der Kriterien der amerikanischen Rheumagesellschaft aufweisen muß, so sind es 2,5% Männer und 6% Frauen. Die chronische Polyarthritis nimmt mit dem Alter auf 5 bzw. 16% bei über 65jährigen zu. Einflüsse der geographischen Lage, der Höhe, des Klimas, des Berufs, Stadt oder Land gelten als nicht gesicherte Faktoren, die Manifestation oder Verlauf beeinflussen. Jedoch kommt eine familiäre Häufung von Rheumafaktoren und von manifester chronischer Polyarthritis vor: Die Häufigkeit von Erkrankungen in Familien von Kranken mit chronischer Polyarthritis ist zwei- bis dreimal höher als in Vergleichsfamilien. Da dies für die prognostisch ungünstigeren seropositiven Formen gilt, sind mehrere Fälle in der Familie ein prognostisches Risiko für den einzelnen Kranken. Wahrscheinlich treffen hier mehrere genetische Anlagen zusammen. Zwillingsstudien unterstreichen, daß die Wirkung von Umweltfaktoren hinter der Bedeutung von spontan wirksamen Faktoren zurücktritt: In 33% der Fälle von seropositiver chronischer Polyarthritis haben beide eineiige Zwillinge die Krankheit.

Die epidemiologischen Studien umfassen die behandlungsbedürftigen klinisch manifesten Fälle, außerdem aber die Kranken, die geringfügige subjektive Symptome mit deutlichen objektiven Zeichen der Rheumafaktoren, Rheumaknötchen, röntgenologischen Veränderungen an Gelenken und Halswirbelsäule haben, aber auch diejenigen Gesunden, die nur die objektiven Zeichen, aber keine Beschwerden haben. Die Bedeutung dieser Tatsache wird durch die Beobachtung demonstriert, daß röntgenologische Zeichen der chronischen Polyarthritis bei Männern und Frauen gleich häufig sind: 5–6%. Sie sind aber bei Frauen schwerer ausgeprägt. Die klinische Erkrankung wird bei Frauen 3–4mal häufiger manifest als bei Männern. Ähnliches gilt für Rheumafaktoren. Sie finden sich bei Männern und Frauen etwa gleich häufig. Bei Frauen müssen also geschlechts- oder umweltspezifische Einflüsse die Manifestation der Krankheit begünstigen.

Die Anwesenheit von Rheumafaktoren hat für die Manifestation der Krankheit und für die Prognose nur begrenzten Wert. Das zeigt folgende Beobachtung: Städtische Bevölkerungen haben doppelt so häufig einen positiven Waaler-Rose-Test wie ländliche, aber die Krankheit kommt in beiden Bevölkerungen gleich häufig vor.

Die Faktoren, die zur Steigerung der physiologischen Bildung von Anti-γ-Globulin-Antikörpern führen, sind also nicht die gleichen, die den Ausbruch der Krankheit bedingen. Diese Aussage ist zu unterscheiden von der prognostisch ungünstigen Bedeutung hoher und ansteigender Titer für Rheumafaktoren bei Erkrankten. In Bevölkerungsstudien ist der Prozentsatz der sero-positiven Fälle bei Menschen, die die Kriterien der sicheren oder wahrscheinlichen chronischen Polyarthritis erfüllen, wesentlich niedriger als bei einem klinischen Krankengut. Schwere und Verlauf, z. B. die Notwendigkeit der Behandlung in einer Klinik, hängen also mit der Bildung von Rheumafaktoren statistisch zusammen. Sie bestimmen wesentlich den Verlauf, weil sie die Entstehung von Gewebsnekrosen, z. B. an Gefäßen und in Rheumaknötchen, begünstigen. Das geschieht durch Bildung von Immunkomplexen, d. h. Bindung von Rheumafaktoren an Eiweißkörper der Bindegewebe.

Die prognostischen Schlüsse aus der Analyse von Kollektiven sind auch durch die Auswahl der Patienten beeinflußt: Klinisches Krankengut, ambulantes Krankengut, Bevölkerung, Berufsgruppe usw. Sie sind auch abhängig davon, ob ein Kollektiv oder ein Individuum über Jahre wiederholt untersucht wird, unabhängig davon, ob es Beschwerden hat und behandelt wird oder nicht. Denn die Krankheit kann langsam progredient oder intermittierend verlaufen. In der Gruppe der Intermittierenden finden sich die Fälle mit sogenannter benigner Polyarthritis und guter Prognose.

Epidemiologische Nachuntersuchungen haben folgende Ergebnisse gehabt: Auf die Prognose des Spontanverlaufs weist eine wichtige Beobachtung in England hin. Bei Bevölkerungsuntersuchungen geben 5% der Männer und 7% der Frauen typische Symptome einer vorübergehenden chronischen Polyarthritis zwischen dem 5. und 24. Lebensjahr an. Bei 5% dieser Gruppe, die eine Mitralstenose hatten, mußten die Gelenksymptome einem rheumatischen Fieber zugewiesen werden. Bei 26% fand man Restsymptome von chronischer Polyarthritis ohne Krankheitswert. Auch mehrere Schübe sind möglich. Es entwickelt sich keine chronische Krankheit. Solche Ereignisse wurden als benigne Polyarthritis bezeichnet.

Cobb untersuchte 331 Angestellte über 28 Monate 20mal. Bei der ersten Untersuchung entdeckte er 2% chronische Polyarthritis — in Übereinstimmung mit allen bisherigen Bevölkerungsuntersuchungen. Bei jeder Nachuntersuchung aber kamen neue Fälle hinzu, so daß am Ende der Studie 5% die Kriterien für chronische Polyarthritis erfüllten und 15% für definitive und wahrscheinliche zusammen. COBB berechnete, daß 11% der von ihm untersuchten Angestelltengruppe während 10% des Beobachtungszeitraumes eine aktive chronische Polyarthritis hatten. LINCOLN und COBB fanden in einer ähnlichen Studie eine Kumulation der chronischen Polyarthritis von 6 auf 14% in 2 Jahren.

BEHREND hat 1968 eine Bevölkerung nachuntersucht, die sie 1963 schon einmal untersucht hatte. Sie fand für die Bevölkerungen einer deutschen und zweier englischer Gemeinden eine Zuwachsrate von 5% für Männer und 6% für Frauen, wenn sie die Kriterien 1 u. 2 der New Yorker Vereinbarung von 1968 verwendete (Tab. 2).

Tabelle 2. Zuwachsrate (Incidence) an chronischer Polyarthritis in Oberhörlen, Leigh und Wensleydale
Altersgruppe zum Zeitpunkt der Erstuntersuchung
New York-Kriterien 1 u. 2

Männer: Altersgruppe (in Jahren)	15–24	–34	–44	–54	–64	65+	Ungewog. Mittel
Untersucht	36	52	57	57	74	49	
Initial mit chr. P.	0	1	1	5	8	3	
Initial ohne chr. P.	36	51	56	52	66	46	
Neue Fälle von chr. P.	1	0	5	0	4	3	
5 Jahres-Incidence	2,8%	0%	8,9% ns	0%	6,1%	6,5%	4,0%
Frauen:							
Untersucht	26	72	69	85	69	75	
Initial mit chr. P.	0	2	3	5	12	7	
Initial ohne chr. P.	26	70	66	80	57	68	
Neue Fälle von chr. P.	0	0	1	9	6	7	
5 Jahres-Incidence	0%	0%	1,5% ns	11,2%	10,5%	10,2%	6,0%
Männer und Frauen:							
Untersucht	62	124	126	142	143	124	
Initial mit chr. P.	0	3	4	10	20	10	
Initial ohne chr. P.	62	121	122	132	123	114	
Neue Fälle von chr. P.	1	0	6	9	10	10	
5 Jahres-Incidence	1,6%	0%	4,9%	6,8%	8,1%	8,8%	5,0%

ns = nicht signifikant

VALKENBURG hat die jahreszeitlichen Schwankungen der Arthritisepisoden gezeigt, die bei epidemiologischen Studien über abortive Verläufe berücksichtigt werden müssen.

Die *Summe dieser Erfahrungen* zeigt eine große Zahl klinisch symptomloser, leichter, vorübergehender, rudimentärer, unbehandelter Formen, die offenbar eine gute Prognose haben. Ihr Anteil am Vorkommen der Krankheit in der Bevölkerung liegt sicher über 50%.

Aussagen über die Prognose der chronischen Polyarthritis aus Statistiken werden dadurch erschwert, daß unter dem sozialmedizinischen und morbiditätsstatistischen Begriff „Rheuma" alles subsumiert wird, was Menschen mit Schmerzen in Gelenken, Muskeln, Knochen, Sehnen und mit Behinderungen der Bewegung zum Arzt führt. Davon leiden aber nur etwa 15% an einer chronischen Entzündung. Am Krankengut der Krankenhäuser ist die chronische Polyarthritis mit etwa 0,6–1,2% beteiligt.

Mortalität

Die Mortalität der chronischen Polyarthritis ist für Männer mit 0,5 und für Frauen mit 0,6 pro 200 000 Einwohner gering. Nach BJÖRKMANN beträgt sie in vergleichbaren Altersgruppen 24,4‰, verglichen mit 18‰ für Gesunde. Sie ist nicht durch die Arthritis bedingt, sondern durch deren Komplikationen wie Carditis, Arteriitis, Polyserositis, durch Amyloid und Zerstörungen des Atlantooccipitalgelenkes (Tab. 3).

Tabelle 3. Cause of death in rheumatoid arthritis

Cause	No. of cases	Percentage	Percentage in American series[a]
Heart disease	27	36.0	19.0
Infection	11	14.7	41.0
Nephritis	13	17.3	11.5
Cancer	10	13.3	7.0
Cerebral accident	4	5.3	2.0
Gastro-intestinal disease	6	8.0	5.5
Pulmonary embolism	3	4.0	7.0
Accident	1	1.3	0.5
Miscellaneous	—	—	6.0
Total	75		

[a] COBB, ANDERSON and BAUER (1953).

Nach ROSENBERG starben von 30 Autopsiefällen 30% an Herzkomplikationen, 37% an Lungenkrankheiten. COBB gibt 19% für Herzkrankheiten und 41% für Infektionen an, DUTHIE 36% für Herztodesfälle, 14,7% für Infektionen. Hinzu kommen Komplikationen der Therapie mit Steroiden: Magenblutungen und Infektionen.

Auf die Bedeutung der entzündlichen Komponente weist die höhere Mortalität im Vergleich zur degenerativen Arthrose in der Altersgruppe 45–64 Jahre hin. In dieser Altersgruppe stehen chronisch-rheumatische Krankheiten an dritter Stelle der Häufigkeit von Krankenhausbehandlungen. In der ärztlichen Praxis stehen sie in dieser volkswirtschaftlich wichtigen Altersgruppe sogar an erster Stelle. Diese Zahlen umfassen entzündliche und degenerative Gelenkerkrankungen. Aber in dieser Altersgruppe hat die entzündliche Form ihren Gipfel.

Sozialmedizinische Bedeutung

Für die von der Therapie unabhängige Prognose interessieren sich außer Kranker und Arzt die Volkswirtschaft, die Arbeitgeber, die Krankenkassen und die Versicherungen. Maßstäbe der Urteilsbildung sind Häufigkeit der Arbeitsausfälle sowie Beginn und Häufigkeit der Invalidität. Für Westdeutschland und Jugoslawien sind diese Daten für Arbeitsausfälle zusammengestellt: Der chronische Rheumatismus ist mit 9,6% der Fälle und mit 10,7% der ausgefallenen Arbeitstage beteiligt (Tab. 4).

Nach Belart ist die Gesamtheit der sogenannten rheumatischen Beschwerden an den Arbeitsausfällen mit 15–21%, an den Krankmeldungen mit 5–12% beteiligt. Die durchschnittliche Dauer der Arbeitsunfähigkeit beträgt 19,8–24,6 Tage pro Jahr. Dabei nimmt er ein Verhältnis von 1 : 3 des entzündlichen zum degenerativen Rheumatismus an.

Lawrence hat 1965 für England den Arbeitsausfall auf ½ Tag/Jahr pro Einwohner berechnet. Das sind 28 Millionen Arbeitstage. In der Schweiz werden 1½ Tage/Einwohner/Jahr geschätzt.

An den Frühinvalidisierungen sind die rheumatischen Beschwerden mit 19–25% beteiligt. Die volkswirtschaftliche Bedeutung der chronischen Polyarthritis ist also erheblich, das Interesse an einer Verbesserung der Prognose groß. In den USA sind 2,5 Mill., in Schweden 25 000 Menschen jährlich wegen chronischer Polyarthritis teilweise oder ganz berufsunfähig.

Spontanverlauf und natürliche Prognose der chronischen Polyarthritis

Die chronische Polyarthritis kann in jedem Stadium zur Ruhe kommen, d. h. klinisch ausheilen. Das ist aber selten, sicher weniger als 10% der Fälle, wenn man die benignen Formen ausscheidet. Häufiger sind langdauernde Remissionen und Stillstände (Tab. 5). Short sah sie in 80 von 293 Fällen der Vorcortison-Ära. Dauer der Attacken und Remissionen sind prognostisch zuverlässiger als Schwere des Schubs. 50% dieser 80 Fälle hatten kurze Attacken und kurze Remissionen, 40% kurze Schübe und lange Remissionen, 10% lange Attacken und lange Remissionen. Die Regel ist ein langsames, kontinuierliches oder sprunghaftes Fortschreiten. Die dabei auftretenden Schäden am Knorpel sind irreversibel. Rückbildungsfähig sind dagegen die Erosionen am subchondralen Knochen (Tab. 6).

Bei etwa der Hälfte der Fälle läßt sich im Laufe von 10–15 Jahren eine schwere Beeinträchtigung der Gebrauchsfähigkeit der erkrankten Gelenke nicht vermeiden. Nach Reah verkürzt sich die Lebenserwartung eines Kranken, der die chronische Polyarthritis vor dem 50. Lebensjahr erwarb, von 73 auf 55 Jahre.

Eine wesentliche prognostische Bedeutung hat die Anwesenheit von Rheumafaktoren und ihr Verhalten unter der Behandlung. Seronegative Fälle haben eine ungekürzte Lebenserwartung.

In einer Studie von Duthie u. Mitarb. blieben mehr als ein Drittel der seronegativen Patienten in einem Beobachtungszeitraum von 12 Jahren ohne Funktionseinbußen der erkrankten Gelenke, aber nur 9% der seropositiven Fälle. Rheumafaktoren spielen offenbar keine Rolle bei Beginn der Krankheit. Aber sie verschlechtern die Prognose, weil sie wesentlich an den Gewebsnekrosen in Rheumaknoten und in Gefäßen beteiligt sind, also Form und Schwere der Gewebsschädigung und die viscerale Beteiligung bestimmen. Wenn im Laufe der Behandlung die Rheumafaktoren abnehmen und verschwinden, verbessert das die Prognose. Eine die Rheumafaktoren senkende Wirkung wird von d-Penicillamin

Tabelle 4

Country	Disease	Intern. class. No.		Cases		Cas	Days		Jours
				Absolute figures Chiffres absolus	Rate per 100 popul. insured Taux pour 1000 pers. assurées	Percentage distribution Repartition en pour-cent	Absolute figures Chiffres absolus	Rate per 100 popul. insured Taux pour 1000 pers. assurées	Percentage distribution Repartition en pour-cent
Germany: République fédérale † 1957	All causes		T	6 450 000	903	100,0	154 170 000	21 159	100,0
			M	4 090 000	891	100,0	96 600 000	21 046	100,0
			F	2 360 000	925	100,0	57 570 000	22 576	100,0
	Rheumatism	400–402	T	620 000	87	9,6	16 480 000	2 308	10,7
		720–727	M	420 000	92	10,3	5 830 000	2 320	11,0
		730–749	F	200 000	78	8,5	27 711 385	2 286	10,1
Yugoslavia †1956	All causes		T	1 937 897	738	100,0	20 295 930	10 556	100,0
			M	1 459 102	737	100,0	7 415 455	10 265	100,0
			F	478 795	739	100,0	1 678 558	11 442	100,0
	Arthritis and rheumatism, except rheumatic fever	720–727	T	134 054	51	6,9	1 327 449	639	6,1
			M	110 935	56	7,6	351 109	671	6,5
			F	23 119	36	4,8	509 719	542	4,7
	Arthritis and spondylitis	720–725	M	26 975	14	1,8	509 719	258	2,5
			F	6 985	11	1,5	166 390	257	2,2
	Muscular rheumatism and rheumatism unspecified	726–727	M	83 959	42	5,8	817 730	413	4,0
			F	16 134	25	3,3	184 719	285	2,5

behauptet. Jedoch reichen die Erfahrungen noch nicht aus, um seine die Prognose verbessernde Wirkung beurteilen zu können.

Auch eine Studie von HILL zeigt die prognostische Bedeutung der Rheumafaktoren. Er konnte von 114 Fällen nach 3 Jahren 67 nachuntersuchen. Davon hatten 21 (9 Männer und 12 Frauen) eine wahrscheinliche seropositive, 36

Tabelle 5. Functional effects of rheumatoid arthritis

	Number of patients followed	Complete functional recovery (%)	Minimal or moderate crippling (%)	Severe crippling (%)	Deaths (%)
LAAKSONEN (1966)	544	30.1	40.2	29.7	4
PICKARD (1947)	35	40	25.7	25.7	8.6
LAURIN and FAUVREAU (1963)	31	50	25	25	—
BARKIN (1952)	51	41	—	39	20
NORCROSS, LOCKIE, and MACLEOD (1958)	62	77.4	17.8	—	4.8
LINDBJERG (1964)	75	36	35	22	7
BREWER (1966)	100	33	51	11	5
SURY (1957)	151	39	32	29	—
CALABRO (1965)	50	74	10	14	2

Tabelle 6. Results of 1954 follow-up study-patients of present series who were available for observation in 1937, 1947, and 1954 evaluated with respect to disease status

Status of disease	1937		1954		1947	
	No.	Per cent	No.	Per cent	No.	Per cent
In remission	41	17.2	23	13.2	38	16.9
Moderately improved	30	12.6	23	13.2	35	15.6
Slightly improved	58	24.3	15	8.6	50	22.2
Stationary	64	26.8	4	2.3	26	11.6
Worse	46	19.2	109	62.6	76	33.8
Total	239	100.1	174	99.9	225	100.1
Total improved	129	54.0	61	35.0	123	54.7

(14 Männer und 22 Frauen) eine seronegative chronische Polyarthritis, 8 (3 Männer und 5 Frauen) eine seropositive und 34 (12 Männer und 22 Frauen) eine seronegative mögliche chronische Polyarthritis, 12 (9 Männer und 3 Frauen) eine seropositive und 3 (2 Männer und 1 Frau) eine seronegative „episodische" Arthritis. Nach 3 Jahren hatte keiner der seronegativen Fälle eine definitive chronische Polyarthritis entwickelt. Von der seropositiven waren 8 wahrscheinliche, 2 mögliche und 6 episodische in eine endgültige chronische Polyarthritis übergegangen. Die Schlußfolgerung aus diesen Befunden lautet: Der Waaler-Rose-Test

für Rheumafaktoren ist ein zuverlässiger Maßstab für die Voraussage, ob eine Polyarthritis gelenkzerstörend fortschreitet oder nicht. Wenn eine seronegative in eine seropositive chronische Polyarthritis übergeht, verschlechtert sich natürlich die Prognose (Tab. 7).

Tabelle 7. Manifestation einer definitiven chronischen Polyarthritis in Abhängigkeit von Rheumafaktoren (nach HILL)

Wahrscheinliche c.p.:	Fälle ♂	Fälle ♀	Nach 3 Jahren nachuntersucht	Übergang in definitive c.p.
seropositiv	9	12	11	8
seronegativ	14	22	22	2
Mögliche c.p.:				
seropositiv	3	5	5	2
seronegativ	12	22	18	0
Arthritis-Episoden:				
seropositiv	9	3	8	6
seronegativ	2	1	3	0

Im Verlauf der Krankheit zeigen hohe und ansteigende Werte für die Rheumafaktoren eine schlechte Prognose und schlechte Kontrollierbarkeit der entzündlichen und gelenkzerstörenden Prozesse durch die Therapie an. Niedrige Werte, gleichbleibende oder absinkende Titer signalisieren eine Besserung der Prognose. Jedoch besteht kein Einfluß der Medikamente auf den Titer an Rheumafaktoren, auch dann nicht, wenn diese befriedigend oder gut antirheumatisch wirksam sind, d. h. Schmerzen und Entzündungssymptome beeinflussen.

Die wichtigste Studie über den Verlauf der chronischen Polyarthritis in einem ambulant überwachten Krankengut, das behandlungsbedürftig war, aber nur durchschnittlich 5,9 Tage im Jahr pro Patient in der Klinik verbringen mußte, stammt aus Rotterdam von DEN OUDSTEN, PLANTEN und POSTHUMA. Sie umfaßt einen Zeitraum von 15 Jahren. Jeder Patient, der aus einem Stadtteil mit etwa 25 000 Einwohnern in die regionale Rheumaambulanz kam, wurde einmal im Jahr klinisch röntgenologisch und serologisch untersucht. Die Zahl der Kranken mit sicherer und wahrscheinlicher chronischer Polyarthritis betrug 321 (47 klassische, 121 sichere, 153 wahrscheinliche). Der Übergang der einzelnen Schweregrade ist in der Tabelle zusammengestellt (Tab. 8). Der Übergang vollzieht sich mit einem Maximum in 4–11 Jahren. Nach 15 Jahren haben sich 60% der Fälle verschlimmert. Man muß bei der prognostischen Auswertung davon ausgehen, daß diese Patienten in dieser Zeit sachverständig überwacht und behandelt wurden mit den therapeutischen Strategien, die zwischen 1950 und 1965 als optimal galten.

Die prognostischen Parameter sind der folgenden Tabelle zu entnehmen: Die BKS ist ein unzuverlässiger Hinweis. Am zuverlässigsten sind Gelenksteifigkeit, Gelenkschwellung, Greifkraft und Rheumafaktoren (Tab. 9).

Tabelle 8. Conversion of possible RA to probable or definite RA and of probable RA to definite RA in the Rotterdam RA study

Observation period	Possible RA			Probable RA		
	Number of patients	Converting to probable or definite RA		Number of patients	Converting to definite RA	
		(number)	(%)		(number)	(%)
< 1 year	382	0	0	231	0	0[a]
1– 2 years	360	16	4	211	14	7
2– 3 years	339	39	11	192	23	12
3– 4 years	303	47	15	175	34	19
4– 5 years	274	49	18	154	41	27
5– 6 years	248	61	25	135	38	28
6– 7 years	229	61	27	127	46	36
7– 8 years	200	61	30	107	43	40
8– 9 years	173	58	33	93	41	44
9–10 years	150	58	39	73	37	51
10–11 years	128	54	42	58	31	53
11–12 years	94	35	37	46	28	61
12–13 years	78	36	46	32	23	72
13–14 years	63	31	49	23	16	70
14–15 years	48	29	60	17	11	65

[a] Patients changing from possible to probable or definite RA and from probable to definite RA within a year of diagnosis were not defined as convertors.

Tabelle 9. Rotterdam RA study — Comparison of certain characteristics in patients with possible RA in relation to subsequent changes in diagnosis

Characteristic	Converted to probable or definite RA		Remained only possible RA		Significance of difference
	(number[a])	(%)	(number[a])	(%)	
Morning stiffness (> 15 min. duration)	34	27	84	33	$P > 0.1$
Joint tenderness	120	96	229	89	$P < 0.05$
Joint swelling	60	48	85	33	$P < 0.01$
ESR (Westergren) ♂ > 10 mm., ♀ > 15 mm.	73	58	185	72	$P < 0.01$
Rheumatoid factor (Waaler-Rose, > 1 : 8)					
— initially	11 (108)	10.2	14 (254)	5.5	$P > 0.1$
— on retesting in 1965	40 (108)	37.0	24 (254)	9.4	$P < 0.001$
Grip strength < 350 mm. Hg	52 (71)	73	93 (173)	54	$P < 0.01$
Haemoglobin ♂ > 15 g.%, ♀ > 14 g.%	71 (83)	86	167 (200)	83	$P > 0.5$
Total sample	125		257		

[a] Values in parentheses denote the number tested when this is less than the total sample.

Prognose des klinischen Krankengutes

Die klassische Studie über den Wert klinischer Zeichen für die Prognose der chronischen Polyarthritis stammt von Short et al. (1957). Ihre Bedeutung liegt darin, daß sie repräsentativ für die Ära vor Einführung der Steroidtherapie ist. Es handelt sich zwar um Patienten, die so schwer krank waren, daß sie in die Klinik aufgenommen werden mußten. Aber sie wurden im wesentlichen nur mit Salicylaten, Bettruhe, krankengymnastischen Übungen und orthopädisch behandelt. Es wurden 300 Patienten in die Studie aufgenommen, die zwischen 1930 und 1936 in das Massachusetts General Hospital eingewiesen wurden. Von 1938 an wurden 293 Patienten weiter beobachtet. Zwischenergebnisse wurden 1947 und 1954 zusammengestellt und veröffentlicht und von Short 1968 noch einmal prognostisch ausgewertet.

Wesentliche Schlüsse für die Prognose lassen sich aus der Form des Beginns der chronischen Polyarthritis und aus dem Verlauf im ersten Jahr ziehen. Ein akuter exsudativer Beginn signalisiert eine gute Prognose. Ihm folgt häufiger ein intermittierender Verlauf (31,2%) als ein progressiver (18,3%). Wenn ein rheumatischer Schub länger als 1 Jahr dauert, so verschlechtert das die Prognose.

Symmetrischem Beginn folgt ein schwererer Verlauf als asymmetrischem. Fehlen von Ergüssen und röntgenologischen Zeichen verspricht einen günstigen Verlauf.

Wenn Patienten im ersten Jahr der Erkrankung in eine Verlaufsstudie aufgenommen werden, so sind 40% von ihnen nach 12 Jahren inaktiv. Patienten, die im 2.–5. Jahr bei Beginn der Beobachtung und Therapie waren, wurden in nur 11% im gleichen Zeitraum inaktiv (Duthie).

In der Studie von Short waren von Patienten, die im ersten Jahr der Erkrankung in die Behandlung genommen wurden, bei Kontrolle 74,1% im Stadium der Besserung, 37% im Zustand der Remission.

Patienten, die später als ein Jahr nach Beginn der Erkrankung in die Behandlung kamen, waren 10 Jahre später nur in 43,2% gebessert, nur in 4,7% frei von Gelenksymptomen.

Diese Zahlen lassen zwei Deutungen zu: Entweder haben die akut einsetzenden Arthritiden, die den Patienten schnell zum Arzt führen, eine bessere natürliche Prognose, oder die Frühbehandlung, die bei diesen Fällen einsetzt, hat Vorteile gegenüber der späteren Behandlung, die bei Patienten wirksam wird, bei denen ein langsamer undramatischer Beginn den Gang zum Arzt lange hinauszögert.

Unter den klinischen Zeichen gibt es prognostisch günstige und ungünstige. Sie sind in der folgenden Tabelle zusammengestellt (Tab. 10). Die Zeichen stehen untereinander in Häufigkeitszusammenhängen. Deswegen sollte ihre Zusammenstellung als prognostisches Muster gelesen werden. Ein einzelnes Symptom ist unzuverlässig.

Short gibt als Typ des prognostisch günstigen Kranken folgende Kriterien an: Männliches Geschlecht, unter 40 Jahre alt; akuter, unilateraler oder monartikulärer Beginn in einem großen Gelenk; Dauer 1 Jahr; Fehlen von Rheumaknoten, Arteriitis und röntgenologische Zeichen von Gelenkzerstörung; ständig niedrige BKS; gute Moral; negative Rheumafaktoren.

Über die Beobachtungszeit bis 1947 sagt Bauer, daß sie als Kontrollgruppe für spätere Studien dienen könnte. Die in dieser Zeit angewandte Therapie hat zwar die Beschwerden gemildert, nach seiner Auffassung aber den Verlauf der Krankheit nicht beeinflußt. 53% hatten sich gebessert, aber 34% waren schlechter geworden. Unter den gebesserten waren mehr Männer (67,2%) als Frauen (49,7%). Beginn im Alter unter 40 Jahren verspricht häufigere Besserung (60,2%) nach 10 bis 15 Jahren als Start der Krankheit im 5. Lebensjahrzehnt oder später (45,3%).

1954 nach etwa 15jähriger Beobachtungsdauer standen für eine Nachuntersuchung 174 Kranke zur Verfügung. Das wichtigste Ergebnis ist eine bedeutende Zunahme der Fälle, deren Befund sich verschlechtert hatte (62,6%). Gebessert

Tabelle 10. Muster prognostischer Zeichen bei chronischer Polyarthritis

Hinweis auf wahrscheinlich günstigen Verlauf	Hinweis auf wahrscheinlich laufende Verschlechterung
Akuter Beginn ohne Prodromi	Langdauernde Prodromi: Appetitlosigkeit, Gewichtsabnahme, kalte und morgens steife Hände, Kälteempfindlichkeit
Beginn im frühen Lebensalter (< 40)	Schleichender Beginn
Einseitiger Beginn	Muskelatrophie
Monartikuläre Form	Fieber
Fehlen von Gelenkerguß	Anämie
Fehlen von Röntgen-Zeichen	Befall vieler Gelenke
Niedrige Rheumafaktoren	Symmetrischer Befall der Finger- und Handgelenke
Niedrige BKS	Röntgenologische Veränderungen (Gelenknahe Osteoporose, Gelenkspaltverschmälerungen, Erosionen, Luxationen)
Intermittierender Verlauf	Rheumafaktoren
	Rheumaknötchen
	Progressiver Verlauf

oder in Remission waren 35%. Einflüsse einer zwischen 1947 und 1954 verbesserten Therapie auf den Verlauf sind also nicht erkennbar. Das ist um so wichtiger, als RAGAN 1949 eine Verlaufsstudie über 374 Kranke veröffentlichte, die im Durchschnitt 11 Jahre beobachtet wurden. 201 von ihnen hatten eine Goldtherapie erhalten, 173 eine Behandlung, die mit der in der Studie von SHORT vergleichbar war. RAGAN fand keinen Unterschied in seinen beiden Gruppen, also auch keine die Prognose verbessernden Einflüsse der Goldbehandlung. Der Verlauf seiner Kranken ist ähnlich dem in Boston: Nach 11 Jahren waren 48% gebessert und 26% ohne Symptome einer Arthritis, also im Zustand der Remission.

Eine vergleichbare Studie legte DUTHIE 1961 vor. Er stellte zwischen 1948 und 1951 eine Gruppe von 307 Krankenhauspatienten zusammen, die mit Bettruhe, hyperämisierenden Pflastern an den erkrankten Gelenken, Physiotherapie und maximalen Aspirin-Dosen behandelt wurden. Nach etwa 10 Jahren konnten 200 Kranke nachuntersucht werden (Tab. 11). Die Ergebnisse stimmen im wesentlichen mit denen von SHORT und RAGAN überein: Von den Fällen mit akutem

Beginn waren nach 9 Jahren 52,9% im Stadium geringer Bewegungsbehinderung, aber nur 13,9% der Kranken, deren Krankheit langsam begonnen hatte.

Interessant ist der prognostische Wert des Behandlungserfolges bei der ersten Krankenhausbehandlung, der natürlich mit der Schwere der Krankheit an ihrem

Tabelle 11. Prognostischer Wert des Behandlungserfolges bei der 1. Krankenhausbehandlung der chron. Polyarthritis (nach DUTHIE und Mitarbeitern)

Entlassung mit Störung der Gelenkfunktion	Zustand nach 9 Jahren gebessert	inaktiv nach 9 Jahren
Leicht	80%	
Mittel	65%	
Schwer	37%	
aktiv		18%
inaktiv		36%

Tabelle 12. Dauer der chronischen Polyarthritis vor der 1. Krankenhausbehandlung und Verlauf der Krankheit (nach SHORT, BAUER und REYNOLDS)

Dauer der Krankheit vor Krankenhausaufnahme	Zahl der nach 10 Jahren nachuntersuchten Patienten	Gebessert in %	Totale Remission
	250	53,2	
< 1 Jahr	81	74,1	37
> 1 Jahr	169	43,2	4,7

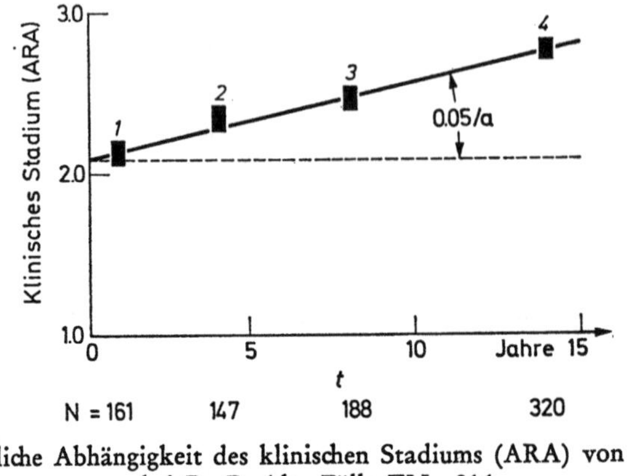

Abb. 1. Durchschnittliche Abhängigkeit des klinischen Stadiums (ARA) von der Krankheitsdauer bei P.c.P. Alte Fälle $\Sigma N = 816$

Beginn in Zusammenhang steht: Ein guter Erfolg verheißt einen milden Verlauf und eine gute Prognose.

Die jüngste Studie stammt von JACOBY et al. Sie ist prospektiv an 100 Patienten angelegt, die im ersten Jahr der Krankheit waren. 83 wurden 3–11 Jahre danach nachuntersucht. 5 waren an Folgen der Krankheit oder Behandlung verstorben. 18 seronegative Fälle wurden während eines Schubes seropositiv. Es fand sich eine

Korrelation zwischen Waaler-Rose-Test, Zahl der erkrankten Gelenke und Schwere der an großen Gelenken röntgenologisch sichtbaren Zerstörungen. Obgleich die Aktivität der Krankheit in der Regel zurückging, schritt die Funktionseinschränkung doch voran. Als Grund dafür wird ein mit dem Krankheitsverlauf interferierender Altersprozeß an den Gelenken diskutiert. Daraus ist zu lernen, daß zunehmende Gebrauchsunfähigkeit von Gelenken bei Kranken mit chronischer Polyarthritis im 4. und 5. Lebensjahrzehnt und später nicht ausschließlich auf die chronische Polyarthritis bezogen werden kann.

Ein zusammenfassendes Urteil über die Prognose der chronischen Polyarthritis und ihre Beeinflußbarkeit durch Therapie gibt eine Untersuchung von JOSENHANS, der 816 behandelte und unbehandelte Fälle auswertete: Die Krankheit schreitet mit oder ohne Behandlung gesetzmäßig fort. Es befinden sich immer etwa gleichviele Patienten in den verschiedenen Schweregraden und Stadien der Erkrankung (Abb. 1). Die Prognose wird nicht so sehr durch die Therapie bestimmt als durch die Art des Beginns und die Form des frühen Verlaufs signalisiert. Die Therapie beeinflußt aber das Maß der Gebrauchsfähigkeit der erkrankten Gelenke. Die Bewertung von Verlauf und Prognose mit Funktionskriterien z. B. nach STEINBROCKER hat ein günstigeres Ergebnis (Tab. 13). Wahrscheinlich ist es richtig zu sagen: 50–60% der Kranken erhalten die Gebrauchsfähigkeit ihrer Gelenke, 10–15% heilen klinisch aus, der Rest verkrüppelt. BARNES gibt folgende Werte an:

Tabelle 13

Pat. mit Kriterien, die nicht den Arzt aufsuchen	30%
Kurze Aktivität mit Ausheilung	20%
Leichte bis mäßige Dauerschäden	25%
Daueraktivität mit Exacerbationen	45%
Schwerer, gelenkzerstörender Verlauf	10%

Diese relativ schlechte Prognose muß jedoch ergänzt werden durch den Hinweis auf die relativen Verbesserungen der Gebrauchsfähigkeit erkrankter Gelenke durch gelenkchirurgische Maßnahmen einerseits und psycho-therapeutische ärztliche Führung und Lebenshilfen andererseits.

Den prognostischen Zusammenhang von Verlauf und röntgenologischen Zeichen gibt die folgende Tabelle nach FREYBERG (Tab. 14):

Tabelle 14. Verlauf der chronischen Polyarthritis und Auftreten irreversibler Gelenkzerstörungen (nach FREYBERG 1969)

Betroffene Gelenke		72 Kranke unter optimaler Therapie: 56 Frauen, 16 Männer					
		Destruierende Gelenkveränderungen	Beginn von klinischer und röntgenologischer Gelenkzerstörung				
			3 Jahre	4 Jahre	5 Jahre	6 Jahre	10–20 Jahre
Fingergrundgelenke	72	52	3	6	10		33
Handgelenke	72	49	7	3	6	15	18
Ellenbogengelenke	56	21	1	5	3		12
Kniegelenke	67	26	1	1	5	2	17

Psychische Haltung. Sozialpsychologische Situation und Prognose

Auf das Schicksal der Kranken, d. h. auf Zeitpunkt und Ausmaß ihrer Invalidität hat ihre Haltung zur Krankheit, ihr Widerstand gegen die Versteifung der Gelenke, ihr Wille zur Selbsthilfe und ihr Ertragen von Schmerzen einen wesentlichen Einfluß. Deswegen ist es in der Therapie so wichtig, den Schmerz schnell zu beseitigen, die Gelenke zu bewegen, die Muskeln zu entkrampfen und zu üben und auf diese Weise das Vertrauen der Kranken in die Gebrauchsfähigkeit des Bewegungsapparates zu erhalten und zu stärken. Denn die Kranken mit chronischer Polyarthritis neigen zur Resignation. Es ist schwer zu sagen, ob es sich um die Aktualisierung latenter Charaktermerkmale handelt oder um Reaktionen auf das Verhalten der Umgebung oder ob das mit der Tatsache zusammenhängt, daß es sich meist um Frauen am Ende der familien-aktivsten Lebensperiode handelt, die die gemeinsame Existenz mit dem Mann aufgebaut und die Kinder großgezogen haben und die sich dann selbst der Familie zur Pflege übergeben. Vielleicht verhilft die Einsicht in die Bedeutung des Bewegungsapparates für das typische menschliche Dasein zu erklärenden Erkenntnissen: Der Bewegungsapparat ist Instrument der Weltbewältigung, er dient sowohl der Bewegung, der Inbesitznahme, der Verteidigung und Selbstbewahrung in Rückzug u. a., er dient aber auch der Wahrung der aufrechten Haltung, also der typisch menschlichen Lage zur Umwelt. Sie bedeutet eine gewisse statische Labilität, aber auch die Möglichkeit zur Überschau. Bewegungsbehinderung bedeutet Einengung des menschlichen Aktions- und Orientierungsfeldes. Sie bedeutet auch Gefährdung der Selbstbewahrung. Sich bewegen können bedeutet Aktivität, Freiheit, Entfaltung. Der Bewegungsapparat wird sehr früh, zwischen dem 8. und 18. Lebensmonat, in der Kindheit mit Werten besetzt: Angriff und Verteidigung mit dem Wert der Feindseligkeit, Haltung und Geltung mit dem Wert der Selbstbehauptung. Am chronischen Rheumatiker sind folgende Züge als charakteristisch aufgedeckt worden: Zwanghafte Gewissenhaftigkeit, Fügsamkeit, ja Unterwürfigkeit; masochistisch-depressive Züge von Selbstaufopferung und Selbstbestrafung; Bedürfnis nach körperlicher Aktivität vor der Krankheit.

Diese Haltungen sind Abwehrreaktionen gegen den Ausbruch von Feindseligkeit. Im Umgang mit Mitmenschen benimmt sich der Kranke mit chronischer Polyarthritis mit „böser Demut" und „liebevoller Tyrannei" (Cremerius).

Biographisch werden Enttäuschungs-Aggressionen als kindliche Fügsamkeit, Helferhaltung und Opferbereitschaft verarbeitet. Die moralische Legitimation, die für diese Haltung ausgebildet wird, ist sekundär und verdeckt den Wunsch, feindselig zu sein. In der mitmenschlichen Beziehung schafft das Kontaktschwäche und Verletzlichkeit. Die Hilfsbereitschaft des Kranken, der zu chronischer Polyarthritis neigt, verpflichtet den, dem geholfen wird, zu einer eigentümlichen, ihm unangenehmen Abhängigkeit. Es wird eine penetrante Form von Herrschaft ausgeübt, besonders auch, wenn die Krankheit ausgebrochen ist: „Die Mütter beherrschen in ihrer Fürsorge die Kinder so, wie später die Patienten selber mit ihrer Opferbereitschaft die Umgebung tyrannisieren" (Beck). Die Mütter der Kranken werden als gleichzeitig überfürsorglich — overprotective —, streng und kalt beschrieben. Das dämmt den protesthaften Bewegungssturm des Kindes zurück. Die natürliche Beziehung von Bewegungsdrang und Bewegungsapparat wird gestört.

Im späteren Leben können Affektstürme in den Bewegungsapparat durchbrechen, wenn die verdrängten Aggressionen aktualisiert werden oder wenn ihre Kontrollmechanismen entfallen, z. B. die Bezugspersonen von Dienen und Herrschen sich von dem Rheumatiker trennen.

Diese biographischen und sozial-psychologischen Konstellationen bedingen die eigentliche Passivität, Resignation und mangelnde Kooperationsbereitschaft der Kranken. Damit scheinen sie sich selbst zu strafen, Rache an ihrer Umgebung zu nehmen, oder diese sich zu Diensten zu machen. Rimon hat gezeigt, daß vor allem depressive Syndrome das Ansprechen auf die Therapie negativ beeinflussen. Wir wissen jedoch nicht, ob diese Form der Depression mit einer erhöhten Suicidgefahr verbunden ist.

Der Verlauf der chronischen Polyarthritis wird ungünstig beeinflußt durch latente Abhängigkeits- und Versorgungswünsche und Inaktivitätstendenzen, Herrschaftsimpulse und masochistische Selbstbestrafungsneigungen.

So entsteht leichter als bei anderen Krankheiten ein sekundärer Krankheitsgewinn. Nutzen die Kranken ihn unbewußt voll aus, so richten sie sich in und mit der Krankheit ein. Beck hält das in bezug auf Heilungsmöglichkeit für ein schlechtes prognostisches Zeichen. Die Krankheit chronifiziert nach Halliday öfter aus psychoneurotischen als aus körperlichen Gründen und führt so zur Arbeitsunfähigkeit.

Diese Erkenntnisse sind für die Verbesserung der Prognose der chronischen Polyarthritis noch nicht hinreichend erforscht und geprüft. Jedoch unterstreichen sie die Notwendigkeit, den Patienten aus seiner Passivität herauszuführen, seinen Widerstand gegen die Versteifung der Gelenke zu stärken, ihm Vertrauen zur Gebrauchsfähigkeit zu geben und seine Kraft zur Selbsthilfe zu unterstützen.

Prognose gelenkchirurgischer Maßnahmen

In den vergangenen 15 Jahren haben gelenkchirurgische Methoden die Prognose der Bewegungsfähigkeit und der Gebrauchsfähigkeit der Gelenke verbessert.

Die Synovektomie vermag ohne Zweifel ein entzündetes Gelenk für viele Jahre, bei guter Technik für mindestens zwei, zu beruhigen, von Entzündung und Erguß, sowie von Schmerzen freizuhalten. Entscheidend ist, früh genug möglichst die gesamte Synovialis zu entfernen. Unter dieser Bedingung können sich sogar bereits nachweisbare Erosionen wieder mit Knochen auffüllen. Man hat jetzt Erfahrungen über die Prognose für einen Zeitraum von 10 Jahren nach der Synovektomie. Am besten geeignet ist das Kniegelenk. Es folgen Hand-, Finger-, Daumen- und Ellenbogengelenk. Wenn die Synovektomie die entzündete Synovialis subtotal entfernt, wird das knorpel- und knochenzerstörende Geschehen so lange unterbrochen, bis die Reste der entzündeten Synovialis sich wieder über das Gelenk ausgebreitet haben. Jakubowski u. Mitarb. haben an 150 Knien von 100 Patienten Synovektomien durchgeführt und diese Patienten 2,6–7 Jahre beobachtet (Tab. 15 u. 16). Pouget u. Mitarb. haben 52 Synovektomien über einen Zeitraum von 2,5 Jahren verfolgt. Die Erfolge hingen davon ab, wie weit es einer medikamentösen Therapie gelang, ein Synovitis-Rezidiv zu verhindern. Die am meisten aufschlußreiche Studie stammt von Nicolle u. Mitarb. 38 Synovektomien des Handgelenkes, 4–5 Jahre lang. Das Krankengut schloß 102 Synovektomien an Metacapophalangialgelenken ein. In dieser Zeit betrug die Zuwachsrate von wieder- und neu aufgetretenen Synovitiden 6%. Bei einer nichtoperierten Vergleichsgruppe betrug sie 84%.

Die totale Gelenkprothese wird heute an schwer deformierten oder versteiften Fingergelenken, Hüftgelenken und Kniegelenken durchgeführt. Prognostische Beurteilung kann hier nicht die gesamte Krankheit und ihren Verlauf ins Auge

Tabelle 15

No. of years with R.A.	No. of followed-up synovect. a. debridem.	Results	
		good	failure
4	29	29	—
5–8	40	34	6
8	31	14	17
total	100	77	23

Tabelle 16

Kind of operation	Number of		Results	
	operated	followed-up	good	failure
Synovectomy	68	58	54	4
Debridement	54	42	23	19
total	122	100	77	23

fassen. Vielmehr geht es um die Wiederherstellung von Gehfähigkeit bei Gelenkersatz in Hüfte und Knien, oder der Greiffähigkeit an den Händen. Wendet man dieses prognostische Kriterium an, sind die bisherigen Ergebnisse gut, weil sie einen bereits eingetretenen Endzustand der Krankheit an bestimmten Gelenken beseitigen.

Die Prognose des Lupus erythematodes

Der Lupus erythematodes galt früher als tödliche Krankheit. Der Name Lupus erythematodes acutus bezeichnet den schnellen und akuten Verlauf. Der spontane, schnell tödliche Verlauf ist heute selten. Das hat zwei Gründe: Erstens vermag eine sich dem Verlauf anpassende Therapie mit Steroiden, Chloroquin und Azathioprin in vielen Fällen den autoimmunaggressiven Prozeß in den befallenen Organen zu kontrollieren und ein Übergreifen auf andere Organe zu verhindern. Zweitens gibt es chronische Verläufe ohne akuten Beginn und mit Befall nur eines oder weniger Organe und Gewebe, z. B. Arteriitis, Nephritis, Polyserositis, Thrombopenie, Neuritis, Arthritis, Myocarditis, hämolytische Anämie. Die Zuordnung eines Krankheitsbildes zum Lupus erythematodes geschieht aufgrund des Nachweises antinukleärer Antikörper mit Hilfe des Lupus erythematodes-Zellphänomens oder des Lupus erythematodes-Komplementtests (LECT) oder durch andere Zellantikörper wie antimitochondriale Antikörper und durch den Nachweis charakteristischer histologischer Veränderungen, z. B. in der Niere; diese sind durch Ablagerung von Immunkomplexen bedingt und durch Bildung von Fibrinoid aus immuncytologisch zerstörten Zellen. Auch bevor es eine Therapie gab, verlief mancher Fall mit Spontanremissionen, aber die Lebenserwartung lag bei akutem Beginn bei 18 Monaten, bei subakutem bei 3 Jahren.

Die Prognose des Lupus erythematodes wird bestimmt durch

1. die Schwere des Organbefalls, insbesondere von „Schlüsselorganen" wie Niere, Herz und Gehirn,
2. die Ausbreitung der dem multiplen Organbefall zugrunde liegenden Vasculitis, deren Progression — früh genug diagnostiziert — heute erfolgreich verhindert werden kann.

Dagegen lassen klinische Symptome des akuten Stadiums wie hohes Fieber, starke Beschleunigung der BSG, Hypergammaglobulinämie keine Rückschlüsse auf den weiteren Verlauf oder auf die Prognose zu.

Es gibt einen langen Streit, ob Lupus erythematodes *visceralis* und Lupus erythematodes *integumentalis* verschiedene Verlaufsformen einer Erkrankung sind, oder ob es sich um zwei gelegentlich in ihrer Hautmanifestation ähnliche, grundsätzlich jedoch voneinander ganz unabhängige Erkrankungen handele. Aufgrund eingehender histologischer und Verlaufsstudien faßt man beide Formen als Einheit zusammen. Mehr als 50% von Kranken mit anscheinend auf die Haut beschränkter Symptomatik zeigen hämatologische und immunologische Hinweise auf einen generalisierten Krankheitsprozeß. Das früher als typisch für die viscerale Form angesehene Schmetterlingserythem ist nur eine der vielen, sehr variablen Hauterscheinungen der Krankheit. Röckl sah unter 143 zehn Jahre lang beobachteten Patienten mit LE in 8,1% den Übergang von der integumentalen zur visceralen Form. Die Konsequenz aus diesen Beobachtungen ist die Notwendigkeit einer jahrzehntelangen intensiven Überwachung von allen Erythematodespatienten unter Einschluß von Methoden, die eine Frühdiagnose einer viszeralen Beteiligung erlauben; die Kontrolle der Nierenfunktion ist hier an erster Stelle zu nennen.

Autoptisch weisen 75% aller Patienten mit Erythematodes visceralis eine Nierenläsion auf (Muehrke et al.). Während frühere Statistiken eine 5-Jahres-Überlebensrate von 20–30% aufwiesen, brachte die Einführung einer konsequenten hochdosierten Therapie mit Steroiden (40–60 mg pro die über Monate) eine entscheidende Besserung der Prognose gerade der Lupus-Nephritis (V. E. Pollak et al.). Neuere Studien unter voller Ausnutzung der heute zur Verfügung stehenden Behandlungsmöglichkeiten zeigen eine 3-Jahres-Überlebensrate von 80% (Siegel et al.), Epstein berichtete kürzlich sogar von 80% Überlebensrate nach fünf Jahren. 50–60% der Patienten erreichen 10 Jahre nach Diagnose der Erkrankung (Siegel et al.). Bei Kranken, die multiple Organsymptome zeigen, wird heute zunächst eine hochdosierte Steroidbehandlung angewandt. Führt diese nicht zum Ziel, ist die sog. immunsuppressive Behandlung mit einer Kombination von Steroiden und Zytostatika am Platze. Die konsequente Anwendung dieser Behandlungsform bringt praktisch in allen Fällen eine klinische Remission (Schubert et al.); die beste Form der Langzeitbehandlung ist noch nicht endgültig geklärt, aber die Mehrzahl der Autoren zieht heute eine Langzeitbehandlung mit einer „immunsuppressiven" Kombination vor, weil auf diese Weise eine sichere Einsparung von Steroiden erreicht werden kann (Sztejnbok et al.). Die meistgebrauchte Kombination von Steroiden mit Azathioprin erwies sich in einer kontrollierten Studie von Sztejnbok et al. der einfachen Steroidbehandlung als überlegen, was die Gesamtsituation der Patienten anging. Ob die entscheidende Organläsion, die Lupus-Nephritis, in ihrem Verlauf unter der Behandlung mit dieser Kombination besser beeinflußt wird als durch Steroide allein, ist allerdings aufgrund einer weiteren kontrollierten Studie von Donadio et al. zu bezweifeln. Wenn die Steroid-Azathioprin-Kombination versagt, kann mit Erfolg Cyclophosphamid angewandt werden (Steinberg et al.), in Einzelfällen auch andere zytostatische Präparate (Schubert et al.). Neben den organspezifischen Parametern sind die Titer von Anti-DNS-Antikörpern und insbesondere der Serum-Komplement-Spiegel gute Parameter der Aktivität des Krankheitsprozesses; steigt der DNS-Titer und/oder fällt das Komplement ab, so ist ein Rezidiv zu erwarten. Viele Patienten haben ihr „persönliches" Schlüsselsymptom, z. B. Gelenkschwellungen oder Thrombozytopenie oder Auftreten des Exanthems. Wir haben in den letzten acht Jahren unter 24 Patienten nur eine junge Patientin an einer progredienten Lupus-Glomerulonephritis verloren: sie hatte die laufende Kombinationstherapie längere Zeit gegen ärztlichen Rat unterbrochen und starb im Koma uraemicum.

Eine generelle Richtlinie für die Langzeitbehandlung zu geben, ist heute noch nicht möglich. Man muß nach der Devise „so wenig wie möglich, so viel wie nötig" handeln und dabei immer wieder alle wichtigen klinischen und Laboratoriumsparameter zur Auswertung heranziehen. Hierzu gehört auch die — wenn nötig wiederholte — Nierenbiopsie.

Die früher als typisch angesehene schmetterlingsförmige Rötung über Nasenrücken und Wangen, die der Krankheit den Namen gab, findet sich in weniger als der Hälfte der Fälle und ist kein zuverlässiges prognostisches Symptom. Es kann, muß aber nicht in die akute Form übergehen. In der Regel bleibt die Hautkrankheit ein prognostisch gutartiges Rudiment ohne Generalisierung und Viszeralisierung. Sie ist deswegen prognostisch nicht identisch mit dem systematischen Lupus erythematodes oder, wie man auch sagt, Lupus erythematodes visceralis bzw. disseminatus.

Der akute Verlauf des Lupus erythematodes kann therapeutisch heute in der Regel unter Kontrolle gebracht werden. Der Beginn wird dann 5–10 Jahre überlebt.

Der primär-chronische Verlauf mit rudimentärem Organbefall hat eine gute Prognose, bezogen auf normale Lebenserwartung und Arbeitsfähigkeit, wenn er dauernd behandelt wird. Etwa die Hälfte der Fälle kommt unter Therapie soweit zur Ruhe, daß die Krankheit als klinisch ausgeheilt angesehen werden kann. Ich kenne solche Fälle von Arthritis, Arteriitis, Neuritis, Carditis, Polyserositis. Die Kranken sind aber ständig von Rezidiven bedroht, die durch Infekte, Gravidität oder Sonnenbestrahlung, vielleicht auch durch Toxine und sicher durch Medikamente, wie z. B. Phenylhydantoin ausgelöst werden können. Eine Analyse der durch Therapie beeinflußbaren Veränderungen zeigt, daß zwar klinische Symptome wie Fieber, Gelenkschmerzen, Pleuritis, Exantheme fast regelmäßig zu beseitigen sind und sich auch BKS, Dysproteinämie, Hämoglobin, Blutungszeit in mehr als der Hälfte der Fälle günstig beeinflussen lassen, daß aber der positive Lupus erythematodes-Zellbefund bestehen bleibt — als ständige Warnung.

Die Polyarthritis des Lupus erythematodes führt nicht zu Gelenkzerstörung und Verkrüppelung. In wenigen Fällen wurde eine Nekrose der Oberschenkelköpfe, wahrscheinlich durch örtliche Arteriitis hervorgerufen und beobachtet.

Literatur

Ansell, B. M., Bywaters, E. G.: Prognosis in Still's disease. Bull. rheum. Dis. **9**, 189 (1959).

Baehr, G., Klemperer, P.: Systemic lupus erythematosus. New York-London, 1959

Beall, G., Cobb, S.: The frequency distribution of episodes of rheumatoid arthritis as shown by periodic examination. J. chron. Dis. **14**, 291–310 (1961).

Beck, D.: Psychosomatische Aspekte des chronischen Gelenkrheumatismus. Basel, 1971.

Behrend, T., Lawrence, I. S., Behrend, H., Koch, R.: Eine longitudinale Studie im Hinblick auf rheumatische Erkrankungen in der ländlichen Bevölkerung von Oberhörlen in Hessen. Z. Rheumaforsch. **31**, 153–167 (1972).

Björkman, St.: Diagnose und Prognose des Frühstadiums der progressiven chronischen Polyarthritis rheumatica. Lebensversicher.-Med. **4**, 61 (1953).

Brewer, E. J.: Juvenile rheumatoid arthritis. Philadelphia-London-Toronto, 1970.

Bywaters, E. G. L.: Heberden oration 1966. Categorisation in medicine: A survey of Still's disease. Ann. rheum. Dis. **26**, 185 (1967).

Bywaters, E. G. L., Curwen, M., Dresner, E., Dixon, A. St. J.: Ten-year follow-up of rheumatoid arthritis. Lancet **2**, 1381 (1960).

Bywaters, E. G. L., Dresner, E.: The prognosis in rheumatoid arthritis. Quart. J. Med. **21**, 463 (1952).

Cobb, S.: On the great frequency of mild intermittent rheumatoid arthritis. Atti del X congresso della Lega internationale contro il Reumatismo. Turin, 1961.

Cobb, S., Anderson, F., Bauer, W.: Length of life and cause of death in rheumatoid arthritis. New Engl. J. Med. **249**, 553 (1953).

Cotta, H., Schulitz, K. P., Städler, J.: Unsere Erfahrungen mit der Rotationsprothese. In: H. Cotta und K. P. Schulitz „Der totale Hüftgelenkersatz". Stuttgart 1973.

De Forest, G. K., Mucci, M. B., Boisvert, P. L.: Two-year comparative study of serial hemagglutination tests done on groups of rheumatoid patients. Arth. Rheum. **1**, 387 (1958).

De Forest, G. K., Mucci, M. B., Boisvert, P. L.: The clinical behavior of the hemagglutination test for rheumatoid arthritis. Amer. J. Med. **21**, 897 (1964).

Den Oudsten, S. A., Planten, O., Posthuma, E. P. S.: Longitudnal survey R. A. in an urban district of Rotterdam. In: Population studies of the rheumatic diseases. Ed.: P. H. Bernett und Ph. H. N. Wood, Amsterdam, 1968.

Dixon, A. St. J.: „Rheumatoid arthritis" with negative serological reaction. Ann. rheum. Dis. **19**, 209 (1960).

Donadio, J. V., Holley, K. E., Wagoner, R. D., Ferguson, R. H., McDuffie, F. C.: Treatment of lupus nephritis with prednisone and combined prednisone and azathioprine. Ann. intern. Med. **77**, 829 (1972).

Duthie, J. J. R., Brown, P. E., Truelove, C. H., Baragar, F. D., Lawrin, A. J.: Course and prognosis in rheumatoid arthritis. A further report. Ann. rheum. Dis. **23**, 193 (1964).

Epstein, W. V., Tan, M.: Production of fibrils *in vitro* by action of normal humen kidney enzymes on L-chain proteins. Abstract 43, 36th Annual Meeting of the Amer. rheum. Ass., 1972.

Freyberg, R. H.: Study of the time of onset of disability due to joint pathology in rheumatoid arthritis. Panamerican Pheumatology; Proceedings of the fourth Panamerican Congress of Rheumatology, Amsterdam, Excerpta Medica Foundation, 1969, S. 103.

Goel, K. M., Shanks, R. A.: Follow-up study of 100 cases of juvenile rheumatoid arthritis. Annals of the Rheumatic Diseases 33, 25 (1974).

Halliday, J. L.: Psychological factor in rheumatism. Brit. med. J. 213, 264 (1937).

Hill, A. G. S.: Suspected rheumatoid arthritis; clinical features and prognosis. Atti dell X congresso della Lega internationale contro il Reumatismo. Turin, 1961.

Hill, A., Greenbury, C. C.: Clinical interpretation of serological tests in rheumatoid arthritis. In: Dixon, A. St. J., ed.: Progress in clinical rheumatology. Boston: Little, Brown & Co., 1965, p. 42.

Jacoby, R. K., Cosh, J. A., Jayson, M. I. V.: Prognosis of rheumatoid arthritis. A prospective survey over 11 years. Ann. rheum. Dis. 32, 391 (1973).

Jakubowski, S., Ruszczynska, J., Dubinska, A.: The value of knee joint synovectomy in rheumatoid arthritis (in the light of late observation). Rheumatologia (Warschau) 10, 43–56 (1972).

Jonsson, E.: On the prognosis of rheumatoid arthritis. Acta orth. scand. 30, 115 (1961).

Josenhans, G., Binzus, G.: Behandlungserfolge bei progressiv-chronischer Polyarthritis. – Medizinisch-physiologische Beurteilungsmethoden und Ergebnisse. Verhandlg. dt. Ges. Rheumatologie, 1, 316–322 (1969).

Kellgren, J. H., O'Brien, W. M.: On the natural history of rheumatoid arthritis in relation to the sheep cell agglutination test. Arthr. Rheum. 5, 115 (1962).

Kellgren, J. H., Lawrence, J. S., Aitken-Swan, J.: Rheumatic complaints in an urban population. Ann. rheum. Dis. 12, 5 (1953).

Kjevekjarto, M. v.: Zur Persönlichkeitsstruktur des Rheumatikers. Rheuma und Nervensystem. Basel, 1969.

Laaksonen, A. L.: A prognostic study of juvenile rheumatoid arthritis. Analysis of 544 cases. Acta paed. scand. 1, 173 (1966).

Lawrence, I. S.: The epidemiology and genetics of rheumatoid arthritis. In: Rheumatology population studies and genetics. Ed.: J. Roststein, Basel, 1969.

Lawrence, J. S., Bennett, P. H.: Benign polyarthritis. Ann. rheum. Dis. 19, 20 (1960).

Lincoln, T. A., Cobb, S.: The prevalence of mild rheumatoid arthritis in industry. J. Occup. Med. 5, 10 (1963).

Merrel, M., Schulman, L. E.: Determination of prognosis in chronic diseases, illustrated by lupus erythematosus. J. chron. Dis. 1, 12 (1955).

Miescher, P.: Immunsuppressive Therapie. Verhdlg. Dtsch. Ges. Innere Medizin 174, 1084 (1968).

Mohing, W.: Erfahrungen mit Synovektomien bei rheumatoider Arthritis. Med. Klin. 65, 2158 bis 2163 (1970).

Muehrke, R. C., Kark, R. M., Pirani, C. L., Pollak, V. E.: Lupus nephritis: a clinical and pathologic study based on renal biopsies. Medicine (Baltimore) 36, 1 (1957).

Nicolle, F. W., Holt, P. J. L., Calnau, J. S.: Prophylactic synovectomy of the joints of the rheumatoid hand; clinical trial with 4 to 8 year follow up. Ann. rheum. Dis. 30, 476–480 (1971).

Otten, H. A., Boerma, F. W.: Significance of the Waaler-Rose test, streptococcal agglutination and anti-streptolysin titre in the prognosis of rheumatoid arthritis. Ann. rheum. Dis. 18, 24 (1959).

Plügge, H.: Anthropologische Beobachtungen bei primär-chronischen Polyarthritikern. Z. Rheumaforsch. 12, 231 (1953).

Pollak, V. E., Priani, C. L., Schwartz, F. D.: The natural history of the renal manifestations of systemic lupus erythematosus. J. Lab. clin. Med. 63, 537 (1964).

Pouget, G., Benoist, M., Deburge, A., Cauchoi, C. J.: Synovectomy in rheumatoid arthritis. Presse méd. 79, 621–626 (1971).

Ragan, C.: The general managment of rheumatoid arthritis. J. Amer. med. Ass. 141, 124–127 (1949).

Ragan, C., Farrington, E.: The clinical features of rheumatoid arthritis. Prognostic indices. J. Amer. med. Ass. 181, 663 (1962).

Reah, T. G.: The prognosis of rheumatoid arthritis (183 patients followed up over 13 years). Proc. roy. Soc. Med. 56, 813 (1963).

RIMON, R.: A psychosomatic approach to the rheumatoid arthritis. Acta rheum. scand. Suppl. 13 (1969).

RÖCKL, H., METZ, G.: Der Wandel in Klinik und Prognose des Erythematodes. Fortschr. Med. 91, 271 (1973).

ROSENBERG, E. F., BAGGENSTOSS, A. H., HENCH, P.: Causes of death in 30 cases of rheumatoid arthritis. Ann. Inter. Med. 20, 903 (1944).

ROURKE, M. D., ERNSTENE, A. C.: A method for correcting the erythrocyte sedimentation rate for variations in the cell volume percentage of blood. J. Clin. Invest. 8, 545 (1930).

SCHREIBER, A., JANSSEN, G.: Züricher Erfahrungen mit der Hüfttotalendoprothese (1962–1970). In: H. COTTA.

SCHUBERT, J. C. F., SCHUBERT, H., HOLTZ, G., MARTIN, H.: Immunsuppressive Langzeittherapie des Lupus erythematodes visceralis. Dtsch. med. Wschr. 95, 1769 (1970).

SCHULHOF, O.: On the various types of course in rheumatoid arthritis. Atti del X Congresso della Lega Internazionale contro il Rheumatismo 1, 115 (1961).

SHARP, J. T., CALKINS, E., COHEN, A. S., et al.: Observations on the clinical, chemical and serological manifestations of rheumatoid arthritis, based on the course of 154 cases. Med. 43, 41 (1964).

SHORT, C. L.: Long remissions in rheumatoid arthritis. Med. 43, 401 (1964).

SHORT, C. L.: Rheumatoid arthritis: Types of course and prognosis. Medical clinics of North America 52, 549 (1968).

SHORT, C. L., BAUER, W.: The course of rheumatoid arthritis in patients receiving simple medical and orthopaedic measures. New Eng. J. Med. 238, 142 (1948).

SHORT, C. L., BAUER, W., REYNOLDS, W. E.: Rheumatoid arthritis. A definition of the disease and a clinical description based on a numerical study of 293 patients and controls. Cambridge, Mass., Harvard University Press, 1957.

SIEGEL, M., GWON, N., LEE, S. L., RIVERO, I., WONG, W.: Survivorship in systemic lupus erythematosus: Relationship to race and pregnancy. Arthritis Rheum. 12, 117 (1969).

SIEVERS, K.: The rheumatoid factor in definite rheumatoid arthritis. An analysis of 1279 adult patients, with a follow-up study. Acta rheum. scand., Suppl. 9 (1965).

STEINBERG, A. D., KALTREIDER, H. B., STAPLES, P. J., GOETZ, E. J., TALAL, N.: Cyclophosphamide in lupus nephritis. A controlled trial (DECKER, J. L.). Ann. intern. Med. 75, 165 (1971).

SZE, T. S.: Mortality and morbidity from chronic rheumatic diseases in the United Kingdom and Western Europe. In: The epidemiology of chronic rheumatism. Ed.: J. H. KELLGREN, M. R. JEFFREY and J. BALL: Oxford, 1963.

SZTEJNBOK, K., STEWARD, A., DIAMOND, H., KAPLAN, D.: Azathioprine in the treatment of systemic lupus erythematosus. Arthritis Rheum. 14, 639 (1971).

VALKENBURG, H. A.: Observer variance and prevalence of rheumatoid arthritis and osteoarthrosis in a longitudinal population study in the Netherlands. In: Population studies of the rheumatic diseases. Ed: P. H. BENNETT and PH. H. N. WOOD, Amsterdam, 1968.

The Diagnosis of Rheumatoid Arthritis and Allied Disorders

Dr. Francis Bach

During the past century, the general improvement in living standards, and the development of modern medicine have eliminated infectious disorders as a major cause of mortality in Great Britain. What are described as socially induced disorders are taking their place. The increase in lung cancer, much of it almost certainly due to cigarette smoking is an example, but accidents, drug addiction and suicide are also taking an increasing toll, especially among the young. In our industrial society, traffic and industrial accidents are now the commonest cause of death among older adolescents and young adult males. The introduction of the breathalyser, and the setting of an upper limit to the permissible amount of alcohol in the blood was followed by an appreciable reduction in deaths from traffic accidents. The general life expectancy has been considerably extended, so that the great majority of people now survive to become liable to the chronic conditions associated with advancing years. Chronic bronchitis, coronary disease, stroke, cancer, and rheumatism are the most common of these.

The rheumatic diseases are among the most widespread causes of ill-health in the United Kingdom. In a Government survey published last year, Harris showed that over one million people in the United Kingdom have rheumatic disorders which cause significant physical impairment. David Taylor, the research sociologist in the Office of Health Economics has estimated that in the United Kingdom in 1972, about 12% of the total working time lost in the industry through sickness was the result of rheumatic diseases. In a society in which there is full or nearly full employment, rheumatic and arthritic people, although absent because of ill-health for short periods of time are more likely to stay in, and keep their jobs. Although in times of unemployment the conscientious individual sufferer from arthritis thinks it wrong or inexpedient to stay at home because of relatively mild aches and pains, and even painful and swollen joints, in general in our more affluent society, absenteeism due to this type of disease is more acceptable. The fact that an increasing number of middle-aged and older women are employed in industry, who expect compensation if they cannot work, may also be a factor in increasing the total amount of sickness absence due to arthritis and rheumatism.

Rheumatism, as a cause of medical consultation is secondary only to the respiratory diseases. Between 1954—1959 a series of special surveys were carried out in Northern England on the prevalence of rheumatic complaints. Amongst men the commonest cause of rheumatic diseases was intervertebral disc degeneration and arthrosis, and in women rheumatoid arthritis. Wood, in a survey pub-

Table 1. Causes of death

Case No.	Sex and Age		Cause of Death	Interval from Onset of Rheumatoid Arthritis to Death
1	F.	70	Septicaemia, septic arthritis, steroid treatment [a]	16 Months
2	M.	61	Carcinoma of lung	19 Months
3	M.	76	Myocardial infarct	2 Years
4	M.	62	Heart block	3 Years
5	M.	35	Vasculitis, neuropathy, malignant hypertension [a]	5 Years
6	F.	59	Angina. Sudden death	5 Years
7	M.	61	Myocardial infarct	5 Years
8	F.	57	Bronchopneumonia, heart failure, carcinoma breast	5 Years
9	F.	64	Peritonitis, strangulated hernia	6 Years
10	M.	60	Myocardial infarct	6½ Years
11	F.	67	Uraemia, nephrotic syndrome, ?amyloid [a]	7 Years
12	F.	60	Constrictive rheumatoid pericarditis: post-operative death [a]	7 Years
13	F.	69	Rheumatoid heart disease, pulmonary emboli [a]	8 Years
14	F.	68	Cerebral thrombosis	8 Years
15	F.	67	Uraemia, congestive heart failure	8 Years
16	M.	72	Myocardial infarct	9 Years
17	F.	78	Myocardial infarct	12 Years

[a] Patient died as a result of rheumatoid arthritis (Cosh 1973).

Table 2. Relative Importance of Rheumatic Complaints. — The data on sickness benefit were compared with those for certain other conditions

Cause of Sickness	Spells current during year		Days of certified incapacity	
	(thousand)	(%)	(million)	(%)
All causes	9,207.2	100.0	288.86	100.0
Bronchitis	1,005.2	10.9	39.25	13.6
Rheumatic complaints (listed above)	876.9	9.5	29.82	10.3
Accidents	810.8	8.8	20.91	7.2
Diseases of stomach and duodenum	540.6	5.9	12.56	4.3
Psychoneurosis and psychosis	297.1	3.2	26.54	9.2
Influenza	1,202.5	13.1	13.88	4.8

Thus, of chronic conditions, the rheumatic complaints came second only to bronchitis among the principal causes of loss of time from work, and they accounted for one-tenth of the total sickness incapacity (Ann. Rheum. Disease, 1969).

lished in 1971, established that half a million people in Great Britain suffer from rheumatoid arthritis, 400,000 of whom are women.

In 1930 in a survey of London school children in which I took part we found that 1.2% suffered from juvenile rheumatism with rheumatic heart disease. During the last forty years this figure has been reduced to 0.2%. The death rate from heart disease from rheumatic fever in Great Britain has decreased from 20,000 in 1928—1930 to less than 4,000 in 1971. Improvement in housing, diet, education and the prophylactic use of penicillin, as well as early recognition and treatment of these children has played a major role in this improvement.

As you will realise we must be cautious in "assessing" the value of national statistics. Values vary with economic conditions.

Confusion both among the medical profession and among "laymen" has been caused by the vague and inconsistent use of medical labels and terms. "Rheumatism" is a generic name for pain and stiffness of joints, muscles and related structures. In the past invariably, and still in some countries this term is used to include rheumatic fever, and sub-acute rheumatism. "Arthritis" refers more specifically to the inflammation of the joints although it is still often used in cases where inflammation does not occur. "Arthrosis" is a more accurate description of the latter type of condition, and the term arthrosis now usually replaces the term osteo-arthritis. "Fibrosis" is a vague term, now no longer used by the majority of physicians.

To-day we have been listening to our colleagues telling us about that form of rheumatism which they as experts term rheumatoid arthritis and allied disorders. We must realise however, that the family doctor and the epidemiologist and general physician usually include a large variety of arthritic conditions under the label rheumatoid arthritis when they fill in their medical attendant report, and the medical report when they examine an applicant for assurance.

As KELLGREN has pointed out: — "In rheumatoid arthritis we are still very ignorant of causation, and have only limited therapeutic possibilities". From the standpoint of diagnosis the classic cases with chronic inflammatory poly-arthritis of peripheral joints, X-ray evidence of articular erosions and positive serological tests for rheumatoid factor are no problem. Such cases present a rather uniform picture, characterised as they are by a fluctuating but generally progressive course by destructive arthrodes often accompanied by nodules, and vasculitis, to which BUNIN first drew our attention, and less frequently by visceral lesions, and multiple immunological abnormalities such as anti-nuclear factors, and L. E. cells. But when we are faced with the full spectrum of the disease, we are faced with dilemmas. Should we include all arthritis not obviously due to definite disease such as gout or bacterial infections. Should we be studying a pathological process characterised by immunological abnormalities, nodules, and vasculitis which might present with arthritis, but might also be present with a variety of syndromes affecting different organs, as does syphilis. Is there a specific rheumatoid joint disease that we can recognise in all grades of severity? *As yet,* we are *unable to give* an agreed answer to questions such as these. Were we wise many years ago, when in our Rheumatic Unit at St. Stephens Hospital, we labelled people as suffering from rheumatoid disease, and talked about the "rheumatoid lung".

The diagnostic criteria which we rheumatologists now accept are major steps in definitions but unfortunately these criteria present a compromise between differing views about the nature of rheumatoid arthritis. In science as KELLGREN has pointed out compromise is no virtue. But I suggest for the clinician especially for one interested in assurance medicine, compromise even if not virtuous is a practical necessity. You will I think agree with me when I say that rheumatoid arthritis does not present clear cut clinical criteria, and the laboratory does not offer us specific laboratory tests.

Long term studies of patients who later in life present the classical form of rheumatoid arthritis have in the experience of all of us shown that rheumatoid factor may not be detectable in early months of the disease, and may disappear again in its later stages, when the anatomical changes are severe, and the disease inactive. Radiological changes may take months to develop, and usually persist indefinitely.

Diseases such a systemic lupus erythematosus, Sjorgren's syndrome without arthritis, liver disease, pulmonary fibrosis, and a variety of chronic infections may be associated with positive serological tests (i. e. S.C.A.T.).

In brief, we are still uncertain how to *define* rheumatoid disease, and we still have no certain method of measuring the prevalence of rheumatoid disease in any population. In the diagnosis of ankylosing spondylitis, and gout, fortunately we have no such problems since both the radiological evidence of sacro-ileitis and the laboratory figures of hyper-uricaemia may manifest themselves at an early age, and are of diagnostic value. Also we have *no reliable means of recognising predisposition to rheumatoid arthritis.* Although some of us think we can recognise the potential rheumatoid or spondylitic person, we still cannot tell which of the unaffected individuals in a given population will later become affected.

Our clinical experience has taught us that rheumatoid arthritis may take many different forms. Rheumatoid arthritis in population studies shows a gradient, the extremes being the so-called "benign" form which undergoes complete recovery and never recurs, and the classical severe progressive mutilating form of the disease. Between these extremes are cases which recur over a period of one or two years, and then remit completely and those which recur for a time, and then become chronic. Those which make a complete recovery may conveniently be grouped together under the heading "benign poly-arthritis". Fortunately this is the form which we see frequently in people who apply for life assurance. Those of us who are hospital consultants, in charge of beds usually have under our care people suffering from the *classical* form of the disease. The family doctor in his practice sees few patients with the classical form, and is usually not responsible at any one time for more than three or four such people. Also we must realise that many people, presenting the clinical signs of rheumatoid arthritis have never consulted a doctor. "Benign poly-arthritis" shows itself commonly in young people between the ages of 5–24, females being more affected than males. It may have an acute or febrile onset resembling rheumatic fever, or run a sub-acute or recurrent course. These attacks usually occur in the winter months, and may follow a sore throat, or a virus infection such as rubella or infective hepatitis, but often arise spontaneously and without an obvious cause. Benign poly-arthritis may leave slight residual damage to joint tissues, radiological residue are found particularly in the cervical spine. Tests for the rheumatoid factor are usually negative. The diagnosis of this "benign" rheumatoid arthritis condition as distinct from true rheumatoid arthritis must be largely retrospective, and it is for this reason that it has come to the notice chiefly of epidemiologists, and hospital clinicians engaged in research. The diagnosis is suggested by the relatively acute onset with high blood sedimentation rate or pyrexia, by the youthful age of the patient, and by the negative serum test, and absence of erosions in hand and foot x-rays. The diagnosis as distinct from rheumatic fever is also difficult, and the more acute forms, and where carditis is not present it may be impossible to make a differential diagnosis. In this benign form there appears to be no evidence to suggest that a genetic factor is involved, and there seems to be no relation to occupation or any other environmental *factor*.

The *classical form* of rheumatoid arthritis has an increasing incidence with age, severe disease reaches a peak at the ages of 45–57, but in males the peak incidence seems to be between the ages of 25–34, and rises again at the age of 65, whereas in women, there is a considerably greater incidence with increasing age. It is of interest and practical value in assurance work to compare the incidence on age of rheumatoid arthritis in men with peak incidence in adolescence of spondylitis and Reiter's syndrome.

In my own clinical experience of rheumatoid arthritis in women it is common among young and middle-aged housewives, and in women doing secretarial and other sedentary work.

One small item: In 1965 Dr. April Kay and I published a survey, which was accepted as "statistically valid". We found lower fertility in rheumatoid women than in the control group. This low fertility was seen not only in women who developed rheumatoid arthritis during the child-bearing age, but in married women who developed rheumatoid disease after the onset of the menopause. Does the endocrine orchestra play a bigger role than at present realised? Fortunately our clinical experience has shown us that rheumatoid arthritis although painful and disabling, is a relatively non-lethal disease, and those who suffer from it may lead relatively normal full family and social lives for very many years.

There are few things more frustrating than trying to make international comparisons of morbidity and mortality rates over a period of time. I will therefore, confine myself to mentioning three studies reported between 1960 and 1973, in Great Britain. These have been careful hospital "Follow-up" of people suffering from rheumatoid arthritis, the number who died and the cause of death. Eric Bywaters and Barbara Ansell a colleague of mine at Mount Vernon Hospital reported in 1960 the follow-up of 250 patients who had been under their care for at least ten years. 125 of these were first seen early in their disease, 125 late in their disease. 25 had died. Those seen for the first time late in the disease fared, as it would be expected less well in regard to their functional status, and had a much higher death rate. The causes of death varied but were similar to the population at large. They did, however, occur at a somewhat earlier age. Among those seen early in their disease, those who were young and male did best. Those whose disease had an acute onset did better than the ones with a slow onset and those with a negative Rose Waaler Test did better than those with a positive Rose Waaler Test. Duthie in 1964, reported on a nine year follow-up of 307 hospitalised patients. His findings were similar. Those with an acute onset did best. Those in whom the disease had periods of "inactivity" tended to have a better prognosis as regards function than those in whom the disease remained active. Mortality was highest among the severely afflicted and higher than in the general population at all ages, and in both sexes, but similar in character to the general death rate.

Cosh and his colleagues in April this year (1973) published a review of 300 early cases. Among his 17 deaths only five were directly attributed to their rheumatoid disease. There was one example each of septicaemia, vasculitis, uraemia secondary to amyloidosis, constructive pericarditis, and rheumatoid heart disease.

Rheumatoid arthritis in childhood and in adolescence is of particular interest to those of us who are interested in assurance medicine. My colleague, Dr. Barbara Ansell, who has been studying and treating children with rheumatoid arthritis, tells me that in a study started fifteen years ago, and which is still in progress, 244 children fulfilled the original criteria for Stills Disease. She believes that there are many forms of juvenile chronic poly-arthritis, the majority have a chronic sero-negative arthritis with a reasonable prognosis, as regards the disease becoming inactive, and the maintenance of function. Those children, who start with the disease at the age of 10 or 11, looking like adult "classical" rheumatoid arthritis, and who are sero-positive tend to fare much worse. Those in the spondylitic group of Stills disease, usually boys aged 9 and 10, in whom irridocyclitis is commonly seen, do the best.

However, in February this year (1973) Hugh Burry read a paper at the Royal Society of Medicine, in London on the kidney and arthritis. He stated that Renal failure is a common cause of death in patients suffering from rheumatoid arthritis. Significant renal changes had been noted in 72% of patients coming to post-mortem, with rheumatoid arthritis. This he states in some cases is the result of drugs used in its treatment such as gold, phenacetin, and aspirin.

I would like to point out that from the point of view of the assurance medical officer, the two laboratory indicator systems in common use, the sheep agglutination test, and the latex test, which although not absolutely specific have become widely accepted as important in rheumatoid arthritis. People who have repeatedly high positive titre, fare worse than those who are repeatedly sero-negative. There is a close association between raised rheumatoid factor titre, and the presence of erosive changes, and of subcutaneous nodules. They are often in a very high titre, where there are prominent visceral manifestations such as arteritis, and Sjorgrens Syndrome. While they may take some months to become positive, they can occur early in the course of the disease. However, there is a tendency to remit to a sero-negative state in a complete remission. In the examination of a so-called "difficult" case the blood count sedimentation rate, S. C. A. T., and Latex may help the examiner, in making his assessment of the severity of the disease and in making a prognosis. But he must realise, that drug therapy, chryso-therapy, and anti-malarial drugs, steroids, and penicillamine administered over a period can cause a temporary fall in the titre of the rheumatoid factor which may mislead the medical examiner who sees the rheumatoid person on one occasion only.

In general when assessing people with rheumatoid arthritis it is important to note age, sex, duration of the disease mode of onset serological state, and if they have any of the "potentially fatal complications". The older the person the more likely he is to have "incidental" disease. Surgery has its risks, major surgery to joints, such as total hip replacement is occasionally associated with a fatal complication, such as fat embolus.

Amyloidosis must be borne in mind as it has been noted as occurring in 5% of patients who have had active rheumatoid arthritis for more than three years.

Amyloidosis tends to progress, and kill by renal failure. Patients with rheumatoid arthritis are more likely to get infections than the general population.

Drugs given for rheumatoid arthritis may affect the alimentary tract adversely and blood dyscrasias are common side effects. Steroid therapy, although of great value has its complications which are well known to all of you.

We still do not know the cause of Rheumatoid arthritis, it may be that the origin of rheumatoid arthritis is attributable to a micro-organism. If it is the resistance of the body to this micro-organism should not in any way be diminished, unfortunately it is this resistance that we physicians are affecting when we use "immuno-suppressive" drugs.

Our basic aim must be to influence the precipitating factors and to arrest them before irreversible changes take place. It does not seem likely that the disease will be controlled until we know a great deal about the mechanism. We do not know the cause of rheumatoid arthritis. We have reason to believe that we do know that there are certain "trigger factors" which may precede the clinical manifestations of this disease, and influence its "natural history". Among these are genetic or hereditary background, geographical and social factors, the effect on the individual of stress, environmental and occupational factors, and so on. We doctors can play our part by understanding the individual, his familiy, his background, and his education. We doctors, and the community as a whole can help by providing "good medicine" which needs to be based on a proper sense of proportion with a wise application of the various medical and surgical procedures that are available to us. I believe that wise preventive medicine, and good rehabilitation is good business. I believe that our National Health Service in Great Britain will in spite of its "growing pains" enable us to practise good medicine, and to make it available to all members of the community. Within my professional life time, the improvement of social conditions has been the main cause of the dramatic reduction in the incidence of morbidity and mortality caused by rheumatic fever.

I believe that within the professional life time of many of you, education, and a better understanding of the "purpose of living" will have a similar effect on the incidence of rheumatoid arthritis, and the reduction in mortality caused by it.

Finally, as most of us know, medical underwriting is based on evidence provided by a large number of cases as well as the "knowledge" of the medical examiner, and the statistical acuity of the actuary or life underwriter. The cases studied are people of different nationalities, living under very varied geographical and social conditions. They are under the care of doctors with very different standards of education and with different clinical training and knowledge as to the methods available to them. The routine insurance medical examination includes the taking of a history, which includes the family background, previous ill-health, habits, employment and so on and then careful physical examination. There is more to be learnt from a quiet talk with the applicant than from a multitude of tests. The computer is only of limited value. With the help of the medical attendant's report, and with his wide knowledge of general medicine, the medical examiner can usually give a fair appraisal of the applicant's present state of health, and is able to report on his expectation of life, and whether or not it is normal or below normal for his age, race, and occupation.

We underwriters, medically or actuarially trained or, life underwriters with just "common sense experience" are grateful to those of our colleagues, among whom I will mention by name only Professor ERNST TANNER, who have compiled the rating manuals to which we refer, and from which we derive great help, and a proper sense of "consistency" in underwriting. But may I remind you that within the last six months, two men presented themselves with "rheumatoid arthritis". These articular manifestations were in the one instance the first clinical signs of carcinoma of the prostate, in the other of carcinoma of the lung. The first has died, the other happily is still alive. The practice of rheumatology, and the practice of insurance medicine, are both the proper application by the internist of reasonably good internal medicine.

Long-Term Treatment with Corticosteroids in Rheumatoid Arthritis over a Period of 19 to 22 Years

A. DRIVSHOLM, M.D., J. BOYE-NIELSEN, M.D.,
and K. BRØCHNER-MORTENSEN, M.D.

The introduction of a new drug in the treatment of a disease or a group of disorders often rises a widespread optimism. Unfortunately, with increasing experience, the optimism very often turns to deep scepticism, especially, when serious side effects occur. The application of corticosteroids in the treatment of rheumatoid arthritis is a typical example of the fact just mentioned.

As a result of the report of HENCH et al. [1] from 1949 — demonstrating, that corticotropin or cortisone therapy brought about an immediate improvement in the condition of many patients suffering from rheumatoid arthritis — a long-term treatment of 50 patients with rheumatoid arthritis was started in Medical Department A, University Hospital of Copenhagen, in August 1950. Sex and age distribution of the patients are shown in Table 1.

All the patients had active progressive rheumatoid arthritis. Previously, the patients had been treated intensively with conventional methods, for example, most of them had received quite large doses of sanocrysin. The duration of disease and stage prior to treatment with steroids are shown in Table 2. Classification according to stage was carried out on the basis of the criteria recommended by the American Rheumatoid Association 1949 [2].

The working capacity prior to treatment with steroids is shown in Table 3. A.C.T.H. was used first, cortisone shortly afterwards and from 1955 onwards prednisone. No other steroids have been used in this material. In addition to the steroid treatment, physiotherapy was given. The use of analgesics was reduced as far as possible. Five patients underwent orthopaedic operations in the course of the period under consideration. Otherwise there has been no other treatment apart from that necessary in manifest complications.

The patients have been followed closely. The main rule — only rarely broken — has been for the patients to have an out-patient examination at least once a month. The control examination has been done by the same doctor, specially chosen for the purpose, and serving over a period of several years at a time. Patients and their relatives received explicit instructions to report immediately to the department on the slightest sign of complications or changes in the patients usual condition.

Table 4 shows the classification of the patients. As seen in the table, 8 patients (group D) are still treated with prednisone, the duration of therapy being 19 to

Table 1. 50 Patients with rheumatoid arthritis treated with steroids

Sex and age distribution			
Age	Number of patients	Males	Females
20—29	6	1	5
30—39	14	5	9
40—49	20	7	13
50—59	8	1	7
>60	2	1	1
Mean 41.8	50	15	35

Table 2. Duration of disease and stage prior to treatment with steroids

Duration years	Number of patients	Males	Females	Stage [a]			
				I	II	III	IV
1/4—1/2	2	1	1	1	1	—	—
1/2— 1	3	1	2	—	2	—	1
1— 2	5	1	4	1	2	2	—
2— 5	16	1	15	—	8	5	3
5—10	14	7	7	—	2	7	5
>10	10	4	6	—	—	4	6
Average 5.9	50	15	35	2	15	18	15

[a] Classification of *stage* according to the criteria of the American Rheumatism Association 1949.

Table 3. Working capacity prior to treatment with steroids

Class	Number of patients	Males	Females
I Complete ability	—	—	—
II Adequate ability	2	1	1
III Limited ability	34	10	24
IV Incapacitated	14	4	10
	50	15	35

Table 4. Classification of 50 patients with rheumatoid arthritis treated with steroids

Group		
A	Treatment discontinued (unsatisfactory response)	9
B	Treatment discontinued (complications or death)	21
C	Treatment discontinued (remission)	12
D	Treatment continued	8

Table 5. Treatment discontinued because of complications or death (group B)

Sex	Age when treatment was stopped	Duration of treatment (mths)	Reason for discontinuing treatment
♀	36	1.5	
♀	29	2.5	
♀	50	12	Mental disturbances
♀	35	43	
♀	54	90	
♀	53	12	Gastric ulcer
♂	47	12	
♀	51	73	Death from cerebrovascular accident
♀	41	265	
♀	54	96	Death from cardiac insufficiency
♀	62	126	Death from hepatitis
♀	55	156	Death from chron. renal disease
♀	83	212	Death from age
♀	76	234	
♂	47	16	
♂	39	19	
♂	50	84	Death from pneumonia
♀	60	89	
♂	58	111	
♂	39	113	Death from pulmonary complications after operation for gastric ulcer
♂	71	115	Death from coronary occlusion

Table 6. Side effects in 50 patients with rheumatoid arthritis treated with steroids

	Number of patients
Haemorrhagic diathesis	19
Decalcification of the bony skeleton	16
Mental disturbances	12
Gastric or duodenal ulcer	11
Acute adrenocortical insufficiency	8
Death in consequence of treatment with steroids	7
Pneumonia	7
Spontaneous fractures	4

Table 7. Capacity for work (group D)

Class	Before treatment	During treatment
I Complete ability	0	0
II Adequate ability	1	6
III Limited ability	3	1
IV Incapacitated	4	1

22 years. Withdrawal of the steroid treatment in all these patients has been tried several times.

In 12 patients (group C) the steroid treatment was withdrawn following gradual reduction of the dose because of complete or almost complete remission. One of the 12 patients showed signs of renewed activity $1^1/_2$ years after withdrawal of steroid treatment, but complete remission has later occurred.

The treatment was discontinued in 9 patients (group A) as sufficient effect was not obtained at a reasonable level of dosage. These patients were almost all in a rather late phase of the disease, and characterized by irreversible changes in the joints.

In 21 patients (group B) the treatment was discontinued because of complications or death. Table 5 shows details concerning these 21 patients in group B.

As seen in Table 5, the treatment was discontinued in 7 cases because of complications. Five of these patients developed mental disturbances, two gastric ulcer. The mental disturbances were mainly in the form of depression or pronounced restlessness and disappeared in all cases on withdrawal of the treatment.

Seven of the 21 patients in group B died of diseases, which in all probability could *not* be related to the rheumatoid arthritis or the treatment with steroid, as shown in Table 5.

The remaining 7 patients of group B died under the circumstances which probably are related to the treatment with steroids. 5 of these 7 patients died of pneumonia, the other two died of pulmonary complications and coronary occlusion respectively as a complication to operation for gastric ulcer. Three of the five patients who died of pneumonia did not receive a necessary extra supplement of cortisone and were not transferred to the hospital in spite of instructions provided, the remaining two died in the department of a complicated staphylococcal pneumonia and of shock respectively.

The more serious side effects in the 50 patients are shown in Table 6.

As a matter of fact it is difficult to record side effects. Are the complications due to the treatment with steroids, are they caused by the disease itself or are they without relationship to the disease itself or the treatment? In many cases this question can't be answered. A number of undesirable side effects are hardly of great significance such as moon face (which was observed periodically in all our patients), slight increases in weight and disturbances of menstruation and are not shown in Table 6. Concerning the four patients with spontaneous fractures, all of them had compression fractures of the spine.

Various methods can be used in evaluating the result of steroid treatment. We have used the capacity for work and Table 7 shows the working capacity in the 8 patients (group D), who still are treated with steroid.

Before the treatment only one of these 8 patients was able to work, in contrast to 6 patients now. 4 patients were completely incapacitated, in contrast to one now.

In conclusion: On the basis of a close follow-up of 50 patients with severe rheumatoid arthritis on long term treatment (19 to 22 years) with corticosteroids it must be concluded, that it is possible to carry out long-term treatment with adrenocorticosteroids and obtain an improvement in the working capacity of the patients. However, the risk of complications is so considerable that the treatment should generally be avoided and employed only as a last resort with patients with severe activity for whom all other forms of treatment have failed.

References

1. HENCH, P. S., KENDALL, E. C., ULOCUMB, C. H., POLLEY, H. F.: The effect of a hormone of the adrenal cortex (17-hydroxy-11-dehydrocorticosterone: compound E) and of pituitary adrenocorticotrophic hormone on rheumatoid arthritis. Proc. Mayo Clin. 24, 181 (1949).
2. STEINBROCKER, O., TRAEGER, C. H., BATTERMANN, R. C.: Therapeutic criteria in rheumatoid arthritis. J. Amer. med. Ass. 140, 659 (1949).

IV Sesión

Tema: Enfermedades tropicales

Presidente: Dr. Manuel Martinez-Báez, México

Spätfolgen bei den verschiedenen Malariaformen und Frage der Einschränkung der Lebenserwartung durch das Überstehen einer Malaria

Dr. W. Mohr

Vorwiegend 3 Tatsachen haben die Malaria in ihren verschiedenen Formen auch wieder in den Blickkreis des Arztes im zentraleuropäischen Raum gerückt, aus dem sie längere Zeit praktisch verschwunden war:

I. Die Zunahme des interkontinentalen Flugverkehrs;
II. Der Austausch von Arbeitskräften und der Einsatz mitteleuropäischer Arbeitsgruppen im tropischen Raum;
III. Der Tourismus, der in zunehmendem Maße auch tropische Gebiete einbezieht.

Dieser Massentourismus birgt vielleicht die größte Gefahr in sich. Diese Personengruppe reist sehr häufig *ohne* genügende Vorbereitung und *ohne* jede Kenntnis der möglichen gesundheitlichen Gefahren in tropische Gebiete aus.

Lange Jahre hindurch, praktisch bis zum Beginn des 2. Weltkrieges, war für den mitteleuropäischen Raum die Malaria eine kaum mehr bekannte Krankheit. Nur ganz bestimmte Berufsgruppen waren ihr ausgesetzt; sie war eine ausgesprochene Berufskrankheit. Zu diesen betroffenen Berufsgruppen gehörten in erster Linie die Seeleute, sodann Personen des Überseehandels, die Missionare und Mitglieder kirchlicher Organisationen, die in den Tropen arbeiteten, sowie in geringem Maße Mitglieder des Auswärtigen Amtes, die in tropischen Ländern Dienst taten. Alle Angehörigen dieser Gruppen wußten, unter welchen Voraussetzungen sie in die Tropen gingen und hatten Gelegenheit, sich vorzubereiten und sich draußen entsprechend zu verhalten.

Mit der sprunghaften Zunahme des interkontinentalen Flugverkehrs stieg auch die Versuchung, die früher aufgestellten Regeln für die Gesunderhaltung in den Tropen außer acht zu lassen. So kam es, besonders in der ersten Zeit nach dem 2. Weltkrieg, als viele Firmen Arbeitsaufträge, Bauvorhaben und Montagen in Übersee übernahmen, zu einem Anstieg der Malaria-Erkrankungsfälle in diesem Personenkreis. Sehr bald allerdings setzte dann schon für diese Personengruppe die Aufklärung ein und die Bemühungen, durch entsprechende richtige Informationen der hinausgesandten Personen eine Häufung von Krankheitsfällen zu vermeiden. Damit wurde erreicht, daß diese Gruppe in malariagefährdeten Gebieten eine regelmäßige Malaria-Prophylaxe betrieb. Dadurch wurde allerdings nicht in jedem Fall das Auftreten einer Malaria verhindert, aber die Zahl der Malariafälle doch wesentlich eingeschränkt. Mit der Einschaltung einer regelmäßigen

Medikamenten-Einnahme ergab sich aber nun auch das Problem, inwieweit diese Medikamente vertragen wurden, Nebenwirkungen hatten oder sogar Schäden zu setzen in der Lage waren.

Die Fragen, die die Lebensversicherungsmedizin bei der Malaria interessieren müssen, betreffen also nicht nur die Malaria selber, sondern auch die zu ihrer Behandlung angewandten Medikamente.

Daraus ergeben sich folgende Hauptpunkte für diese Ausführungen:

1. Welche Form der Malaria ist in der Lage, so intensive Schäden zu setzen, daß es zu Spätfolgen kommen kann, oder daß gar die Lebenserwartungen nachhaltig herabgemindert werden können?
2. Welche Form von Spätschäden kann auftreten?
3. Welche Kriterien sind für die Anerkennung von Schädigungsfolgen zu erwarten? Eine Frage, die dann schon mehr die Versorgungsmedizin angeht.
4. Kann es u. U. durch eines der Malaria-Medikamente zu einer Spät- oder Dauerschädigung von Organen kommen und damit zur Beeinträchtigung der Lebenserwartung?

Zu 1. An den Anfang der Ausführungen zu Punkt 1 ist die Tatsache zu stellen, daß es *4 verschiedene, für den Menschen pathogene Plasmodien-Arten gibt.* Diese führen zu *drei,* auch im klinischen Bild und in der Prognose recht unterschiedlichen Krankheitsabläufen.

Plasmodium vivax und Plasmodium ovale (vorwiegend Westafrika) führen zu dem gleichen klinischen Krankheitsbild.

Nur eines der drei klinischen Krankheitsbilder ist wirklich lebensbedrohend und kann gesundheitliche Dauerschäden hinterlassen, die u. U. die Lebenserwartung beeinträchtigen können. Es ist dies die Malaria tropica, hervorgerufen durch *Plasmodium falciparum.* Die anderen 3 Parasitenarten führen zu zwar im Augenblick sehr dramatischen Krankheitszuständen, doch sind diese niemals lebensbedrohend und verschwinden mit der Beseitigung der Parasitämie.

Das durch Plasmodium vivax und Plasmodium ovale hervorgerufene Krankheitsbild der *Malaria tertiana* führt nach einem uncharakteristischen Initialfieber zu typischen Anfällen mit heftigem Schüttelfrost, hohem Fieberanstieg, Fieberabfall unter starkem Schweißausbruch und nach 24stündigem praktischem Wohlbefinden zu erneutem Schüttelfrost mit erneutem, hohen Fieberanstieg. Dieser Fieberrhythmus kann sich aber auch ändern. Unter der Einwirkung der Abwehrkräfte des Organismus ereignet sich eine Phasenverschiebung in der Parasitenentwicklung, so daß es zu täglichen Fieberanfällen kommen kann (Malaria tertiana duplicata). Zwar verursacht diese Malariaform in der akuten Fieberphase leichte Elektrokardiogramm-Veränderungen, ein Absinken des Blutdruckes, gelegentlich auch Fieberdelirien, jedoch niemals Dauerschäden oder Spätfolgen.

Es kommt bei dieser Form der Malaria auch zu Milz- und Leberschwellung, doch haben die bioptischen Untersuchungen der Leber — durchgeführt von verschiedenen Autoren — gezeigt, daß die beobachteten Veränderungen des Lebergewebes nach Beseitigung der Parasitämie sich völlig wieder zurückbilden können. — Auch die sich entwickelnde Anämie regeneriert sich nach Beseitigung der Parasiten außerordentlich schnell. In keinem Fall kommt es zu einer bleibenden Anämie oder einer bleibenden Leberschädigung.

Nach durchgeführter Behandlung heilt diese Malariaform stets folgenlos aus; allerdings können in einem bestimmten Zeitraum Rückfälle auftreten. Diese Rückfälle sind innerhalb von 2 bis 2½ Jahren möglich, selten bis zu 3 Jahren. Allerdings haben wir in letzter Zeit in dem Fall einer Plasmodium-ovale-Infektion noch nach 4½ Jahren das Auftreten eines Rückfalles — und zwar nach einer Stress-Situation — beobachten können. Nach der bisherigen Kenntnis stellte diese Beobachtung aber ein Novum dar.

Auch die *Malaria quartana* — hervorgerufen durch Plasmodium malariae — verursacht im allgemeinen keine schwerwiegenden Komplikationen. Sie kann allerdings noch über Jahrzehnte zu Rückfällen führen, die von den schwer zu bekämpfenden, sekundären Gewebsformen in der Leber ausgehen. Diese sekundären Gewebsformen haben in einzelnen Fällen bis 40 Jahre nach der Erstinfektion Rückfälle verursacht. Um solche späten Fieberanfälle aber als „Malaria quartana-Anfälle“ anzuerkennen, ist ein Parasitennachweis durch Blutuntersuchung unbedingt zu fordern!

Mit der Milz- und Leberschwellung verhält es sich hier ähnlich wie bei der Malaria tertiana; Elektrokardiogramm-Veränderungen werden gelegentlich gesehen, sind aber geringgradig und nur passager; bleibende Störungen im Sinne von Narben im Myokard treten *nicht* auf.

Vorwiegend bei den Einheimischen in Malariagebieten, in denen Malaria quartana vorkommt, werden besonders bei Kindern und Jugendlichen *Nierenbeteiligungen* beobachtet im Sinne einer Nephrose ohne stärkere Blutdrucksteigerung, aber mit der Tendenz des sehr chronischen Verlaufs und dadurch doch einer erheblichen Gefährdung des Befallenen. Bei den Mechanismen, die bei dieser Komplikation zum Tragen kommen, handelt es sich wohl um einen Vorgang ähnlich wie er von VOLLER und EHRICH bei experimenteller Tier-Malaria erzeugt werden konnte, und bei dem es zu Ablagerungen in den Epithelzellen der glomerulären Blutgefäße von IgG und IgM, sowie beta-i-c kommt. Auffallend ist, daß die Nierenveränderungen *nicht mit der Schwere* der Infektion zusammenzuhängen scheinen, sondern *mit der Dauer* der Infektion. Von einigen Autoren wird die mangelnde Antigenität der Malaria-quartana-Parasiten als Ursache angenommen; außerdem aber spielt es sicher eine Rolle, ob Behandlungsmaßnahmen durchgeführt wurden oder nicht.

Beim europäischen Kranken wird man es mit dieser letztgenannten Komplikation außerordentlich selten zu tun haben. In den Verbreitungsgebieten der Malaria quartana hat man beobachtet, daß mit Intensivierung der Bekämpfungsmaßnahmen der Malaria auch diese Komplikation eine rückläufige Tendenz zeigte.

So kann man zusammenfassend sagen, daß auch diese Malariaform praktisch nicht zu bleibenden Schäden führt und die Lebenserwartung kaum beeinträchtigt. Auch sind Minderung der Erwerbsfähigkeit oder gar Invalidität durch diese Malariaform — ebenso wie bei der Malaria tertiana — *nicht* zu erwarten.

Grundsätzlich anders liegen die Verhältnisse bei der *Malaria tropica*. Sie ist diejenige Form der Malaria, die lebensbedrohend werden kann und bei der es, wenn die Behandlung nicht rechtzeitig und ausreichend durchgeführt wird, zu Spätschäden bzw. Folgezuständen kommen kann.

Hier schließt nun der 2. Punkt an. Welche Form der Spätschäden kann bei der Malaria tropica auftreten?

Bei einer massiven Malaria-tropica-Infektion ist stets eine hochgradige Parasitämie zu beobachten. Diese starke Parasitämie kann verschiedene Folgen haben:

Der Befall der Erythrozyten mit einem oder mehreren Parasiten, wie er bei der Tropica zu beobachten ist, führt zu einer Veränderung der Viskosität der Zellen, sie werden klebriger und haften eher an der Wand der Kapillaren, so daß es zur Stase in den kleinsten Blutgefäßen kommt. Diese Stase hat dann z. B. im Hirnbereich die Bildung von Dürckschen Granulomen zur Folge, die in multipler Aussaat über das ganze Gehirn verteilt sein können (Flohstich-Enzephalitis).

Tabelle 1. Symptome von 25 Patienten mit cerebraler Malaria bei der Aufnahme in die Klinik des Bernhard-Nocht-Instituts, Hamburg (in Prozenten ausgedrückt)

Kopfschmerzen	80
Verwirrung	64
Schmerzen in den Gliedmaßen	64
Übelkeit	56
Ausgesprochen comatös	44
Taubheitsgefühl in Beinen u. Armen	36
Erbrechen	36
Durchfälle	28
Nackensteifigkeit	20
Ikterus	48
vergrößerte Milz	84
vergrößerte Leber	80
Oligurie	44
Anurie	18

Diese multiplen enzephalitischen Herdchen können ein sehr buntes neurologisches Bild verursachen, das u. U. schwer zu deuten ist. Bei ungenügender oder zu spät einsetzender Behandlung können sich bleibende Folgen entwickeln, wie wir das in einigen — glücklicherweise wenigen — Fällen beobachteten. So sahen wir

psychomotorische Erregungszustände,
Aphasie,
Halbseitenlähmung
und epileptiforme Bilder, wenn auch sehr selten.

Wird ein solcher Krankheitsfall, bei dem es schon zu zentralnervösen Erscheinungen gekommen ist, nicht behandelt, dann kommt es zum zerebralen Koma. Patienten, die länger als 36–40 Std. im Koma liegen, sind im allgemeinen nicht mehr zu retten oder sie behalten nach der Ausheilung Dauerschäden, auch wenn eine intensive Behandlung dann noch eingeleitet wird.

Unter den heute zur Verfügung stehenden therapeutischen Möglichkeiten ist es allerdings selten, daß ein solches Koma auftritt. Unter 500 Malaria-tropica-Fällen bei „Nicht-Immunen" — meist Europäern — sah mein Mitarbeiter Volkmer in 4 Jahren in einem westafrikanischen Minenhospital nicht einen Todesfall bei rechtzeitig einsetzender Behandlung. — In den letzten Jahren haben wir 6 Malaria-tropica-Todesfälle in unserer Klinik beobachten können, bei denen in 2 Fällen das zerebrale Koma zum Tode führte. — Unter unserem Beobachtungsgut von über 500 Malaria-Fällen der Nachkriegszeit — davon 278 Malaria-tropica-Fälle — sahen wir nur einmal die Entwicklung eines zentralnervösen Folgezustandes mit Verlust der Merkfähigkeit, Verlangsamung, Herabsetzung der geistigen Fähigkeiten, so daß eine Umschulung vorgenommen werden mußte. — Bei einem Kind mit zerebralen Erscheinungen im akuten Anfall waren im Elektroenzephalogramm noch nach 2 Monaten deutliche Veränderungen festzustellen und nach 2 Jahren noch leichte Abweichungen von der Norm.

Vegetative Störungen konnten wir in einem gewissen Prozentsatz noch längere Zeit nach Überstehen der Malaria tropica beobachten, jedoch verloren sich diese auch nach einem bestimmten Zeitraum.

Tabelle 2. Komplikationen von seiten des Herzens und Kreislaufs bei Malaria tropica (in Prozenten ausgedrückt)

Tachycardie	86
Hypotonie	72
Veränderung der Repolarisation	76
Extrasystolie	20
Radiologisch faßbare Vergrößerung des Herzens	16
Systolisches Herzgeräusch	10

Ein anderes Organ — *das Herz* — kann bei der Malaria tropica auch in Mitleidenschaft gezogen werden. Auch hier kann es zur Stase in den Kapillaren kommen und damit zur Hypoxaemie mit Insuffizienzerscheinungen, sowie schließlich zum Bild einer interstitiellen Myocarditis. Zur Entwicklung von Dauerschäden kommt es allerdings hier auch nur dann, wenn die Behandlung zu spät einsetzt. Einer von den Todesfällen, die wir beobachten konnten, der leider auch zu spät zu uns in die Behandlung kam, konnte zwar parasitenfrei gemacht und auch durch Peritoneal-Dialyse aus der prä-urämischen Situation herausgeholt werden, ist dann aber an einem ganz akuten Herzversagen verstorben. Die Histologie des Herzmuskels zeigte dabei eine interstitielle Myokarditis.

Von unserem Beobachtungsgut von über 500 Fällen in der Nachkriegszeit zeigten 27 Malaria-tropica-Patienten noch kürzere oder längere Zeit Elektrokardiogramm-Veränderungen, teils Rhythmusstörungen, wie Tachycardie, Extrasystolie, Tachyarrhythmie, sowie Veränderungen des ST-Stückes und der T-Zacke. Auch hier spielte der Zeitpunkt des Einsetzens der Therapie eine entscheidende Rolle. — Beobachtungen während des letzten Krieges an einigen Tausend Malariafällen ergaben nur ganz vereinzelt länger persistierende Elektrokardiogramm-Veränderungen. Immer wieder zeigte sich, daß eine frühzeitig einsetzende Behandlung solche Spätfolgen verhindert. Die Veränderungen sind bei nicht vorgeschädigtem Organismus auch nicht so, daß es zu einer Beeinträchtigung der Lebenserwartung kommen könnte. Gefäßkrankheiten, etwa eine Raynaudsche Gangrän, die im älteren Schrifttum gelegentlich der Malaria zugeschrieben wurden, sind nach einmaliger Malaria-Infektion außerordentlich selten und werden im neueren Schrifttum nicht mehr beschrieben.

Leber- und Milzschwellung gehören zum Bild der Malaria tropica genau so wie zu dem der übrigen Malariaformen. Jedoch gilt auch für diese Veränderungen, die histologisch durch Leberbiopsien studiert werden konnten, daß es bei rechtzeitig einsetzender Behandlung zu keinen bleibenden Schäden kommt. Die tödlich endenden Malaria-tropica-Erkrankungen können allerdings erhebliche Veränderungen in der Leber aufweisen, und zwar in Form von Vermehrung und Schwellung der Kupferschen Sternzellen, die mit Malariapigment, Parasiten und Erythrozytenresten beladen sein können. Die Leberzellen selber enthalten kein Malariapigment, wohl aber Hämosiderien und Gallenpigment. In schweren Fällen findet sich eine Verfettung der Zellen in den Läppchenzentren. *Dauerschäden allerdings im Sinne einer chronischen Hepatitis oder gar einer Leberzirrhose als Malariafolge* sind aufgrund der heutigen Auffassung über die Art der Leberschädigung *nicht möglich.*

Tabelle 3. Veränderungen der Leberfunktionstests bei Malaria (Überblick über 110 Fälle)

	Malaria tropica	Cerebrale Malaria tropica	Malaria tertiana
SGOT	leicht erhöht	leicht erhöht	kaum erhöht
SGPT	kaum erhöht	leicht erhöht	kaum erhöht
LDH	deutlich erhöht	deutlich erhöht	kaum erhöht
gamma-Globuline	deutlich erhöht	deutlich erhöht	leicht erhöht

Auch die Veränderungen an der *Milz* sind reversibel und führen nur bei sehr oft widerholten Malariainfektionen zu einer chronischen Vergrößerung dieses Organs mit Fibrose, u. U. auch einmal zu Kalkeinlagerungen in der Milzkapsel nach einer Perisplenitis.

An den *Nieren* können Veränderungen auftreten, die ähnlich denen sind, wie sie bei der Quartana beobachtet werden. Nur daß sie bei der Tropica sehr viel akuter in Erscheinung treten. Während das Bild der febrilen Albuminurie mit Mikrohämaturie fast stets den akuten heftigeren Malariaanfall begleitet, kann es bei den sehr massiven Infektionen dann zu schwereren Nierenschädigungen kommen mit Oligurie, Anstieg des Harnsäurespiegels im Blut, des Harnstoff-N- und Kreatininspiegels und schließlich Auftreten einer Anurie, die eine Peritoneal-Dialyse erforderlich macht, mit deren Hilfe manchmal noch diese Situation zu überbrücken ist; in anderen Fällen ist aber auch damit keine Hilfe mehr möglich.

Daß es nach Ausheilen der Malaria tropica zu bleibenden Nierenschäden im Sinne einer chronischen Glomerulonephritis kommt, ist allerdings nicht beobachtet worden. Durch sofort nach dem Tod vorgenommene Nierenbiopsien haben wir in einem unserer Fälle durch die Mithilfe von Herrn Prof. Fischer (Kinderklinik des Universitäts-Krankenhauses Hamburg-Eppendorf) nachweisen können, daß es zu Ablagerungen in den Tubuli gekommen war und damit zu einer Funktionsbehinderung.

Zusammenfassend ist also zu sagen, daß Spätschäden nur durch die Malaria tropica auftreten können. Bei rechtzeitig einsetzender Behandlung sind sie zu vermeiden, so daß auch die Malaria tropica meistens ohne Hinterlassung von Dauerschäden oder Spätfolgen ausheilt.

Diese Feststellung gilt natürlich *nur* für einen vorher gesunden Organismus!

Anders liegen die Verhältnisse, wenn die Malaria tropica einen schon vorher geschädigten Organismus trifft; dann ist es durchaus möglich, daß die vorhandenen Schäden — z. B. am Herzmuskel oder auch an der Leber — verstärkt werden, zumal die Regenerationsfähigkeit des vorgeschädigten Organs nicht mehr so gut ist wie die des gesunden.

Für die Anerkennung von Schädigungsfolgen nach Malaria tropica, wie es für die Versorgungsmedizin von Interesse ist, sind gewisse Kriterien zu fordern:

I. Die Diagnose der Malaria muß durch Parasitennachweis gesichert sein.

II. Im akuten Malariaanfall müssen schon Schäden an dem betreffenden Organsystem aufgetreten sein, z. B. epileptiforme Anfälle, Elektrokardiogramm-Veränderungen, etc.

III. Die Störungen müssen sich von dem Malariaanfall ab mit Brückensymptomen verfolgen lassen. Nur wenn *das* der Fall ist, sind Folgeerscheinungen anzuerkennen.

Zu dem 4. Punkt — der Frage der Schädigung des Organismus durch die angewandten Malaria-Therapeutika — ist zu sagen, daß eine solche Schädigung bei den heute üblichen Behandlungsmethoden nicht gegeben ist.

A. Das am meisten angewandte *Chloroquine* oder *Resochin* (4-Aminochinolinderivate) verursacht — wie eine millionenfache Erfahrung gezeigt hat — in der zur Malaria-Prophylaxe und zur Malaria-Therapie angewandte Dosis *keine Schädigung*.

Im deutschen und ausländischen Schrifttum ist in letzter Zeit wiederholt von Schädigungen durch Resochin gesprochen worden. Dazu ist festzustellen:

1. *Augen*schädigungen durch Resochin werden nur dann beobachtet, wenn die Augen schon *vor*geschädigt waren und es sich um die Therapie eines rheumatischen Geschehens handelt, bei dem eine sehr viel höhere Dosierung angewandt wird, als es in der Malaria-Prophylaxe und -Therapie der Fall ist.

2. Schädigungen der *Leber* durch die Malaria-Therapie mit Resochin treten nicht auf.

3. Ebenso wenig ist das *Bestehen der Schwangerschaft* durch Resochin-Prophylaxe oder Resochin-Therapie einer Malaria gefährdet. Im Gegenteil, diese Resochin-Behandlung bewahrt die Mutter vor dem Ausbruch einer sie schädigenden Malaria.

4. Die Entwicklung des *Feten im Mutterleib* wird weder durch die Resochin-Prophylaxe noch durch die Resochin-Therapie einer Malaria bei der Mutter gefährdet (MAEGRAITH, WOODRUFF, MOHR, u. a.).

5. Auch von den anderen 4-Aminochinolin-Derivaten sind keine bleibenden Schädigungen zu erwarten, die sich etwa einschränkend auf die Lebenserwartung auswirken könnten.

B. Auch das *Paludrin* verursacht als Prophylaktikum oder Therapeutikum keine Schäden.

C. Vom *Daraprim* wurden allerdings bei Überdosierung und Langzeit-Behandlungen in zu hoher Dosierung Knochenmarkschäden gesehen, doch sind das Dosierungen, die weder bei der Malaria-Prophylaxe noch bei der -Therapie gegeben werden.

D. Lediglich beim *Chinin* sind gewisse Schädigungen in der therapeutischen Dosis möglich. Da dieses Medikament aber heute weitgehend nicht mehr angewandt wird, ist dieses Problem nicht mehr aktuell. Früher wurden Hörstörungen, Herzrhythmusstörungen, Neigung zu petechialen Blutungen, „Chinin-Fieber“ und andere allergische Reaktionen gesehen, die sich u. U. ungünstig — auch als Dauerschaden — auswirken konnten.

Zusammenfassend kann man sagen, daß die Malaria in ihren verschiedenen Formen bei rechtzeitig einsetzender Therapie *keine Lebensbedrohung mehr darstellt;*

daß das Überstehen einer Malaria nach richtig und rechtzeitig durchgeführter Behandlung *keine Einschränkung der Lebenserwartung mit sich bringt,* wenn die Malariaerkrankung einen vorher gesunden Organismus befällt; und daß durch die *Malaria-Therapeutika keine Schädigung des Organismus zu befürchten ist.*

Diesen Ausführungen haben wir eine einmalige Malaria-Infektion eines in die Tropen Reisenden zugrunde gelegt. Sie gingen ferner von der Voraussetzung einer rechtzeitig gestellten Diagnose und einer modernen Therapie aus.

Aber auch heute ist die exakte Diagnose in vielen tropischen Gebieten noch nicht möglich! Für die dort im Arbeitseinsatz Stehenden ist es dann erforderlich, um Schäden zu vermeiden, auf den Verdacht „Malaria“ hin eine Malaria-Therapie durchzuführen. So kann auch in solchen Fällen eine ernste Gefährdung vermieden werden.

Repercusión económica del absceso hepático amibiano *

Dr. Bernardo Sepúlveda

5 Figuras

Si bien el análisis de las consecuencias económicas y sociales de cualquier padecimiento tiene siempre interés general, ese análisis adquiere singular importancia en el caso del absceso hepático amibiano en la República Mexicana. Varias razones apoyan esta afirmación.

El absceso hepático amibiano es un padecimiento a la vez grave y frecuente en nuestro país. En efecto, la frecuencia de la amibiasis invasora del hígado en México es una de las más altas del mundo (Tabla 1 [1]) y la gravedad puede juzgarse por la elevada mortalidad y morbilidad del padecimiento.

Tabla 1. Procesos morbosos atendidos con mayor frecuencia en el Servicio de Gastroenterología del Hospital General del Centro Médico Nacional [a]

	Promedio anual No. de pacientes	Por ciento de los ingresos al Servicio
Litiasis biliar	657	19.5
Hemorragia profusa del tubo digestivo alto	592	17.4
Cirrosis del hígado	564	16.5
Absceso hepático amibiano	240	7.0
Pancreatitis agudas	208	6.1

[a] Promedio anual de ingresos al Servicio en el período 1968–1972: 3,400 enfermos.

Para dar idea de lo anterior, basta citar algunos datos. En el Servicio de Gastroenterología de nuestro Hospital, los procesos morbosos que predominan por su mayor frecuencia, son: la litiasis biliar, las hemorragias profusas del tubo digestivo alto, la cirrosis del hígado, el absceso hepático amibiano y las pancreatitis agudas. En esta enumeración, los mencionados procesos están arreglados en orden decreciente de frecuencia; por tanto, el absceso hepático amibiano ocupa el cuarto lugar entre los diversos cuadros patológicos atendidos en el Servicio. Los datos anteriores se presentan en forma numérica en la Tabla 1.

Estos mismos datos se presentan en forma gráfica en la Fig. 1.

* Trabajo presentado en el XI Congreso Internacional de Medicina del Seguro de Vida. México. Octubre 7–11, 1973.

Por lo que se refiere a la mortalidad del padecimiento, a pesar de que tiene tendencia a descender en algunos centros médicos, oscila entre el 4 y el 15 por ciento en adultos atendidos en hospitales del Seguro Social en el país (Fig. 1 [2]). En el Hospital General de la Secretaría de Salubridad y Asistencia en la ciudad de México, el absceso hepático amibiano ocupa el cuarto lugar entre las causas de

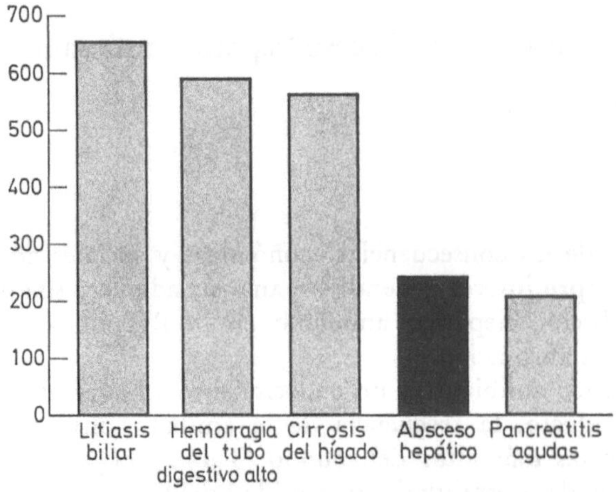

Fig. 1. Número de casos (anuales) de las cinco principales enfermedades del servicio de gastroenterología Hospital General del C.M.N. 1971

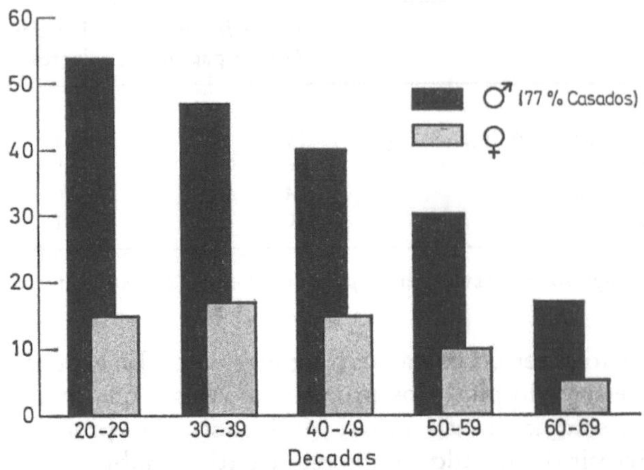

Fig. 2. Número de pacientes afectados, tomando en consideración edad y sexo

muerte. Las tres primeras son: cáncer, cirrosis del hígado y tuberculosis, en ese orden (Tabla 2, Fig. 2 [3, 4]).

En cuanto a la morbilidad, el padecimiento requiere un largo período de hospitalización y convalescencia, que frecuentemente alcanza un lapso de ocho semanas.

Otro hecho que confiere singular importancia a esta enfermedad, es el predominio con que afecta al sexo masculino en la edad adulta. En efecto, las tres cuartas partes de los pacientes son varones entre los 20 y los 49 años (Fig. 3 [5]). La gran mayoría de ellos son jefes de familia y, como es obvio, se encuentran en la edad más productiva de la vida.

Tabla 2. Datos investigados en el grupo de pacientes

- Edad, sexo y estado civil
- Clasificación dentro del Seguro Social (asegurado o beneficiario)
- Categoría de salario en los trabajadores asegurados
- Número de días de estancia hospitalaria
- Evolución del padecimiento (defunción o curación)
- Número de días de incapacidad, en caso de ser trabajador asegurado
- Número de días de ausencia del trabajo, calculado para los cinco años

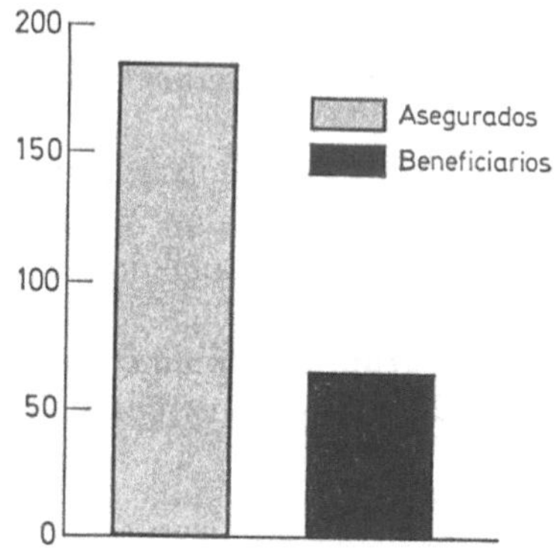

Fig. 3. Número de pacientes, tomando en consideración si son asegurados o beneficiarios. 250 casos de 1968–1972

Recientemente, hicimos un estudio sobre las repercusiones económicas del absceso hepático amibiano, que se refiere en especial a los renglones principales del gasto que el padecimiento significa para el Instituto Mexicano del Seguro Social. A continuación, se presentan los aspectos más interesantes del estudio.

Enfermos y método

En los cinco años transcurridos de 1968 a 1972, inclusive, se atendieron en el Hospital 1200 enfermos con absceso hepático amibiano. De este grupo, se revisaron 250 casos, a razón de 50 por año, que fueron obtenidos del archivo clínico del Hospital por el procedimiento de números aleatorios. Esta muestra, que corresponde al 20 por ciento del total, se consideró representativa del universo motivo del estudio.

En cada uno de los casos, se investigaron los datos siguientes (Tabla 2).

Para el cálculo del costo de hospitalización se hizo un promedio del costo día-cama en los cinco años mencionados; la cifra resultante fue de 688 pesos por día-cama. Por lo que se refiere al pago de incapacidades, el cálculo se basó en las normas establecidas por la Ley del Seguro Social, según las cuales la institución suministra al trabajador el 60 por ciento de su salario, a partir del cuarto día de incapacidad y por toda la duración de la misma.

Resultados

En el grupo estudiado, la edad de los pacientes varió entre 18 y 76 años; el 75 por ciento de ellos, estuvo comprendido entre los 20 y los 49 años. Ciento noventa y cinco enfermos, o sea el 78 por ciento, fueron del sexo masculino; el 77 por ciento de los varones eran casados. En la Fig. 2 se presentan en forma gráfica los datos anteriores.

Por lo que se refiere a la clasificación dentro del Seguro Social, 181, que corresponde al 72 por ciento, eran trabajadores asegurados; el resto, o sea el 28%, eran beneficiarios (Fig. 3). El salario de los trabajadores varió entre 40 y 150 pesos por día; el promedio de salario fue de 66 pesos diarios. En cuanto al número de días de estancia hospitalaria, osciló entre 9 y 32, con un promedio de 20 días.

De acuerdo con el número de enfermos incluidos en el grupo, y con el costo día-cama ya mencionado, la estancia hospitalaria significó una erogación de 3,250,000 pesos.

En lo que respecta a la evolución del padecimiento, se registraron 8 defunciones; y por lo que toca al número de días de incapacidad en los trabajadores asegurados, varió entre 18 y 51, con un promedio de 40 días. El pago de estas incapacidades ascendió a la cantidad de 350,000 pesos. En total de trabajadores enfermos incluidos en el presente grupo, el número de días de incapacidad arriba expresado, representó unos 12,000 días de ausencia del trabajo, a lo largo de los cinco años (Fig. 4).

Fig. 4. Costo por concepto de hospitalización y pago de incapacidades, y número de días de ausencia al trabajo, de pacientes asegurados incluidos en el estudio

Discusión

Los resultados anteriores demuestran la importancia que desde el punto de vista económico, tiene el absceso hepático amibiano en la población atendida en nuestro Hospital. La información obtenida es valiosa por sí misma; pero reviste mayor interés, si se trata de extender los resultados de la investigación a otras unidades hospitalarias del Seguro Social.

Los datos recogidos por medio de encuestas clínicas y seroepidemiológicas en distintas regiones del país, comprueban que la amibiasis invasora, y en particular el absceso hepático amibiano, afectan en proporción aproximadamente igual a la población asistida en los hospitales del Seguro Social en todo el país (Figs. 1, 4 [2, 6]). De acuerdo con estos datos, la incidencia de la enfermedad es independiente de la zona geográfica y de las condiciones climatológicas; en cambio, está relacionada estrechamente con el nivel económico y los hábitos higiénicos de la población. En efecto, el padecimiento predomina en los grupos sociales de menor ingreso monetario y que viven por consiguiente en malas condiciones sanitarias.

Como ejemplo de lo anterior, está el hecho de que el 82 por ciento de los enfermos con absceso hepático amibiano atendidos en nuestro Hospital, son trabajadores con salarios muy bajos (promedio 56 pesos diarios); además, las visitas domiciliarias han comprobado las condiciones higiénicas deplorables en que viven los pacientes y sus familiares en la mayoría de los casos.

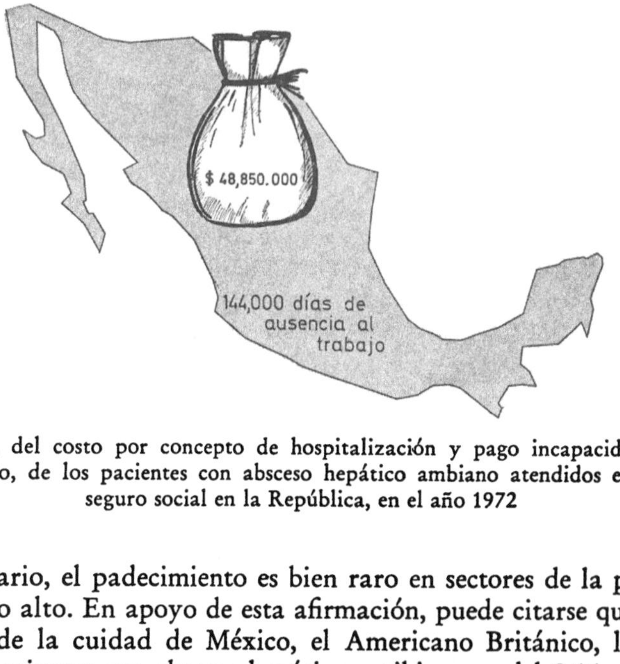

Fig. 5. Estimación del costo por concepto de hospitalización y pago incapacidades, y días de ausencia al trabajo, de los pacientes con absceso hepático ambiano atendidos en hospitales del seguro social en la República, en el año 1972

Por lo contrario, el padecimiento es bien raro en sectores de la población con nivel económico alto. En apoyo de esta afirmación, puede citarse que en un Hospital privado de la cuidad de México, el Americano Británico, la proporción registrada de pacientes con absceso hepático amibiano es del 0,16 por ciento del total de enfermos admitidos en un año (Fig. 5 [7]); mientras que es del 2 por ciento aproximadamente, en distintos hospitales generales del Seguro Social en la República, incluyendo el nuestro.

Por las razones expuestas, y tomando en cuenta además el conocimiento de los carácteres propios del padecimiento, es legítimo deducir que los resultados obtenidos en la presente investigación, son aplicables en términos generales a otras unidades hospitalarias del Seguro Social. Es obvio que la estimación resultante será solo aproximada; entre otras circunstancias, debe tomarse en consideración que los hospitales de las grandes ciudades, con mejores recursos para el diagnóstico y el tratamiento, tienen las tasas más bajas de morbilidad y mortalidad; pero, por otra parte, tienen los costos más altos por concepto de estancia hospitalaria. De cualquier manera, es conveniente hacer algunas generalizaciones sobre la base del presente estudio, para tener una idea, así sea aproximada, sobre la magnitud de los gastos originados por el padecimiento.

De acuerdo con las informaciones de diversas fuentes obtenidas por el Centro de Estudios sobre Amibiasis [8], se calcula que el promedio anual de pacientes *adultos* con absceso hepático amibiano atendidos en los hospitales del Seguro Social en la República, sobrepasa la cifra de 3000. Aun aceptando conservadoramente el número de 3000 enfermos por año, ésto significaría un gasto aproximado de 48,000,000 pesos por año, sólo por concepto de costos de hospitalización y pago de incapacidades (Fig. 5). La suma resulta de impresionante magnitud, y más todavía si se considera que probablemente está por debajo de la realidad.

Por añadidura, en el presente estudio no se han tomado en cuenta otras repercusiones económicas del padecimiento, como son las derivadas de la ausencia del paciente en su centro de trabajo durante el período de incapacidad. Como se ha dicho, este período es de 60 días en promedio en nuestro Hospital; suponiendo que el número de días de incapacidad fuera semejante para los enfermos del resto de las unidades hospitalarias del Seguro Social, ésto significaría aproximadamente — 144,000 días de ausencia del trabajo, por año. Tampoco se han considerado las consecuencias que desde el punto de vista social, representa la pérdida del jefe de la familia en los casos de fallecimiento. Estos y otros aspectos igualmente importantes, deberán ser motivo de análisis en investigaciones futuras.

Finalmente, es preciso insistir en que el absceso hepático amibiano afecta sobre todo a los sectores sociales mas desprovistos de recursos y que viven en las peores condiciones higiénicas. Tales sectores incluyen a la mayor parte de la población mexicana; por ello, adquiere todavía mayor importancia el estudio de esta plaga nacional.

Bibliografía

1. ELSDON-DEW, R.: The epidemiology of amebiasis. En: Advances in parasitology. B. Dawes (Ed.). New York: Academic Press, p. 1 (1968).
2. ALVAREZ ALVA, R. y DE LA LOZA SALDÍVAR, A.: Frecuencia del absceso hepático amibiano en hospitales del Instituto Mexicano del Seguro Social en la República Mexicana. Arch. Invest. Med. (Méx.) 2, Supl. 1, 327 (1971).
3. ALBORES SAAVEDRA, J.: Comunicación personal.
4. BRANDT, H. y PÉREZ TAMAYO, R.: Amibiasis. México: La Prensa Médica Mexicana p. 10. 1970.
5. GONZÁLEZ MONTESINOS, F., LEE RAMOS, F. y AGUIRRE GARCÍA, J.: Influencia del sexo y la edad en la amibiasis invasora del hígado. Arch. Invest. Med. (Méx.) 2, Supl. 1, 395 (1971).
6. LANDA, L., SEGOVIA, E., DÍAZ BARROSO, G., AUBANEL, M. y SEPÚLVEDA, B.: Encuesta seroepidemiológica de la amibiasis. Informe preliminar. Presentado en el Quinto Seminario sobre Amibiasis. México. Febrero de 1973.
7. JINICH, H. y SCHNAAS, F.: Frecuencia del absceso hepático amibiano en clientela particular. Comunicación preliminar. Arch. Invest. Méd. (Méx.) 2, Supl. 1, 333 (1971).
8. Centro de Estudios sobre Amibiasis. México. Datos no publicados.

Coccidioidomicosis

Dr. Dámaso Fernández Lira *, Dr. Sergio de la Garza ** y
Q. F. B. Lilia L. Cortes ***

La Coccidioidomicosis es producida por el hongo denominado Coccidioides-immitis. Este hongo exige determinadas condiciones de clima que se encuentran en el norte de México. Maddy [10] refiere que esta micosis es endémica en la región titulada „The Lower Sonoran Life Zone" de los Estados Unidos de América cuyas características son temperaturas superiores a 25° C en verano y 1,7° C en invierno y promedio de lluvias menor a 20 pulgadas.

Ecología

Las zonas endémicas de esta micosis, tienen las características de vegetación y fauna de las regiones áridas. En particular en ellas se desarrolla un arbusto llamado „gobernadora" *(Larrea-tridentata)* que coincide en las zonas de endemicidad según Maddy en Estados Unidos y González Ochoa [7, 8] en México.

Epidemiologia

Las encuestas de reactores a la coccidioidina realizadas originalmente por González Ochoa y García [6], han permitido precisar las zonas endémicas en nuestro país. Las principales son: la „del norte" que ocupa los estados fronterizos, la del „Pacífico" y la „central", existen además 2 pequeñas regiones tropicales en el centro y sur del país.

Estudios realizados por otros grupos médicos [4, 12, 13] han encontrado posivilidades variables entre el 5 y el 50%, datos que coinciden con los de Edwards y Palmer [3] en el sur de los Estados Unidos.

Datos micológicos

El Coccidioides immitis presenta dos ciclos vitales distintos: uno saprófito en la naturaleza, o en el medio de cultivo y otro parasitario en el huésped humano o animal. *El ciclo saprofítico* corresponde a un hyfomiceto que se desarrolla en el suelo o quizá también sobre los vegetales de la región y que se reproduce por

---

* Director de la Unidad de Neumología del IMSS. Monterrey N. L.

** Profesor jefe de servicio de Patología del Hospital Universitario Dr. J. E. Gonzalez. Monterrey, N. L.

*** Servicio de Bacteriología del laboratorio de la Unidad de Neumología del IMMS. Monterrey, N. L.

esporas, las que al penetrar al organismo humano producen la infección. Dickson y Gifford [2] demonstraron que se adquiere el hongo por inhalación. Posiblemente pueda el hongo penetrar al organismo por otras vías, particularmente a través de una lesión cutánea. Hasta ahora no hay evidencia de infección directa de hombre a hombre o de algún animal al hombre.

El *ciclo parasitario* puede observarse en las lesiones de los tejidos humanos o animales. Inicialmente el hongo aparece como una esférula muy pequeña, corresponde a la endospora recien liberada, y mide 2 a 3 micras. Esta pequeña espora puede hallarse libre o en el interior de células fagocíticas; al crecer desarrolla una cápsula de doble contorno y posteriormente muestra una vacuola central, al llegar a su madurez el protoplasma del hongo se segmenta y aparecen las endosporas características.

La esférula al romperse deja en libertad a las endosporas y éstas se diseminan y vuelven a crecer, repitiéndose el ciclo.

Los productos estudiados en nuestro laboratorio fueron los siguientes: esputo, contenido gástrico, pus de absceso, material de lavado bronquial obtenido por broncoscopía, material necrótico de tumoraciones, líquido de derrame pleural, piezas operatorias y de autopsia. En este material se practicó examen en fresco para investigar la presencia de esférulas, cultivo e inoculación en animales.

Datos anatomopatológicos

La forma primaria es una neumonitis exudativa cuya evolución habitual es a la resolución. Sin embargo, algunos casos evolucionan a la progresión por dos posibles caminos: 1o. Progresión de la forma primaria pulmonar hacia lesiones residuales formando principalmente nódulos, cavernas y abscesos. 2do. De la lesión pulmonar primaria el hongo se disemina a otros órganos utilizando la vía sanguínea y en ocasiones la linfática. Los sitios atacados con más frecuencia son piel y tejido subcutáneo, huesos y meninges. En los casos más graves la diseminación produce lesiones multisistémicas.

Al microscopio se observa una mezcla irregular de un proceso exudativo no específico que tiende a la supuración y a la necrosis y de un proceso granulomatoso similar al producido por el bacilo tuberculoso. Se identifica por la presencia en estas lesiones de esférulas con sus endosporas características.

Presentacion de casos

En este reporte se reúnen dos grupos de casos clínicos: 100 pacientes estudiados en la Unidad de Neumología del I.M.S.S., y 64 por el Dr. Sergio de la Garza en el Departamento de Patología del Hospital Universitario Dr. J. E. González, en Monterrey Nuevo León.

Sexo	
Femenino	47
Masculino	117
	164

Edad	
0 a 10	16
11 a 20	27
21 a 30	51
31 a 40	31
41 a 50	19
51 a 60	12
61 a 70	6
71 a 80	1
81 a 90	1
	164

Edad mínima	20 días
Edad máxima	89 años

Procedencia

Los pacientes nacieron en los estados del norte de la República, con excepción de dos. Once pacientes radicaron en los estados de Texas y California de E.U.A., zona endémica. El resto se consideran casos autóctonos.

Ocupación

La mayor parte de estos pacientes laboraban en fábricas y oficinas en la ciudad de Monterrey. Sin embargo, casi todos son originarios del campo.

Obreros	39
Oficinistas	22
Agricultores	20
Hogar	15
Escolares	11
Mineros	1
No se precisó	56

Diagnóstico

Los procedimientos de diagnóstico practicados en estos pacientes fueron los siguientes:

Biopsia		101
Cultivo		64
Autopsia		17
Inoculación a cobayo		20
Reacción a la Coccidioidina		95
Positivas	71	
Negativas	24	

Según la clasificación de WINN [24] los casos correspondieron a:

C. Primaria pulmonar	11
C. Pulmonar residual	87

C. Diseminada	66
Multisistémica	34
Cutáneas	10
Oseas	20
Nerviosas	2

Lesiones radiológicas pleuropulmonares

En los 100 casos estudiados en la Unidad de Neumología del IMSS. se observaron las siguientes lesiones radiológicas pleuropulmonares.

Caverna única	36
Infiltrado nodular	33
Nódulo único	13
Neumonía	9
Hidroneumotórax	3
Absceso pulmonar	2
Miliar	2
Pleuresías	2
	100

Tratamiento médico

Se trataron 17 pacientes con anfotericín. Todos presentaron formas diseminadas; Cinco tenían lesiones multisistémicas, todos fallecieron; de 12 con lesiones localizadas se obtuvieron resultados satisfactorios en 6 (óseas 2 y cutáneas 4), falleció uno con lesión cerebral y se desconoce en 5. No se administró en formas primarias pulmonares. Tampoco fué utilizada en el pre o post-operatorio en las intervenciones quirúrgicas.

Tratamiento con anfotericín

Tabla 1

Lesiones	Resultados			
	Satisfactorio	Desconocidos	Fallecieron	Total
C. Multisistémica	0	0	5	5
Oseas	2	2	0	4
Cutáneas	4	2	0	6
Nerviosas	0	1	1	2

Tratamiento quirúrgico

La resección pulmonar fué practicada en 58 pacientes. La principal indicación fué la caverna persistente con hemoptisis de repetición. En el resto de los pacientes para precisar el diagnóstico, en particular en aquéllos que presentaron nódulo único para descartar la posibilidad de cáncer.

Cirugía pulmonar

Lobectomía	32
Segmentaria	22
Nodulectomía	4
Toracotomía y biopsia	1
	59

Otras cirugías

Legrado óseo	10
Drenaje céfalo-raquídeo con válvula de Pudenz	5
Resección de Coccidioidoma cerebral	1
Laminectomía vertebral	1
Epididectomía	1
Drenaje de absceso osifluente	1
	78

Resultados

Los resultados observados en los pacientes son los siguientes:

Tabla 2

Resultados:	Satisfactorio	Desconocidos	Fallecieron	Total
C. Primaria pulmonar	7	3	1	11
C. Pulmonar residual	64	21	2	87
C. Diseminada:				
Multisistémica	0	13	21	34
Oseas	5	15	0	20
Cutáneas	6	4	0	10
Nerviosa	0	1	1	2
			Total de pacientes	164

Comentarios

La Coccidioidomicosis es un padecimiento endémico que requiere condiciones de clima de tipo semi-desértico. Su transmisibilidad es directa por la inhalación de polvo de las zonas endémicas. Es excepcional su paso a través de materiales como algodón cosechado en esas regiones [1]. Tampoco es aceptada la transmisión directa de paciente a paciente.

En las personas de piel oscura produce formas graves e incapacitantes [5].

El porcentaje de incapacidades en nuestra región, considerada de mediana endemicidad, es bajo.

Desde el punto de vista clínico, se confunde con la tuberculosis pulmonar. En el resto del organismo, es un padecimiento de polimorfismo clínico que simula múltiples enfermedades.

Es indispensable introducir en los laboratorios clínicos las investigaciones serológicas que faciliten su diagnóstico y eliminen el elevado riesgo de los cultivos para el personal técnico.

El tratamiento quirúrgico resuelve las lesiones residuales pulmonares en un alto porcentaje. Sin embargo su indicación cada vez la hacemos con menos frecuencia y preferimos la conducta conservadora de observación, aún en presencia de lesiones cavitadas [9].

El anfotericín es un medicamento que produce frecuentes reacciones secundarias, algunas de ellas severas, y de pobres resultados. Es de desearse el descubrimiento de nuevos fármacos que controlen esta micosis.

Bibliografía

1. Albert, B. L., Sellers, T. F., Jr.: Coccidioidomycosis from fomites. Arch. Int. Med. **112**, 253–261 (1963).
2. Dickson, E. C., Gifford, M. A.: Coccidioides infection (Coccidioidomycosis) II. The primary type of infection. Arch. Int. Med. **62**, 853–871 (1938).
3. Edwards, P. Q., Palmer, C. E.: Prevalence of sensitivity to coccidioidin, with special reference to specific and non-specific reactions to coccidioidin and histoplasmin. Dis. Chest. **31**, 35–60 (1957).
4. Fernández, L. D., Cortés, L. L., Guadalajara, M. J., Costilla, S. A., Chapa, G. R., Salinas, V. R., Pacheco, P. L., Cantú, G. R., Iglesias, O. T., Posadas, M. R.: Coccidioidomicosis Pulmonar. Neumol. Cir. Tórax, México. **28**, 161–172 (1967).
5. Fiese, M. J.: Coccidioidomycosis. 253 pp. Springfield/Illinois: Charles C. Thomas, 1958.
6. González-Ochoa, A., García, F.: Coccidioidomicosis. Prensa Médica Mexicana. **14**, 245–252 (1944).
7. González-Ochoa, A.: Epidemiología de la Coccidioidomicosis en México. Gaceta Médica de México. **97**, 1383–1391 (1967).
8. González-Ochoa, A.: La importancia médica de la coccidioidomicosis en la frontera entre México y los Estados Unidos de América. Salud Pública de México. Epoca V. **10**, 319–326 (1968).
9. Guadalajara, M. J., Fernández, L. D., Costilla, S. A., Chapa, G. R., Villarreal, R., Chávez, S. A.: Pulmonary Resection as Treatment for Coccidioidomycosis of the Lung. Dis. Chest. **51**, 64–66 (1967).
10. Maddy, K. T.: Ecological Factors Possibly Relating to the Geographic Distribution of Coccidioides immitis. pp. 144–157. In Proc. of Symp. on Coccidioidomycosis. PHS Pub. No. 575, Communicable Disease Center, Atlanta, Ga./USA 1957.
11. Maddy, K. T., Coccozza, J.: The Probable Geographic Distribution of Coccidioides immitis in México. Bull. Pan. Amer. San. Bur. **57**, 44–54 (1964).
12. Madrid, S. G., Contreras, C. J.: Coccidioidomicosis en el estado de Sonora. Neumol. Cir. Tórax, México. **24**, 395–400 (1963).
13. Verduzco, E., Portales, A., Monjardín, S., García, S. R.: Características clínicas y Epidemiológicas de la Coccidioidomicosis en la Comarca Lagunera. Salud Pública de México. Epoca V. **7**, 397–402 (1965).
14. Winn, W. A.: A Working Classification of Coccidioidomycosis and its Application to Therapy. pp. 3–9. Proc. of the 2nd Coccidioidomycosis Symposium. Ajello, L. (ed.). Univ. of Ariz. Press, Tucson, Arizona/USA 1967.

V Sesión

Tema: Seguro de vida en mayores de 60 años

Presidente: Dr. R. Gubner, EE. UU.

Extra Mortality Risk in the Older Insurance Applicant

Richard B. Singer, M. D.

8 Figures

The objective of this paper is to take a critical look at patterns of mortality in the older insurance applicant — the relationships of these patterns to age and policy duration. Mortality rates, both standard and substandard, are compared in terms of their *ratio* — the familiar mortality ratio (MR) which is the basis for developing schedules of underwriting debits — and their *difference*, as extra deaths per 1000 exposed to risk per year (EDR), which is a less common but very useful index of extra mortality. Such risks are examined for substandard policyholders as a group, and also in a number of follow-up studies by individual impairment, including cases of hypertension, post-myocardial infarction patients, subjects with left ventricular hypertrophy pattern in their electrocardiogram, and patients treated for localized cancer.

Various standard mortality rates of significance are shown in Fig. 1, for the age range of 50 to 80 years. Four sets of select rates represent averages for policy duration 1–2 (lowest curve), 3–4, 7–8 and 11–12. In order to compare these curves, one with another and with the others displayed in Fig. 1, I have plotted the rates by *attained age*, not age at entry. The select rates have been derived from an annual age graduation of the Intercompany 1955—1960 Basic Select Tables for males [1]. Each point used to construct the select curves represents an average of four rates; for example the average for entry ages 50 and 51 and policy durations 1 and 2 corresponds to an attained age of 51; the average for the same entry ages and policy durations 3–4 corresponds to an attained age of 53, etc. The attained age calculated in this fashion can be matched as a close approximation to the tabular age for the upper curves shown: mortality rates for males as given in the Intercompany 1957—1960 Basic Ultimate Tables (policy durations 15 years and up), a table of graduated rates for the Framingham study for the period 1950—1968, and U.S. Life Tables 1959—1961. Note that the curve for Framingham men follows the curve for ultimate insured rates quite closely, and these rates are considerably lower than rates for all U.S. white males.

Our original intention was to utilize the experience of standard male insureds with New England Mutual Life Insurance Company with biennial ages and durations starting at age 50, in an entry period from 1945—1970 inclusive, followed to the 1971 policy anniversary [2]. However, even after graduation, the curves for successive policy durations 1–2, 3–4, 5–6, etc. did not follow a completely consistent pattern, especially at attained age 66 up, where the numbers of deaths were very small.

It was therefore not feasible to ulitize curves at the longer policy durations to extrapolate select rates at durations 1–2 above age 70, and the graduated Intercompany experience was substituted. The only data from the New England Life experience shown in Fig. 1 are the *ungraduated* select rates at policy durations

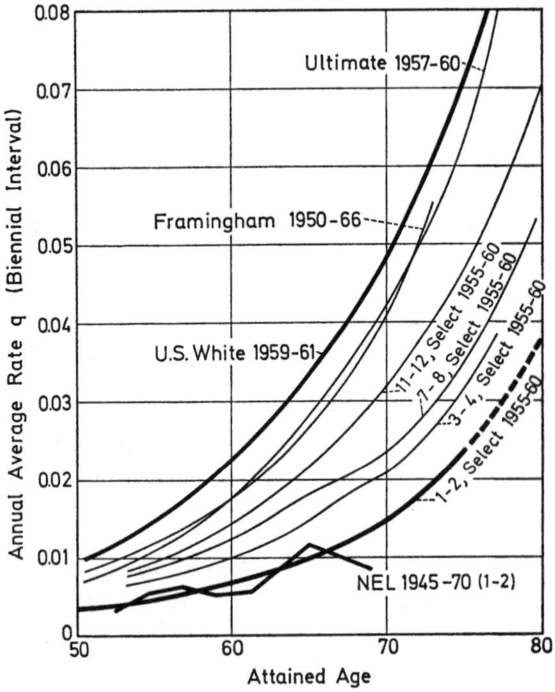

Fig. 1. Male mortality rate age 50 up

1–2. All exposures and deaths age 66 up were combined, with an average attained age of 69 for the highest age shown. At policy durations 1–2 the average mortality ratio was very close to 100 per cent, based on the 1955—1960 Intercompany rates. The curves from age 51–65 are quite similar, the New England Life rate at age 69 (based on only 14 deaths) being somewhat below the Intercompany curve. Important characteristics of the select mortality rates at these older ages are as follows:

1. Despite the high mortality rates only 4.3 per cent of *total* death claims available in the 1955—1960 Basic Select tables were on entrants age 60 up, in the first two years of policy duration, about one quarter the volume of death claims for those age 50–59. When this small fraction is examined 68 per cent of the claims are for entrants age 60–64, 29 per cent age 65–69 and only 3 per cent age 70 up. The aggregate volume of exposure and claims is small for new policyholders age 60 up, the volume decreases sharply with age and becomes extremely small at age 70 and above.

2. Graduation procedures are always more difficult and uncertain in determination of the upper end of the smooth mortality curve, where the data approach a vanishing point just above age 70. The dotted portion of the lower curve in Fig. 1 from age 75 to 79 is an extrapolation I have made, based on the trend of the ratio of q for durations 1–2 to the ultimate q (the volume of death claims in the ultimate experience is, of course, very great at ages 60–80). A similar method was actually used to obtain the graduated select rates for age 70 up in the 1955—1960 Basic Tables.

3. Average age is lower than the central age of the quinquennial age groups at the older ages: average 61 (not 62) for the quinquennial range 60–64; average 66 for the range 65–69; and average 71 for the group age 70 up, even though there is a scattering of policyholders age 75 or more in this open-ended group.

Table 1. Mortality rates and differences variations with age

(Annual rate or diff.) (1000)	Age				
	30	60	65	70	75
q-select, 1st year	0.56	5.53	8.67	12.68	20.03
Δq 1 yr. age	+0.03	+ 0.55	+ 0.74	+ 1.34	+ 1.75
Δq 1 yr. duration	+0.13	+ 2.48	+ 4.51	+ 5.43	+ 8.59
q-125% 1st year select	0.70	6.91	10.84	15.85	25.04
Δq 100% to 125%	+0.14	+ 1.38	+ 2.17	+ 3.17	+ 5.01
q-ultimate (attained age)	1.15	17.69	27.99	42.90	63.36
Δq 1st yr. select to ultimate	+0.59	+12.16	+19.32	+30.22	+43.33

4. Mortality increases very rapidly at the older ages, as is shown in Table 1 for ages 60, 65, 70 and 75, with data at a much younger age, 30, for comparison. The sharp upward trend in first-year select mortality rates is evident on the first line. The *differences* in mortality rate after the first year, on the next two lines show that the difference for one year of policy duration is several times greater than the difference attributable to a one-year increase in entry age. The table also gives values of mortality rate, q, 25 per cent above the first-year select rate (as a conventional upper limit for standard insurance), the ultimate rate, and their respective differences in excess of the first-year select rate. Thus, at age 70, the lowest possible select rate is estimated from the 1955—1960 Basic Tables to be 12.68 deaths per 1000 exposed to risk per year, and the ultimate rate is 42.90, almost 5 per cent per year. The increase in q to the next policy year is 5.43 per 1000; to age 71 it is 1.34; and to the upper limit of standard, 3.17. These *differences* are equal to *total* first-year mortality rates lying in the age range 40 to 60. It is obvious that the entire background of standard mortality in an applicant age 70 is uncertain and fraught with peril, not only for the underwriter in evaluating the risk, but also for the actuary in establishing equitable premiums and reserves.

Under certain circumstances it may be desirable to measure excess mortality as a difference between the observed rate, q, and the standard rate q′. Such a difference is of the kind just illustrated in Table 1, and to this function I have assigned the notation "EDR", which stands for "extra deaths per 1000 per year". EDR and mortality ratio are different but equally valid indices of comparative mortality, and both will be utilized in the analysis to be made of excess mortality risks in older life insurance applicants. Since the standard mortality rate, q′, is dependent on age, the relationship of EDR to mortality ratio is also dependent on age. This relationship is shown in Fig. 2, which is actually a nomogram or graphic device for showing simultaneous values of one or more dependent and two independent variables. Age is given as one independent variable on the horizontal axis and mortality ratio as the other independent variable on the left-

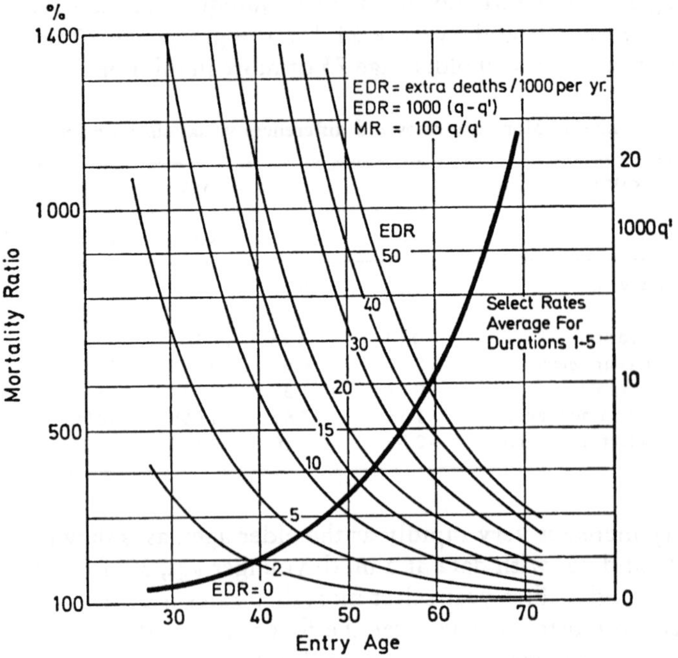

Fig. 2. Mortality ratio and EDR related to age

hand vertical scale. The curves sloping from left to right represent a series of constant values of EDR as the "dependent" variable. Any point on this nomogram gives simultaneous values, which can be read off the scales or curves, for the three inter-related variables, age, mortality ratio and EDR. Values of q are not shown in the nomogram, but the standard mortality rate q′ is represented by the upward sloping curve with its scale of 1000 q′ on the right. In Fig. 2 q′ is an average of the rates for the early part of the select period, durations 1 to 5 years inclusive, not the rate for a particular year. This early part of the select period is a critical one in underwriting because policy reserves are low and death claims therefore entail a high net loss.

It is evident from Fig. 2 that a relatively low value of EDR may correspond to a wide range of values of mortality ratio. For example, consider the curve for an EDR of 5 extra deaths per 1000 per year. At age 30, where the average q′ is only 0.78 per 1000 per year, the mortality ratio is 739 per cent, a declinable level for many companies. At age 50 the mortality ratio has dropped to 203 per cent, and at age 70 to a mere 122 per cent, within the standard range. A flat extra premium of \$ 5 per \$ 1000 per year would cover the extra mortality cost for policyholders with a constant EDR of 5, if commission, expense and interest factors could be ignored. This would be true at any age, despite the very high mortality ratio implied by such an EDR at young ages and the very low ratio at older ages.

Trend in Total Substandard Mortality by Policy Duration. Data to illustrate this trend have been drawn from the male substandard experience of New

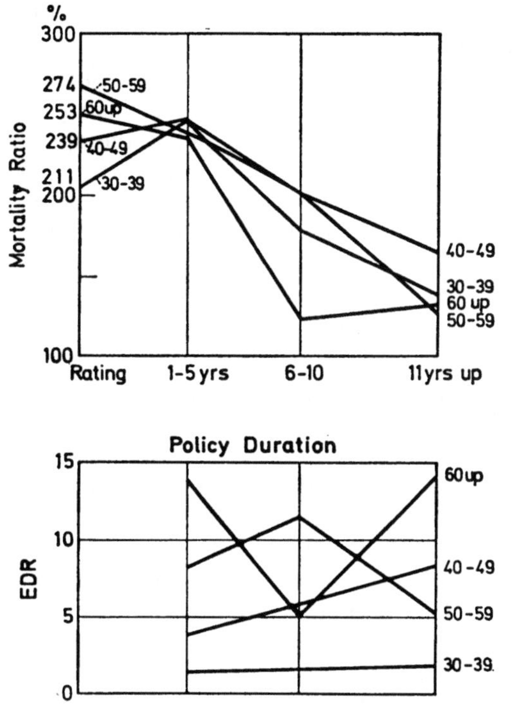

Fig. 3. NEL male substandard mortality '45—68, change with duration

England Mutual Life Insurance Company 1945—1964, followed to the 1968 policy anniversary [2]. Nonmedical issues have been excluded; about 90 per cent of the coded impairments were medical in nature. The experience for older applicants age 60 up is compared with that of three decennial age groups in the range 30–59, at three policy durations, 1–5, 6–10 and 11 years up. Mortality ratios and values of EDR are shown in Fig. 3. These have been calculated against New England Life standard mortality rates, which average significantly lower than the rates in the 1955—1960 Basic Select Tables.

A downward trend in mortality is evident in mortality ratio at all ages, but the trend is more pronounced for policyholders age 60 up, where the mortality ratio decreases from 243 per cent at durations 1–5, (140 deaths) to 122 per cent at durations 6–10 (73 deaths). At 6–10 years 95 per cent confidence limits for the mortality ratio of the oldest age group are 96 to 140 per cent. Mortality ratios for the other age groups at durations 6–10, and for all age groups at durations 1–5 are well above these limits.

Although this decrease in mortality ratio for older policyholders is statistically significant, it should be interpreted with some caution in view of the EDR trends (lower portion of Fig. 3). EDR shows very little change with policy duration in the youngest age group 30–39, but a definite upward trend in the next age group 40–49. The other age groups, 50–59 and 60 up, exhibit irregular but contrasting patterns by duration. It is difficult to conclude whether or not the upward trend for those age 40–49 is also to be found in the older age groups, including those over 60. However, even a moderate upward trend in EDR at the older ages could be accompanied by a decrease in mortality ratio.

Age Trend in Hypertension and Following Myocardial Infarction. In Fig. 4 we have summarized observations from Framingham men [3] and New York Life male applicants with systolic hypertension [4] in the approximate range of 160 to 180 mm. Rates for the Framingham men were compared with the total male population over the intervals between biennial examinations, 1950—1966. BOLT *et al.* utilized the standard rates of the 1959 Build and Blood Pressure Study to calculate expected deaths for each age and blood pressure category, with an average duration of about 7 years. Despite the very different bases for expected mortality results were so similar for the two independent studies that single trend lines were drawn rather than separate ones. Mortality ratio decreases from 400 per cent at age 35 to about 175 per cent at age 70. EDR, on the other hand, shows a clear upward trend from about 4 extra deaths per 1000 per year at age 35 to a rate of 25 at age 70.

Similar trends with age, downward for mortality ratio and upward for EDR, are observed in a 10-year follow-up study of male patients admitted to Veterans Administration Hospitals as a result of acute myocardial infarction [5]. Follow-up experience shown in Fig. 5 commences with survivors at two months after the date of the infarction. The solid circles represent the mortality experience in the interval from 2 months to 5 years, and the open circles, from 5 to 10 years. In the earlier period the mortality ratio decreases from 1100 per cent at age 40 to 200 per cent at age 70; corresponding limits in the 5 to 10 year period are 760 per cent and 150 per cent. A reasonably smooth *upward* trend with age is seen in the earlier observation period for EDR: an increase from 45 extra deaths per 1000 per year at age 40 to an EDR of 69 at age 70. Values of EDR in the period from 5 to 10 years are somewhat scattered, but the general trend is also an increase.

Age Trend in Subjects with Left Ventricular Hypertrophy Pattern in The Electrocardiogram. Quite high levels of excess mortality, with similar age trends are found in Framingham men with this ECG pattern [6]. The starting point for follow-up was the first observation of LVH pattern in the routine ECG's taken at the time of the regular biennial examinations. The solid circles in Fig. 6 give the experience for subjects with definite LVH pattern, and the open circles, possible LVH pattern. Observed mortality rates were compared with rates for Framingham men without LVH pattern in their ECG. Excess mortality is at a very high level for those with definite LVH, as evidenced by a mortality ratio of 920 per cent for men with average age 49, and a corresponding EDR of 55 extra deaths per 1000 per year. There is a sharp decrease in mortality ratio with age, and a relatively smaller but definite increase in EDR. Age trends therefore resemble those found in the two other cardiovascular impairments previously reviewed. Levels of excess mortality for cases with possible LVH pattern are much lower.

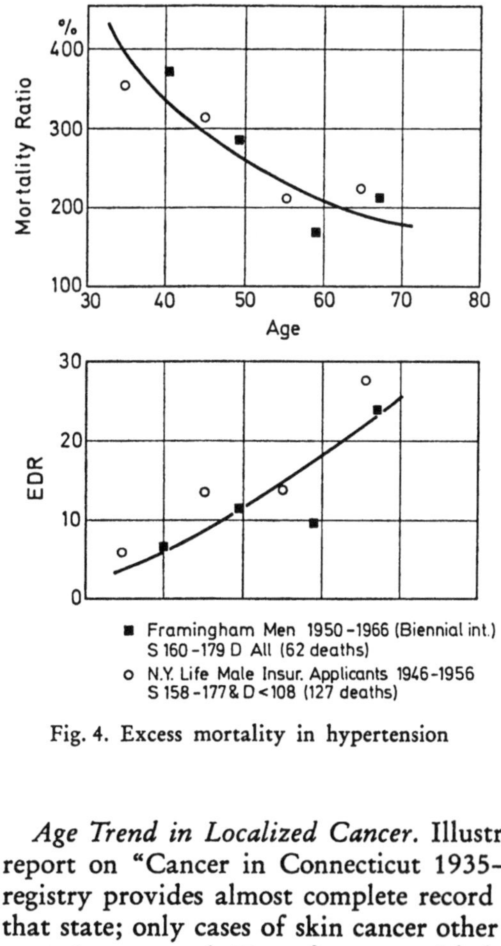

Fig. 4. Excess mortality in hypertension

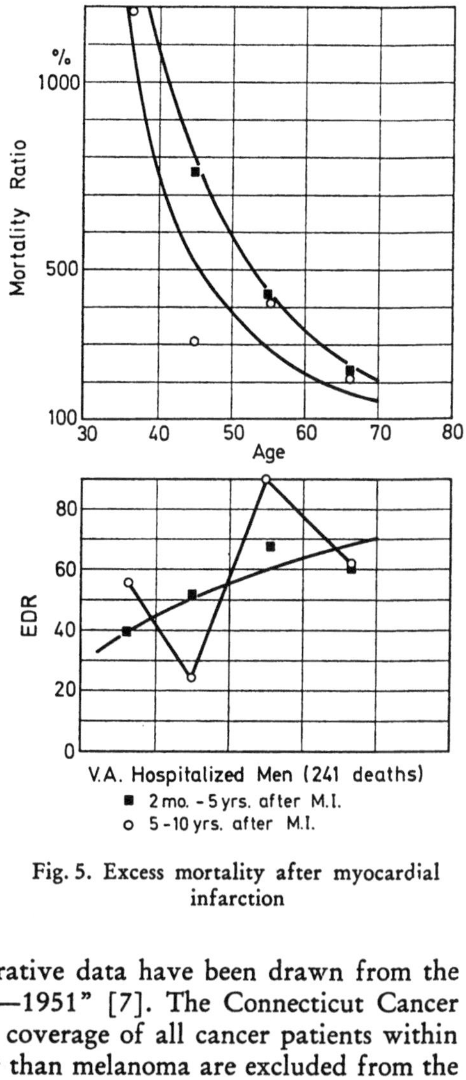

Fig. 5. Excess mortality after myocardial infarction

Age Trend in Localized Cancer. Illustrative data have been drawn from the report on "Cancer in Connecticut 1935—1951" [7]. The Connecticut Cancer registry provides almost complete record coverage of all cancer patients within that state; only cases of skin cancer other than melanoma are excluded from the statistics reported. Data for men with localized cancer, all sites combined are shown in Fig. 7. The solid circles represent experience in the period from 12 to 36 months after diagnosis, and the open circles, experience from 3 to 5 years. In the earlier period of follow-up extremely high levels of excess mortality were observed and provide justification for the general underwriting practice of declining applicants with most types of localized cancer (other than skin cancer) within three or four years of diagnosis and treatment. In terms of EDR excess mortality is at an almost constant level of 100 extra deaths per 1000 per year, although there does appear to be a very slight downward trend with age. Both curves of mortality ratio show the same downward trend with age found for the previous impairments, and the mortality ratio at 3 to 5 years is much lower than it is the earlier period. EDR at 3 to 5 years does show the same upward trend with age found in previous impairments, increasing from a level of 27 at age 40 to about 58 extra deaths per 1000 per year at age 70.

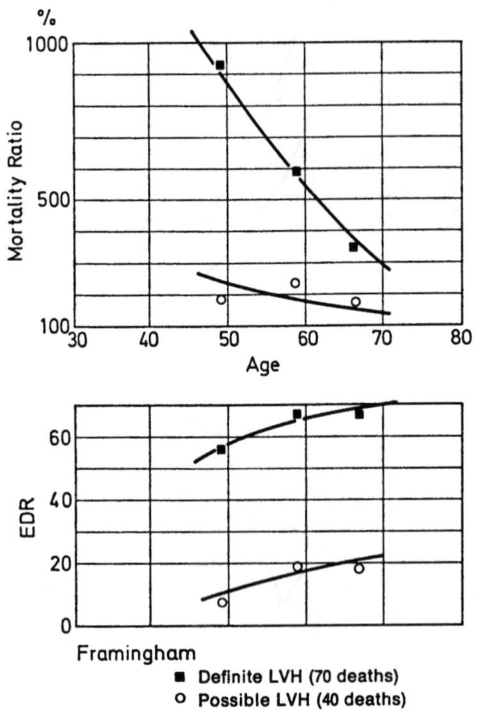

Fig. 6. Excess mortality — LVH pattern in ECG

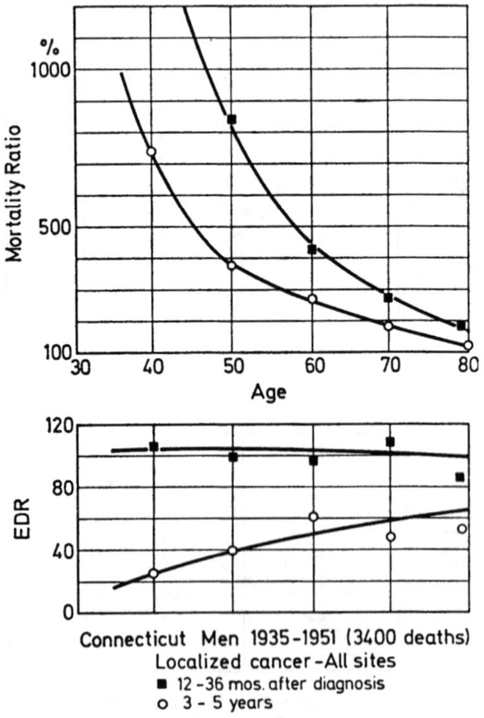

Fig. 7. Excess mortality in cancer

Mortality Ratio and Rating Category. Evidence on this topic is also drawn from our study of New England Life total substandard experience [1], and results for the two oldest age groups, 50–59 and age 60 up are shown in Fig. 8. Within each age group the select experience was divided into two duration classes, 1–5 and 6–15 years, and five rating categories, four of which combine several rating classes to give average ratings of 145, 195, 270 and 410 per cent, respectively. The category with the highest risk is one that has been used in our company since 1948 to provide a graded death benefit to applicants under pension trust plans who would have been declinable as non-pension applicants. Such SD (substandard declined) issues can be followed through the policy record, just as any other paid-for policy. The death benefit was graded by the actuaries on the basis of an estimated mortality ratio of 1000 per cent for applicants under age 50, 750 per cent for those age 50–59, and 500 per cent for those age 60 up. These two SD ratings and the four average ratings within the usual substandard range of 500 per cent are shown at the top of vertical lines marking off the horizontal axis of Fig. 8, while the mortality ratio observed is on the vertical axis and scale at the left. Whenever the observed mortality ratio equals the rating, that point will lie on a 45° line passing through the origin (100 per cent intersection point at the lower left). However, I have substituted for this line in Fig. 8 a band of varying width designated "Underwriting Target Zone". The vertical width of this band has been arbitrarily taken to be one tenth of the mortality ratio, above or below a 45° line. We have considered it to be more reasonable to see if the

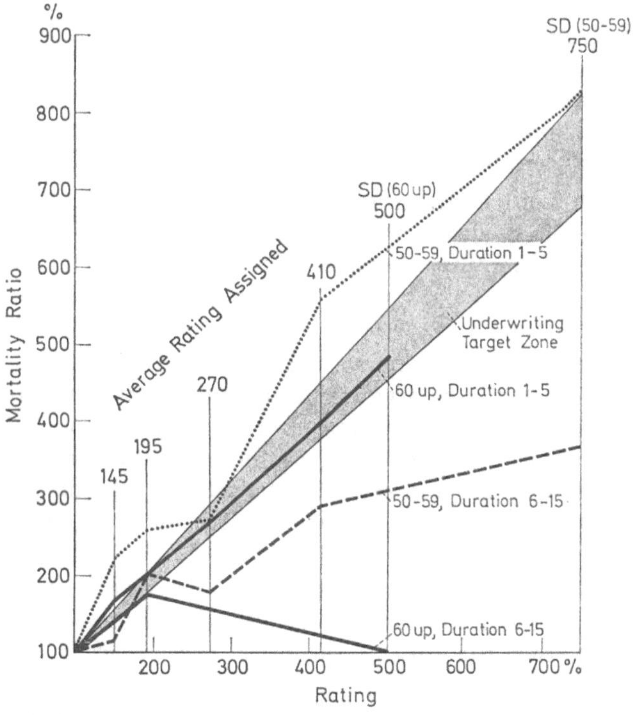

Fig. 8. NEL substandard experience 1955—1968. Mortality ratio observed vs. average rating (male)

mortality ratio observed for an average rating of 500 per cent, for example, is within limits such as 450 to 550 per cent, rather than exactly 500 per cent, which would be a rare and fortuitous occurrence. Points falling within the Underwriting Target Zone could be considered as a satisfactory correspondence of mortality result to selection effort. Mortality ratios above the Underwriting Target Zone reflect liberal underwriting and those below the Zone conservative underwriting, provided that the differences are statistically significant. It should be emphasized that the experience for men age 60 up is based on a total of 140 deaths at policy durations 1–5, and 129 deaths for the balance of the select period, with only 5 to 24 deaths in individual rating categories as shown in Fig. 8. Experience for men age 50–59 was more extensive, with 624 deaths in the early, and 1003 deaths in the later, portions of the select period.

In Fig. 8 observed points for the categories with five or more deaths have been connected by dashed lines for the experience of men age 50–59, and solid lines for men age 60 and up. In the early part of the select period mortality ratios for men age 50–59 are well above the Underwriting Target Zone in most of the rating categories, but the ratios for men age 60 up are generally on target. By way of contrast, mortality ratios beyond the lowest rating categories run well below the Target Zone for both age groups, when the policy duration is 6–15 years. The contrast between the experience in the early and later portions of the select period is especially noteworthy for the SD category, where the more favorable mortality after the first five years represents a difference of high statistical significance, even though there were only 5 deaths among men age 60 up. These changes are consistent with the downward trend of total substandard mortality ratio with quinquennial policy duration intervals previously given in Fig. 3. In older applicants the decrease is especially marked after the first five policy years have been completed.

Some Common-Sense Observations on Underwriting the Older Life Insurance Applicant. These observations will not refer to particular impairment risks but will make use of the mortality characteristics touched on in this review. They will be presented in the form of a series of questions, such as those stated in the abstract, and brief answers as I would give them.

1. Are standard limits of insurance clearly defined for the older applicant? No they are not, because of the large age and duration changes in select mortality rates, and because conventional selection criteria exclude not 10 to 15 per cent but up to 30 per cent of applicants age 60 up from standard consideration. The complexity of this question and the formulation of a rational answer deserve the close attention of any company that issues a significant volume of insurance to applicants over age 60.

2. What are select mortality rates for the older insured applicant? The best approximations available are those from annual graduation of the 1955—1960 Basic Tables, but the reliability of the rates leaves much to be desired at ages 65 up in the first few years of policy duration. The only prospect for more accurate rates would have to come from an intercompany study of pooled standard experience by annual ages starting at 55 or 60, and by annual policy durations, combining entrants from 1950 to as recent a date as possible. This would involve a special study quite different in scope from the annual studies of ordinary insured experience in larger U.S. companies conducted by the Society of Actuaries.

3. Does extra mortality tend to change at the higher ages? The evidence indicates a decrease in mortality ratio with age and policy duration, in the aggregate, and for some individual impairments, probably the majority, although exceptions are known to occur. This change is due primarily to the natural rise in select standard mortality rate with age and policy duration. In terms of EDR extra mortality tends to increase with age, but the pattern of EDR change with duration varies with age and impairment. The trend in EDR may be a more sensitive and reliable predictor of excess mortality in older applicants than the trend in mortality ratio.

4. Is it possible to offer properly evaluated substandard insurance to the older applicant who is an impaired risk? I believe it is possible to do so, subject to due consideration of the special problems involved. However, the risks are sufficiently hazardous to tax all the skills that can be mustered by the medical underwriter and actuary working in close cooperation.

5. What special precautions should be observed with respect to insurance for the older applicant? The following are pertinent in setting up such precautions:

— The need for detailed underwriting information at amount levels lower than for younger applicants (the expense is justified by the high premium).
— The need for careful individual attention to the analysis of all risk factors, which are often multiple, and their contribution to the total mortality risk, and the problem of insurable interest.
— The need for individual actuarial attention to substandard premiums in certain cases.
— The need for a reduction in retention limit that is appropriate to the greatly increased mortality rates in older applicants and any antiselection present in large amount substandard experience.
— The need for a schedule of rating limits that is appropriately graded downward with age. In my opinion the extra risk is too hazardous to insure if the annual substandard extra premium exceeds 10 per cent of the insurance amount.
— The need to keep in mind at all times the magnitude of both the standard and the extra mortality risk, especially during the first five policy years.

References

1. Committee on Mortality: II. 1955—1960 Basic Tables. Trans. Soc. of Act. (1962 Reports Number) p. 44—58.
2. New England Mutual Life Insurance Co. Unpublished Mortality Studies (1971, 1973).
3. Shurtleff, D.: Some characteristics related to the incidence of cardiovascular disease and death: Framingham Study, 16-year Follow-up. Section 26 of The Framingham Study. Ed.: W. B. Kannel and T. Gordon. Supt. of Documents, U.S.G.P.O., Washington, D.C. (December 1970).
4. Bolt, W. R., Bell, M. F., Harnes, J. R.: A study of mortality in moderate and severe hypertension. Trans. Ass. Life Insur. Med. Dir. Amer. 41, 61—100 (1957).
5. Beard, O. W., Hipp, H. R., Robins, M., Verzolini, V. R.: Initial myocardial infarction among veterans: Ten-year survival. Amer. Heart J. 73, 317—321 (1967).
6. Kannel, W. B., Gordon, T., Offutt, D.: Left ventricular hypertrophy by electrocardiogram — prevalence, incidence and mortality in the Framingham Study. Ann. Intern. Med. 71, 89 to 105 (1971).
7. Griswold, M. H., Wilder, C. S., Cutler, S. J., Pollack, E. S.: Cancer in Connecticut 1935—1951. Connecticut State Dept. of Health, Hartford, Conn. (1955).

De la influencia de tres enfermedades frecuentes no malignas y a menudo asintomáticas del aparato digestivo, sobre la mortalidad de personas mayores de 60 años

Dr. MAX L. HEFTI * y Dr. AURELIO OLASCOAGA **

2 Figuras

Introducción

La limitada meta de esta conferencia es la de facilitar al médico de seguros de vida no muy familiarizado con afecciones gastroenterológicas algunas normas seleccionadas sobre la apreciación de anomalías triviales hepato-gastrointestinales, en personas mayores de 60 años.

Dentro de este marco, nos referimos a las investigaciones sobre la influencia de tres enfermedades frecuentes no malignas y a menudo asintomáticas del aparato digestivo, que afectan la mortalidad de personas mayores de 60 años.

Como ejemplo de tales enfermedades, a continuación examinaremos la importancia diagnóstica de la colelitiasis, la hernia hiatal y la diverticulosis del intestino grueso en personas de más de 60 años.

MÜLLER, de Johannesburgo, [6] bautizó con el nombre de „Triada de Saint" la coincidencia de estas tres enfermedades en un mismo paciente (Tabla 1).

Tabla 1. La *Triada de Saint* y las afecciones individuales comprendidas bajo este concepto, presentes en un compuesto policlínico de 713 pacientes

Cuadro patológico	Frecuencia		Edad media al diagnosticarla	Paciente más joven
	Observada	Según cálculo de probabilidad		
Colelitiasis	a) 16,4%		55 años	
Hernia hiatal	b) 14,0%		58 años	
Diverticulosis colónica	c) 18,7%		60 años	
Triada de Saint	3,4%	a)×b)×c) = 0,4%	68 años	50 años

(SEGÚN FOSTER, J. J., KNUTSON, D. L.: J. Amer. med. Ass. **168**, 257 (1958))

* Compañía Suiza de Reaseguros, Zurich/Suiza.
** La Nacional, Compañía de Seguros S.A., México, D.F./México.

Fortes y Knutson [3], en su compuesto policlínico examinado sistemáticamente, han encontrado las enfermedades individuales de la Triada de Saint en un 16,4%, 14,0% y 18,7% de los casos respectivamente.

De acuerdo con el cálculo de probabilidades, debían tener que encontrarse en un 0,4% de los reconocidos las tres enfermedades en forma de la tríada, si la coincidencia fuese el producto del puro azar.

El hecho de que la tríada se haya podido comprobar en un 3,4% de los reconocidos, es decir, en casi diez veces más de lo calculado, habla en pro de la existencia de factores predisponentes.

La comparación de las edades medias obtenidas al diagnosticar las enfermedades individuales con la edad del paciente más joven al diagnosticar la triada, hace suponer que sea el o al menos uno de esos factores predisponentes para la tríada de Saint al aumento de las enfermedades coincidente con la edad.

Este factor „edad" lo examinaremos en su correlación con las tres afecciones individuales de la triada de Saint.

La colelitiasis

La formación de cálculos biliares se ha atribuido a la estasis, irritación y discolia.

Hoy domina la opinion de que los cálculos de colesterina, que constituyen las tres cuartas partes de todos los cálculos biliares [9], son consecuencia de una perturbación del equilibrio entre la colesterina, la leticina y las sales biliares de la bilis producida por el hígado.

En la vesícula biliar desparece la colesterina de la solución saturada y forma los cálculos, que por adición de aún más colesterina y, algunas veces, de calcio se convierten en pequeñas piedras macroscópicas [7].

Las medidas que modifican el equilibrio de la composición biliar a favor de la colesterina, como una dieta de varios años para disminuir la colesterina o un tratamiento prolongado con medicamentos que disminuyen la colesterina, pueden dar lugar a la formación de cálculos [8, 5].

Por el contrario, las medidas que modifican el equilibrio a favor de las sales biliares, como la aplicación durante meses de ácidos de quenodeoxicol, pueden llevar a la disolución de los cálculos [10].

Frecuencia

Tras una hernia hiatal, los cálculos biliares son el hallazgo orgánico más frecuente en la región abdominal superior.

La Tabla 2 muestra la influencia de la edad del paciente sobre la frecuencia porcentual de la colelitiasis.

En el compuesto de autopsias del estudio de Kozoll [4] y colaboradores — que en casi la tercera parte se compuso de casos jóvenes — se han encontrado cálculos en el 6,3% de los autopsiados.

A medida que la edad era más elevada, los cálculos se presentaron con más frecuencia. En el grupo de los mayores de 60 años, los había en el 14,1% de los casos.

En el compuesto de autopsias de Torvik [11] y colaboradores — que en sus 2/3 partes se compuso de casos geriátricos — se encontraron cálculos en el 19,5%

de todos los autopsiados, es decir, tres veces más que en el compuesto de KOZOLL [4].

También en la serie de TORVIK [11] han sido más frecuentes los casos de cálculos conforme era más avanzada la edad. En el grupo de los mayores de 60 años, se comprobó la existencia de una colelitiasis en un 20,6% de los examinados.

Tabla 2. Frecuencia de colelitiasis en por ciento de los casos de autopsias, *según grupos de edades*

Grupos de edades	[a] Estudio de KOZOLL et al.	[b] Estudio de TORVIK et al.
0—19	0,1	} 0,7
20—29	2,1	
30—39	3,7	
40—49	6,4	5,4
50—59	8,7	11,9
60—69	12,5	17,3
70—79	16,3	25,6
≧80	23,8	31,5
Todas las edades	6,3	19,5

[a] KOZOLL, D. D. et al.: Arch. Surg. **79**, 514 (1959).
[b] TORVIK, A. et al.: Acta chir. scand. **120**, 168 (1960).

Si bien no se pueden aplicar sin reserva a la población entera estas observaciones en autopsias, puede no obstante contarse con que del 15% al 20% de los mayores de 60 años presentan cálculos biliares o han sido operados anteriormente por este concepto.

APPLEMAN [1] ha demostrado gráficamente, en relación con la edad, la distribución por sexo de sus casi 5000 pacientes operados a causa de cálculos biliares (Fig. 1).

La línea en la parte superior corresponde a la cuota de las mujeres en cada edad dada; la línea en la parte inferior a la de los hombres.

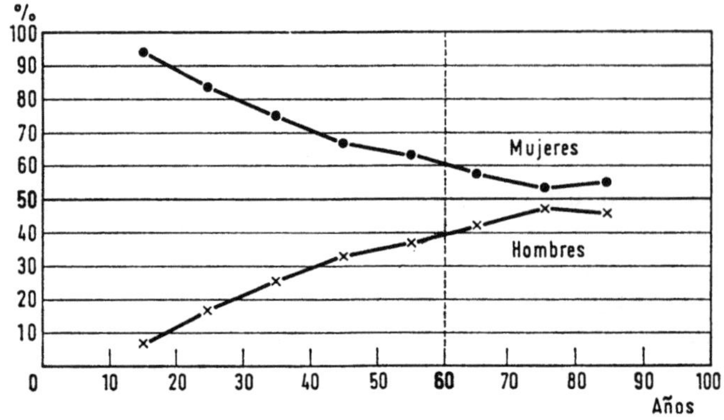

Fig. 1. Frecuencia en por ciento de 4948 pacientes operados a causa de cálculos biliares, *según sexo y edad*. (APPLEMAN, R., et al.: Proc. Mayo Clin. **39**, 473 (1964))

En los operados de 30 a 40 años predominan las mujeres en la proporción de 3:1. A los 60 años, la proporción sigue todavía a favor de las mujeres (3:2). Y conforme avanza la edad, se acerca a la relación de 1:1.

Síntomas

Los cálculos biliares causan síntomas dispépticos relativamente típicos, o cólicos, o ambos conjuntamente.

Sin embargo, parece que una parte de los cálculos biliares quedan silenciosos o al menos quietos. En otros terminos, tales cálculos no causan al paciente molestia alguna o sólo insignificantes y atipicas, que no sugieren la práctica de algún examen apuntado. Son hallazgos accidentales de un colecistograma de rutina, de un examen radiológico de otros órganos abdominales — esto naturalmente sólo cuando sean opacos —, de una laparotomía o una autopsia.

Parece ser que la frecuencia de tales cálculos inactivos aumenta conforme avanza la edad, según comprueban las observaciones hechas en el grupo de pacientes ginecológicas de Truesdell [12] (Tabla 3).

Tabla 3. Frecuencia en por ciento de los *cálculos biliares hallados por casualidad* en 500 operaciones ginecológicas, *según grupos de edades*

Grupos de edades	Números absolutos		%
	Pacientes	Cálculos biliares	Cálculos biliares
≦39	299	20	6,7
40—49	152	20	13,2
50—59	33	5	15,2
60—69	16	5	31,2
Todos los grupos de edades	500	50	10,0

(Truesdell, E. D.: Ann. Surg. **119**, 232 (1944))

En 50 mujeres de entre 500 se hallaron, con motivo de una laparotomía practicada, cálculos biliares antes no supuestos.

En otros términos, se han hallado cálculos biliares antes inactivos en un 10% de todas las operadas y en un 31% de las mayores de 60 años. Considerando, sin embargo, el pequeño número de este último grupo, procede naturalmente aceptar con reserva este dato.

Causas de fallecimientos

Asintomáticos o sintomáticos, los cálculos biliares en sí no constituyen ninguna causa mortal.

Tan sólo produciéndose complicaciones o como consecuencia de una operación pueden poner en peligro la vida del paciente. Según Arianoff [2] las complicaciones en los casos de cálculos solitarios son más frecuentes que en los de múltiples.

La complicación más frecuente hallada en un grupo de autopsiados no seleccionados la constituyó en casi el 50% de los reconocidos la colecistitis [4].

La presencia en por ciento de complicaciones agudas y del carcinoma de la vesícula biliar se ha reunido, según grupos de edad, en la Tabla 4. Otra vez, se trata de hallazgos de autopsia.

Cerca del 3% de todos los portadores de cálculos biliares presentaron una colecistitis aguda con complicaciones secundarias o sin ellas. Su frecuencia no parece estar relacionada con la edad.

Tabla 4. Frecuencia de *complicaciones* y *carcinomas* en por ciento de los casos de cálculos biliares, *según grupos de edades*

Grupos de edades	Frecuencia de complicaciones y carcinomas en % de los casos de cálculos biliares		
	Colecistitis aguda	Coledocolitiasis	Carcinoma de la vesícula biliar
≦29	2,6	0	0
30—39	4,1	8,1	1,0
40—49	2,7	7,3	1,9
50—59	2,9	5,6	4,4
60—69	2,8	5,8	6,5
≧70	2,8	11,7	5,0
Todos los grupos de edades	2,9	7,8	4,6

(KOZOLL, D. D., et al.: Arch. Surg. 79, 514 (1959))

Aproximadamente un 8% de todos los portadores de cálculos biliares, con o sin complicaciones secundarias, sufrieron una coledocolitiasis, de preferencia en combinación con cálculos biliares.

El 5%, aproximadamente, de los portadores de cálculos biliares acusaron un carcinoma de la vesícula biliar. Como era de esperar, se lo encontró con más frecuencia porcentual en personas mayores de 60 años que en los grupos de edades más jóvenes.

Norma para la evaluación del riesgo de colelitiasis entre las personas mayores de 60 años

1. Cada 5° proponente de más de 60 años tiene cálculos biliares o ha sido operado de cálculos biliares.

Con más de 60 años los hombres tienen cálculos biliares casi tan frecuentemente como las mujeres. Alrededor de la mitad probablemente ignoran que tienen cálculos biliares.

2. Cada 10° paciente de cálculos biliares mayor de 60 años tiene también cálculos biliares en el coledoco.

3. El 75% de los cálculos biliares se componen exclusivamente o principalmente de colesterina.

Con la expansión de las dietas y medicamentos para reducir la colesterina no puede excluirse un sensible aumento de frecuencia de los cálculos de colesterina. Por el otro lado, existe la perspectiva de que en el futuro los cálculos de colesterina pueden ser disueltos en parte con medicamentos y sin riesgo.

4. Los cálculos biliares mudos, conocidos desde hace más de 5 años y que se han mantenido mudos, presentan poco peligro de más tarde causar complicaciones.

5. Apenas un 15% de los pacientes de cálculos biliares de más de 60 años tienen una complicacion (sin considerar la colecistitis crónica).

De ellos, alrededor del 10% mueren sea de una complicación interna o de las consecuencias de una operación.

6. Los cálculos biliares solitarios no causan menor complicaciones que los múltiples.

7. En el riesgo de la colelitiasis influyen muy particularmente el estado cardiovascular y la situación del metabolismo de azúcar del paciente.

Hernia hiatal (Definición, patogénesis)

De una manera general, puede definirse la hernia del hiato como el paso de órganos abdominales, a través del hiato, hacia la región tóracica (Fig. 2).

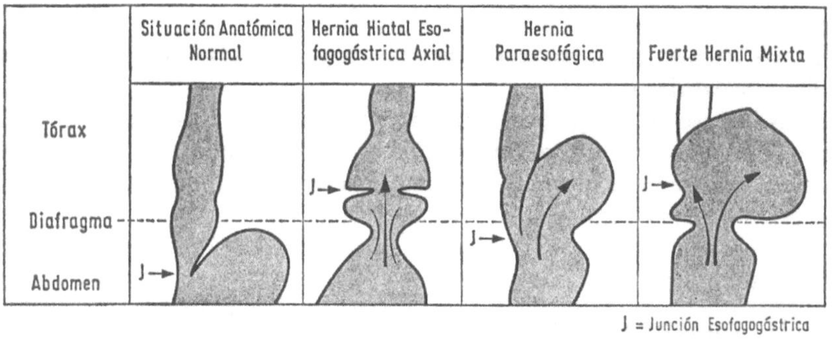

Fig. 2. Mecanismo causante y tipos de la hernia hiatal (sin „short esophagus")

Clásicamente se distingue entre el estómago parcialmente toraxal, por „esófago corto" (short esophagus), la hernia paraesofágica del hiato y la hernia axial esofagogástrica [13].

Frecuencia

La posibilidad del libre deslizamiento alternativo de las hernias esofágicas tiene por consecuencia la de que tales hernias, según la posición del cuerpo del reconocido y la compresión abdominal, se presentan más o menos frecuentemente (Tabla 5).

Las hernias esofagogástricas deslizantes representan $^4/_5$ de todas las hernias hiatales, los dos otros tipos conjuntos una quinta parte más o menos [20] (Tabla 5).

La frecuencia porcentual de las hernias hiatales aumenta con progresión de la edad de la persona. De 590 reconocimientos radiológicos consecutivos de pacientes sin síntomas, Pridie [18] encontró una hernia hiatal en el 29,6% de los casos, y en el de pacientes mayores de 70 años en el 69%.

La relación de 2:3 entre hombre y mujer no mostró influencia de la edad.

Tabla 5. Frecuencia en por ciento de las *diverticulosis colónicas halladas por casualidad, según edad y sexo*

Grupos de edades	Frecuencia de la diverticulosis en %		
	♂	♀	Total
≦40	0	0	0
41—59	14,3	23,1	18,5
60—79	30,0	28,6	29,2
≧80	30,0	55,5	42,1

(Manousos, O. N. et al.: Brit. med. J. **1967 III**, 762)

Hernia hiatal como causa de fallecimiento

Al igual que la colelitiasis sin complicaciones, la hernia hiatal no es en sí causa de muerte.

3/4 de los pacientes con hernias esofagogástricas, si es que tienen síntomas, éstos son mínimos y pasajeros [16].

Síntomas intensos y complicaciones aparecen sólo con la presencia de un reflujo gastroesofágico o una compresión mecánica. En casi todos los casos letales, la causa del fallecimiento estaba en las complicaciones secundarias del reflujo y de la compresión o en la operación.

Reflujo — esofaguitis

Palmer [17] encontró en el 23,9% de los pacientes con hernia hiatal y en el 22% de los pacientes con síntomas de esofaguitis sin hernia hiatal un reflujo gastroesofágico.

En el 77% de casos de „esófago corto" Allison [14] encontró un reflujo.

Mediante sus experimentos, Cohen y Harris [15] pudieron mostrar que la competencia del esfínter esofágico inferior no es influida por su posición anatómica en la cavidad abdominal o torácica.

La causa primaria del reflujo debe ser una disminución de la tonicidad de este esfínter y no de la pérdida del ángulo de His cuando se trata de „esófago corto" y hernia hiatal axial.

La importancia de las hernias hiatales en la aparición de las complicaciones pépticas de reflujo se pone, consiguientemente, en cuestión.

Aproximadamente el 25% de los pacientes con hernia hiatal axial muestran una reflujo-esofagitis [17]. De este porcentaje, alrededor del 10% muestran una úlcera profunda en el paso esofagogástrico y más o menos el 10% una estenosis [14].

Compresión mecánica

La estrangulación de la hernia por el diafragma puede provocar, principalmente en casos de hernias paraesofágicas y hernias combinadas masivas, a gastritis hemostáticas, a úlceras en estómagos herniados y a incarceración de la hernia.

La presión sobre órganos próximos en las hernias grandes puede ocasionar síntomas cardiopulmonares, inclusive modificaciones de EKG.

Perforación

Las perforaciones expontáneas y las iatrogénicas, por ejemplo en caso de esofagoscopía, se presentan en menos del 1% de los casos y, además, casi siempre en personas de más de 70 años.

Hemorragia

En el 10–30% de las hernias hiatiales se observan hemorragias. Muy raramente se trata de hemorragias masivas procedentes del esófago o de la parte posterior del estómago. Casi siempre son hemorragias rezumantes con anemia crónica.

Operación

En total, de un 2,5 hasta un 4% de los pacientes con hernia hiatal son operados.

La mortalidad de la operación selectiva a causa de la reflujo-esofagitis resistente a la terapia es de alrededor del 1%. La mortalidad por operación de las estenosis 5% y de las incarceraciones más del 30% [19].

Norma para la apreciación del riesgo de la hernias hiatales en personas de más de 60 años

1. Prácticamente las hernias hiatales son una manifestación fisiológica de la vejez. 2 de cada 3 candidatos con más de 60 años tienen una hernia hiatal y más de la mitad ignoran el hecho.

2. Los dolores retroesternales o precordiales (principalmente en personas de más de 60 años) no deben ser atribuidos a una hernia no complicada, siempre que no deba excluirse un padecimiento coronario.

3. De 10 hernias hiatales hay 8 de tipo axial esofagogástrico y 2 de tipo combinado paraesofágico.

4. Las hernias hiatales de tipo axial (esofagogástricas y „esófago corto") originan principalmente complicaciones pépticas condicionadas al reflujo. Las hernias del tipo paraesofágico son causa principalmente de complicaciones condicionadas a la compresión.

Las hernias combinadas causan ambas clases de complicaciones.

5. No es la hernia hiatal como tal la responsable de las complicaciones pépticas, sino el reflujo gastroesofágico, independiente de la existencia de una hernia.

6. El 25% de las hernias esofagogástricas y el 75% de las hernias en el caso de „esófago corto" son causa de reflujo-esofagitis. Cuanto más grande sea la parte estomacal herniada, tanto mayor será también la esofagitis.

7. Del 2 al 3% de las hernias esofagogástricas y casi el 10% de las hernias en el caso de „esófago corto" causan una úlcera péptica esofágica.

8. Del 2 al 3% de las hernias esofagogástricas y casi el 10% de las hernias en el caso de „esófago corto" causan una estenosis significante.

9. El 75% de las hernias paraesofágicas y el 25 de las hernias grandes combinadas originan en parte complicaciones de estrangulación con peligro para la vida del paciente.

10. Las hemorragias masivas y las perforaciones son raras.

11. Menos del 5% de todas las hernias hiatales deben ser tratadas quirúrgicamente. La mortalidad por operación de las hernias no complicadas es de aproximadamente el 1%. La proporción de las recaídas es de por lo menos el 5%.

Diverticulosis del intestino grueso

Los divertículos son pequeñas hernias de la mucosa del intestino grueso que como consecuencia de la presión interna forzada del intestino penetran la capa muscular de la pared intestinal donde pasan los vasos.

Los divertículos, por lo tanto, son bolsas de la membrana mucosa situadas fuera de la pared, que siguen unidas con luz del intestino por un cuello delgado.

Los cuellos diverticulares son formaciones intramurales que a menudo están situados en los vacíos vasculares de la capa muscular en contacto muy estrecho con los vasos sanguíneos.

Las condiciones espásticas del intestino o la tumefacción inflamatoria de la mucosa pueden hacer interrumpir la libre comunicación entre divertículo y luz del intestino.

Tal trastorno de la libre comunicación tiene consecuencias diagnósticas y clínicas.

Diagnósticas. Practicarse un examen radiológico con irrigación intestinal mediante bario, los divertículos inflamados a menudo no se llenan con el medio de contraste, de modo que no se ven representados. La posibilidad de ver tales divertículos es mayor en las radiografías tardías de 24, 48 y hasta más horas después de la irrigación con bario, o de una comida.

Clínicas. Existiendo una presión intraluminal aumentada, puede ser que las heces entren en el divertículo por el cuello estrecho sin poder vaciarse posteriormente en la luz del intestino. La consecuencia será una inflamación insidiosa de la bolsa diverticular de la mucosa. Si la inflamación se propaga a los tejidos y estructuras paracólicos adyacentes, se produce la figura de la diverticulitis manifiesta [29].

La diverticulosis afecta en 9 veces sobre 10 al colon sigmoideo y en la mitad de los casos todavía otros segmentos del intestino grueso. En los 503 casos de Horner [26], el 47% de ellos tenían divertículos en el colon sigmoideo sólo y el 48% en el colon sigmoideo y a la vez en otros segmentos intestinales. Sólo en un 5% de los casos estaba libre de divertículos el colon sigmoideo.

La diverticulosis es una enfermedad senil típica que en las personas menores de 40 años prácticamente no se presenta, y en los mayores de 40 años aumenta en cada década de vida (Tabla 6).

En el cuadro asintomático de la población de la región de Oxford de Manousos [28], el 18,5% de las personas de 41 a 59 años presentaban una diverticulosis del intestino grueso, tasa que fue del 29,2% en las personas de 60 a 79 años y del 42,1% en las mayores de 80 años.

Tabla 6. Frecuencia en por ciento de las complicaciones de la diverticulosis del intestino grueso y de la diverticulitis, respectivamente

	Diverticulosis		Diverticulitis		
	Total	De las cuales sin diverticulitis	Total	De las cuales 1 solo ataque	De las cuales varios ataques
	100 %	75,2%	100 %	54,8%	45,2%
Hemorragia (fuerte)	5,4%	4,1%	9,6%	10,0%	9,1%
Obstrucción	5,1%	1,8%	15,1%	2,5%	30,3%
Perforación	5,1%	2,3%	13,7%	10,0%	18,2%
Total de las complicaciones	15,6%	8,1%	38,4%	22,5%	57,5%
Carcinoma	5,4%	4,1%	9,6%	—	—

(Boles, S., et al.: Gastroenterology **35**, 579 (1958))

En resumen, puede estimarse en más del 30% la frecuencia de la diverticulosis en personas mayores de 60 años.

Diverticulosis como causa de muerte.

Al igual que la colelitiasis y la hernia hiatal no complicadas, que en sí no causan la muerte, la diverticulosis colónica tampoco es en sí una causa de muerte.

En prácticamente todos los casos de desenlace letal, son causa de la muerte la diverticulitis y sus complicaciones secundarias u operaciones profilácticas y curativas.

Esta tesis, sin embargo, requiere una reserva al menos desde el punto de vista clínico.

Hemorragias fuertes — es decir, hemorragias en que el paciente se desangraría no efectuándosele transfusiones de sangre de 2000 ml y más en 12 horas — se presentan en casos de diverticulosis sin indicios clínicos o radiológicos de diverticulitis.

En 23 pacientes que han sido operados a causa de una hemorragia intestinal amenazadora para la vida, siendo conocida la existencia de la diverticulosis, Asch y Markowitz [22] encontraron sólo 3 veces una diverticulitis macroscópica. Estudios histológicos apuntados, sin embargo, demostraron que existen también en casos sin diverticulitis visible, erosiones inflamatorias locales de la mucosa diverticular con paso a un vaso adyacente [32].

La *frecuencia de la diverticulitis* aumenta con el tiempo: en diverticulosis conocidas hace 5 años o menos, Horner [26] encontró una diverticulitis en cerca del 10%. En los casos en que la diverticulosis era conocida de entre 6 y 10 años, el respectivo porcentaje aumentó al 25%. Y en aquéllos de una historia de 11 años y más fue del 35%.

La consecuencia indirecta es la de que en personas mayores de 60 años hay que contar con una frecuencia aumentada de la diverticulitis.

Además, la diverticulitis aumenta conforme avanza la diverticulosis.

Finalmente, acrecienta la diverticulitis con la propagación topográfica respectiva de la diverticulosis: si está afectado solamente el colon sigmoideo, la diverticulitis se produce en una sexta parte de los casos, si está afectado el intestino grueso entero, se presenta en cada segundo caso.

En resumen, puede decirse que corren el riesgo de enfermarse de una diverticulitis en más del 50% de los casos los individuos afectados de una diverticulosis conocida desde hace más de 10 años, que se ha extendido con el tiempo y que afecta al intestino grueso entero.

Evolución de la diverticulitis

El *cuadro patológico agudo* de la *diverticulitis* puede evolucionar a semejanza de una apendicitis aguda con signos en el cuadrante inferior izquierdo.

Como operación selectiva de una mortalidad inferior al 2% y una cifra de recidivas del 15% [25], se considera hoy en día la colectomía parcial.

La diverticulitis, sin embargo, puede también — sea primariamente o bien tras la declinación de un ataque agudo — evolucionarse como *cuadro clínico crónico*, cuyos síntomas son a menudo de un parecido sorprendente a los síntomas del colon irritable.

Complicaciones secundarias

Cualquiera que sea la forma de evolución clínica, la diverticulitis es precursora de casi todas las complicaciones graves de la diverticulosis del intestino grueso, las que por lo tanto llamamos *complicaciones secundarias*.

BOLES y JORDAN [23] han observado durante 10 a 30 años unos 294 casos de diverticulosis (Tabla 6).

Una cuarta parte de sus pacientes padecieron, en el curso de los años, una diverticulitis clínicamente manifiesta.

Del 75,2% de los pacientes con *divertículos al parecer no inflamados*, el 8,7% presentó complicaciones, la mitad de los cuales con hemorragias fuertes.

Del 24,8% de los pacientes con *diverticulitis clínicamente manifiesta*, el 38,3%, o sea 5 veces más, presentaron en el mismo lapso una complicación secundaria, el 9,6% una hemorragia fuerte, el 15% una obstrucción y el 13,7% una perforación.

Hemorragias

Las *hemorragias fuertes* se presentan con independencia del número de ataques de diverticulitis y, también sin diverticulosis clínicamente comprobable.

CASARELLA y sus colaboradores [24] han podido demostrar, con la ayuda de la arteriografía selectiva, en 13 de 27 pacientes con hemorragia intestinal importante sin causa conocida, que la fuente de la hemorragia residía en un divertículo no inflamado macroscópicamente. En 12 veces de las 13, el divertículo estaba en situación proxima del ángulo izquierdo y 9 veces de las 12 en el colon ascendente.

Obstrucción

Determinada *obstrucción* existe en toda diverticulosis.

En el compuesto de observación de Boles y Jordan [23], los pacientes con más de un ataque de diverticulitis aguda constituyeron un riesgo doce veces mayor de padecer una obstrucción amenazadora para la vida que los pacientes con un solo ataque.

La mortalidad operatoria de la obstrucción llega a cerca del 15% [27].

Perforación

El concepto „perforación" comprende muy variados cuadros clínicos graves como la perforación cubierta con peritonitis local, la perforación abierta con peritonitis difusa purulenta o fecal y la formación de fístulas en la pared intestinal misma o hacia órganos adyacentes.

La mortalidad operatoria oscila entre el 2,5% para la operación selectiva después de una perforación cubierta, y el 75% para operaciones de emergencia de una perforación con peritonitis fecal.

Carcinoma

Predomina hoy la opinión de que no existe ninguna relación causal entre el *carcinoma colónica* y la diverticulosis.

El problema principal de la combinación diverticulosis/carcinoma colónica lo ha constituido hasta ahora la dificultad de reconocer radiológicamente un carcinoma en un intestino alterado por divertículos e inflamación.

Constituyen al respecto un importante progreso la colonoscopia fibroóptica implantada en los últimos años, y la posibilidad de sacar biopsias apuntadas de todos los segmentos del intestino grueso [34].

Normas para la evaluación del riesgo de la diverticulosis del intestino grueso en individuos mayores de 60 años

1. Cada tercer solicitante mayor de 60 años padece una diverticulosis del colon sigmoideo. Cada sexto solicitante tiene una diverticulosis colónica y del colon sigmoideo. Cerca de la mitad, probablemente no saben que padecen una diverticulosis.
2. Un 25% de las diverticulosis producen una diverticulitis clínicamente manifiesta. Estando afectado el colon entero y existiendo los divertículos más de un año, la cifra de diverticulitis aumenta al 50%.
3. Un 50% de los pacientes que han sufrido un ataque de diverticulitis aguda no experimentarán otro ataque nuevo.
4. Un 5% de las diverticulosis producen una hemorragia copiosa. Los pacientes de arteriosclerosis e hipertensión acusan una cuota de hemorragias mayor y, asimismo, una mortalidad mayor por hemorragias. Una hemorragia puede ocurrir tanto en la diverticulosis asintomática como en la diverticulitis manifiesta y a menudo proviene de divertículos del lado derecho.

5. Un 5% de las diverticulosis producen una obstrucción en la diverticulosis no complicada. Aumenta más y más la cifra de obstrucción con cada diverticulitis padecida.

6. Un 5% de las diverticulosis producen una perforación. Es rara la perforación en la diverticulosis no complicada. Aumenta considerablemente la cifra de perforación con el primer ataque de diverticulitis, y es menos considerable en los ataques posteriores.

7. Un 10% al 15% de las diverticulosis presentan a la vez un carcinoma colónica.

La frecuencia del carcinoma se explica, por un lado, por la dificultad para el paciente de notar los síntomas de carcinoma existiendo ya síntomas de diverticulitis, y para el médico por la dificultad de detectar un carcinoma en el intestino alterado, y, por el otro lado, por el aumento de la frecuencia en ambos cuadros patógenos, dependiente de la edad.

La implantación de la colonoscopia fibroóptica constituye una valiosa ayuda para la selección.

8. La mortalidad operatoria de la colectomía parcial tras la declinación de la fase aguda está actualmente por debajo del 2%.

En pacientes adiposos, dicha mortalidad es sensiblemente mayor.

9. Un 15% de los pacientes resecados parcialmente producen una recidiva de diverticulitis. Todavía no se conoce de modo suficiente la cifra de recidivas de la miotomía del colon sigmoideo.

Para terminar esta exposición quisiera mencionar que por falta de estudios especiales médico-actuariales sobre enfermedades hepato-gastrointestinales con personas de más de 60 años, no ha sido posible proponerles las correspondientes tasas por sobre mortalidad concretas. En lugar de ello, sirviéndome de algunas normas escogidas, he tratado de ser de alguna ayuda para el médico tarificador en la apreciación general de tales riesgos.

Bibliografía

Colelitiasis

1. Appleman, R. et al.: Cholelithiasis and choledocholithiasis: Factors that influence relative incidence. Mayo Clin. Proc. **39**, 473 (1964).
2. Arianoff, A. A. et al.: Etude comparative des mortalités des lithiases biliaires solitaires et multiples. Acta gastro-ent. belg. **25**, 98 (1962).
3. Foster, J. J., Knutson, D. L.: Association of cholelithiasis, hiatus hernia and diverticulosis coli. J. Amer. med. Ass. **168**, 257 (1958).
4. Kozoll, D. D. et al.: Pathologic correlation of gallstones: A review of 1874 autopsies of patients with gallstones. Arch. Surg. **79**, 514 (1959).
5. Leading Article: Diet and cholesterol gallstones. Lancet **1973 I**, 471.
6. Muller, C. J. B.: Hiatus hernia, diverticulosis coli, and gallstones, Saint's triade. S. Afr. med. J. **22**, 376 (1948).
7. Small, D. M.: Prestone gallstone disease — is therapy safe. New Engl. J. Med. **284**, 214 (1971).
8. Sturdevant, R. A. L. et al.: Increased gallstone prevalence in men on serum-cholesterol-lowering diets. New Engl. J. Med. **288**, 24 (1973).
9. Sutor, D. J. et al.: The nature and incidence of gallstones containing calcium. Gut **14**, 215 (1973).

10. Thistle, J. L., Hofmann, A. F.: Efficacy and specificity of chenodeoxycholic acid therapy for dissolving gallstones. New Engl. J. Med. **289**, 655 (1973).
11. Torvik, A. et al.: Gallstones in an autopsy series. Acta clin. scand. **120**, 168 (1960).
12. Truesdell, E. D.: Frequency and future of gallstones believed to be quiescent or symptomless. Ann. Surg. **119**, 232 (1944).

Hernia hiatal

13. Åkerlünd, A.: Hernia diaphragmatica hiatus oesophagei. Acta radiol. (Stockh.) **6**, 3 (1926).
14. Allison, P. R.: Refluxoesophagitis, sliding hiatal hernia and the anatomy of repair. Surg. Gynec. Obstet. **92**, 419 (1951).
15. Cohen, S. et al.: Does hiatus hernia affect competence of the gastroesophageal sphincter? New Engl. J. Med. **284**, 1053 (1971).
16. Mobley, J. E. et al.: Oesophageal hiatal hernia: Prevalence, diagnosis and treatment in an American city of 30,000. Gastroenterology **30**, 1 (1956).
17. Palmer, E. D.: The hiatus hernia — oesophagitis-oesophageal stricture complex. Amer. J. med. **44**, 566 (1968).
18. Pridie, R. B.: Incidence and coincidence of hiatus hernia. Gut **7**, 188 (1966).
19. Schmidt, H. W.: Regurgitant ulceration at the esophageogastric junction. Proc. Mayo Clin. **29**, 153 (1954).
20. Sim, G. P. G.: An evaluation of tests for hiatus hernia. Brit. J. Radiol. **37**, 781 (1964).
21. Spratka, J. L. et al.: aFte of esophageal hiatus hernia. Surgery **36**, 524 (1954).

Diverticulosis del intestino grueso

22. Asch, M. J., Markowitz, A. M.: Diverticulitis coli: a surgical appraisal. Surgery **62**, 239 (1967).
23. Boles, J., Jordan, J. M.: The clinical significance of diverticulosis. Gastroenterology **35**, 579 (1958).
24. Casarella, W. J. et al.: Right-sided colonic diverticula as a cause of acute rectal hemorrhage. New Engl. J. Med. **286**, 450 (1972).
25. Gütgemann, A. et al.: Zur Therapie der Dickdarmdiverticulitis. Langenbecks Arch. Klin. Chir. **302**, 716 (1963).
26. Horner, J. L.: Natural history of diverticulosis of the colon. Amer. J. dig. Dis. **3**, 343 (1958).
27. Localio, S. A., Stahl, W. M.: Diverticular disease of the alimentary tract: Part I: the colon. Current problems in Surgery, 1967.
28. Manousos, O. N. et al.: Diverticular disease of the colon. Brit. med. J. **1967 III**, 751.
29. Morson, B. C.: The muscle abnormality in diverticular disease of the sigmoid colon. Brit. J. Radiol. **36**, 385 (1963).
30. Quinn, W. C.: Gross hemorrhage from presumed diverticular disease of the colon. Ann. Surg. **153**, 851 (1961).
31. Rösch, J. et al.: Selective arterial drug infusions in the treatment of acute gastrointestinal bleeding: A preliminary report. Gastroenterology **59**, 341 (1970).
32. Rosenberg, I. K., Rosenberg, B. F.: Massive hemorrhage from diverticula of the colon with demonstration of the source of bleeding. Ann. Surg. **159**, 570 (1964).
33. Turcolle, M.: Diverticulosis of the colon and complications. Medical Section American Life Convention 1960, p. 177.
34. Wolff, W. I., Shinya: Polypectomy via the fiberoptic colonoscope. Removal of neoplasms beyond reach of the sigmoidoscope. New Engl. J. Med. **288**, 329 (1963).

The Influence of Age on Mortality in Diabetics

Dr. G. Goodkin

2 Figures

Diabetes in the aged is insidious in onset and has become one of our most important geriatric problems. Although the onset of the disease is most common in middle life, the incidence is highest in the geriatric age group because of the increasing longevity of diabetics as a result of better management of the disease and the development of potent therapeutic agents in the treatment of complications.

The Oxford Study of 1947 [1] in which screening tests for diabetics were made for 3245 out of 5089 individuals living in Oxford, Massachusetts, demonstrated that known and newly-detected diabetics totalled 1.7% of the population. If this percentage is applied to the population of the United States, it would indicate a total of 3,400,000 diabetics both known and unknown. Inasmuch as there are nine known diabetics per 1000 population, the known diabetics would total 1,800,000 and the number of ambulant, undiagnosed diabetics about 1,600,000.

In contrast to the Oxford Study, the National Health Examination Survey [2] completed in 1962, where the sample was chosen to be representative of the total population of the United States aged 18 to 79 inclusive, reported data indicating that 1.8% had previously diagnosed diabetes, while one-hour blood sugar levels of 200 mg per 100 ml or higher following challenge with 50 g of glucose occurred in 4% of the population. Although 4% is the general average, there is a great variation in the incidence of diabetes in different ethnic groups in the general population; the highest occurs in the Pima Indians (49.7% based upon glucose tolerance tests) and the lowest in the Alaskan Eskimos (1.5%). It is currently estimated that there are in the USA over 2,000,000 known diabetics, about 2,500,000 chemical and subclinical diabetics, and 5,500,000 prediabetics. The total number of diabetics in the entire world is estimated to be about 50,000,000.

The natural history of diabetes can be divided into four stages of development (Table 1). Progression from the earliest stage may a) never occur, b) proceed slowly over many years or c) be rapid or explosive. Furthermore, these stages are reversible, overt diabetics being known to revert to the prediabetic stage or one of the intermediate stages.

The first stage, prediabetes, consists of the time prior to the onest of identifiable diabetes mellitus. The glucose tolerance test and the cortisone glucose tolerance test give normal results in this stage. Prediabetes cannot be diagnosed with certainty in the current state of our knowledge but may be suspected in the nondiabetic identical twin of a diabetic patient and in the offspring of parents who are both diabetics. Inasmuch as diabetes mellitus is a hereditary disease, prediabetes begins at birth and ends when either the preclinical, chemical or overt stage is identified.

Subclinical diabetes, the second stage, becomes clinically detectable under conditions of stress such as pregnancy or an acute illness. In subclinical diabetes the classical glucose tolerance test is normal but the cortisone glucose tolerance test is abnormal. When the precipitating stress is removed the patient may revert to the prediabetic stage.

Table 1. Natural history of diabetes

	Prediabetes →	← Subclinical diabetes →	← Chemical or latent diabetes →	← Overt diabetes
Fasting blood sugar	normal	normal	normal or elevated	elevated
Glucose tolerance test	normal	ordinarily normal, but abnormal during pregnancy or stress	abnormal	not necessary for diagnosis
Cortisone glucose tolerance test	normal	abnormal	not necessary	not necessary
Insulin like activity	increased	increased	increased	increased
Vascular changes	+	+	+++	++++

The third stage, chemical or latent diabetes, is clinically detectable by the oral glucose tolerance test in the absence of clinical symptoms of diabetes. This is the stage commonly encountered in insurance applicants when, in the absence of symptoms, glucose is discovered in the urine. Confirmation is obtained by securing a glucose tolerance test which gives abnormal results.

Overt diabetes, the fourth and last stage, is ushered in by the classical symptoms and signs of diabetes — polydipsia, polyuria, polyphagia, loss of weight, and a sense of fatigue.

Diabetes at any of the intermediate stages may revert to the earlier stage or advance to the next one. It is not uncommon for a chemical diabetic to revert to the prediabetic state if he loses excess weight or restricts carbohydrates. If he had an abnormal glucose tolerance test in the past, he may show a normal glucose tolerance test currently. This must be kept in mind when assigning a rating to an insurance applicant.

In determining the latent stage in the natural history of diabetes it is necessary to consider the factor of age relative to the normalcy of a glucose tolerance test (Fig. 1). It has been shown that there is an increase, decade by decade, in the incidence of diabetes as detected by the oral glucose tolerance test. The fasting sugar remains normal but the post-glucose tolerance curve rises progressively and then flattens out so that the critical 2-hour post-glucose reading is usually as high as or even higher than the 1-hour reading. Whether this represents an increased incidence of diabetes in the older age groups or is a physiological effect of aging is still in doubt. Dr. Fajans, whose criterion for a definite diagnosis of diabetes consists of a glucose tolerance test with levels exceeding 110 mg when fasting, 170 mg 1 hour after a glucose test meal, 140mg after 1½ hours and 120 mg after 2 hours, has suggested that the 1-hour, 1½- and 2-hour levels be increased by 10 mg for each decade after the age of fifty. The total capacity to metabolize carbohydrate decreases with age because less active muscles and tissues metabolize postprandial hyperglycemia more slowly and glucose tolerance curves tend to rise with successive decades. However, ELLENBERG and RIFKIN [3] showed that in 124 healthy subjects aged between 11 and 70 years the curves for 60-year-olds,

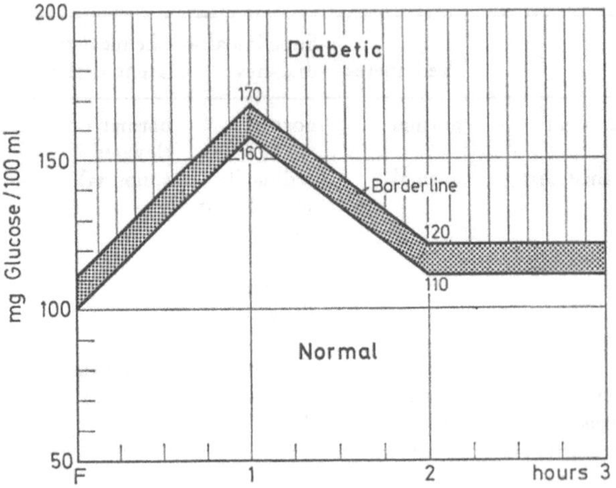

Fig. 1. Glucose tolerance test

although substantially higher than for subjects under 30, were still within normal limits. Their opinion that age impairment of oral glucose tolerance still leaves it well within normal limits contrasts sharply with countless reports of a phenomenal decade-by-decade increase in the frequency of mild diabetes after age 50. These published studies give an erroneous picture of carbohydrate intolerance in elderly people because they were done in sedentary hospitalized patients or in "normally active" inhabitants of old peoples homes and/or because the high carbohydrate priming diet was either omitted entirely or given mere lip service.

Evidence that true hyperglycemia in elderly patients is due to former prediabetics developing diabetes rather than to a physiological process due to aging is the presence of other abnormalities in elderly hyperglycemics, apart from the abnormality in carbohydrate metabolism. BUTTERFIELD in the Bedford Survey [4] reported that 43.3% of hyperglycemics have vascular disease as against 27.9% of normoglycemics. JACKSON and VINIK [5] studied 144 healthy, active elderly subjects living in homes for the aged. Nine were known diabetics; of the rest, 71 were repeatedly investigated and 34 of these (48%) were hyperglycemic on glucose tolerance testing. There was no significantly higher prevalence of cardiovascular disease or neuropathy but, when the ocular fundi were examined, 8 of the 34 hyperglycemics showed true diabetic retinopathy (with at least 2 microaneurysms) while not one microaneurysm was found in the 37 normoglycemics.

The micro-angiopathy of the retina and kidney represent characteristic manifestations of diabetes: the finding of such lesions in older persons with postprandial hyperglycemia would classify them as diabetic, not merely as persons with an abnormality of old age.

Finally, the diminution of mean glucose tolerance with age does not extend beyond 75 to 80 years. This suggests that aging alone does not account for the increased prevalence of hyperglycemia in elderly people and that elevated blood-sugar levels are indicative of latent diabetes.

In old age, the renal threshold is generally raised and considerable hyperglycemia can occur without glycosuria. It is therefore important to secure a glucose tolerance test in aged applicants for life insurance whenever there is a suspicion that diabetes may be present, rather than to rely upon the presence or absence of glycosuria for diagnosis.

Before the introduction of insulin by BANTING and BEST in 1921 there were specific eras of treatment. The Naunyn Era (1897—1914) was characterized by a gradual withdrawal from the rigid carbohydrate diet, and attention was paid to the caloric needs and tolerance of patients. However, some fast days were retained. The usual treatment consisted of a low carbohydrate diet and, when necessary, a low protein diet with the addition of adequate fat to prevent undernutrition. This was followed by the Allen Era (1914—1922). Dr. ALLEN demonstrated the advantage of undernutrition in the treatment of diabetes. He restricted the total diet in addition to limiting carbohydrates. In the Naunyn Era few diabetic children survived to adulthood. The rigid diet of the Allen Era added less than a year and a half to the life expectancy of juveniles. Only after the introduction of insulin in 1921 were mortality rates sharply reduced, and they continued to drop until 1950. Then mortality rates began to rise again in patients between 30 and 45 years of age, reflecting the results of long-term complications.

The experience of the Joslin Clinic (Fig. 2) was that in the Naunyn Era the duration of diabetes among persons who ultimately succumbed to the disease was 4.9 years; this figure increased to 6.1 years in the Allen Era, and 10.3 years after the introduction of insulin. In the 1930s H. C. HAGEDORN in Copenhagen introduced prolonged-action protamine insulin and then neutral protamine Hagedorn insulin (NPH). This resulted in the Hagedorn Era (1937—1949) when the figure advanced to 13.7 years, finally reaching 18.2 years in the Charles H. Best Era (1952—1957). The average age at death also rose during these periods, from 44.5 years in the Naunyn Era to 64.7 in the Charles H. Best Era. The greatest advance was in the younger age groups, and the extension of life in juvenile diabetics rose from 1.3 years to 26.4 years when onset was before age 10.

Much more significant than the duration of diabetes among the deceased in the various eras is the expectation of life among diabetics compared to that of the general population, since this is a measure of the mortality attributable to diabetes itself. The prediction of mortality in any group of impaired lives requires the classification of the group into separate classes representing the degree of risk involved. Classification is by mortality ratio, i. e. the ratio of actual to expected deaths expressed as a percentage. The mortality ratio is the actuarial tool used to measure risk. For example, if out of 1000 standard applicants aged 30, 50 deaths are expected within a 20-year-period and 100 deaths actually occur, then the mortality ratio will be twice that of standard lives, or 200%. If, on the other hand only 25 deaths occur then the mortality ratio will be half of the expected, or 50%.

It was the antibiotic era that provided the opportunity for diabetics to be considered as insurance risks on an experimental basis. In the latter part of the 1940's the Manufacturers Life of Canada and the Lincoln National began to in-

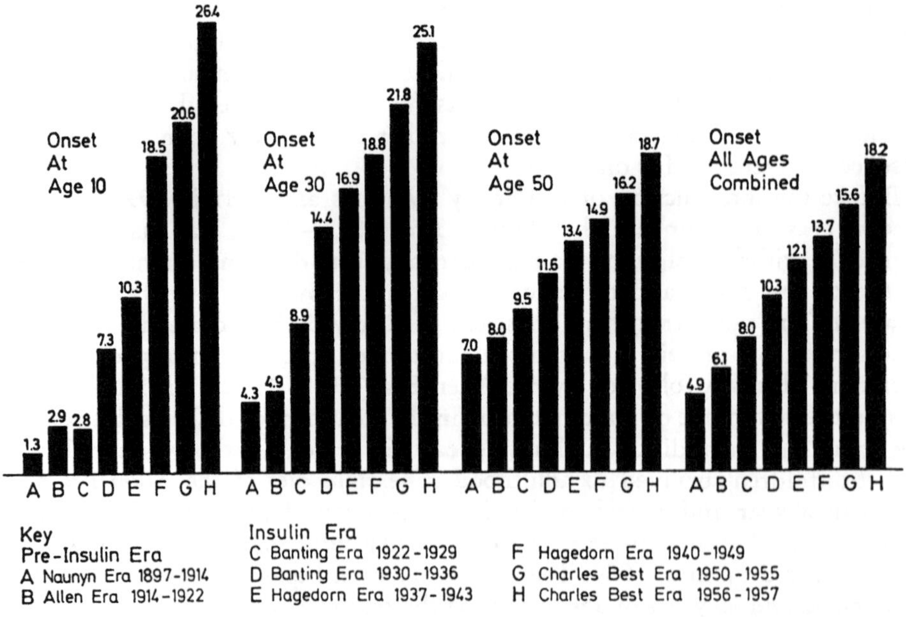

Fig. 2. Duration of life subsequent to the onset of diabetes among 18,055 deceased diabetics in each of the important eras of treatment (experience of Joslin Clinic 1897—1951. (Deaths reported through Dec. 11, 1937)

sure the "best" diabetics. All diabetics were put into the highest substandard class until accumulating mortality experience demonstrated that such diabetics could be put into different classes, depending upon such factors as age of onset, duration and control.

Independent diabetic mortality studies by Lincoln National [6] (1946—1959) and Manufacturers Life [1] (1952—1960) revealed a mortality ratio far in excess of the expected — 382% in the case of Lincoln National, almost four times that of the standard insurance population. But these results applied only to a select and limited group of diabetics, i. e. those who had met the underwriting criteria and were issued policies. What happened to the diabetics who were not accepted or who refused to pay the extra premium assessed for their diabetes? What factor contributed most to mortality — poor control, age at onset, duration? And what was the relative weight of each factor to the mortality risk? Was control really necessary? After all, vascular complications occur in the prediabetic stage before carbohydrate intolerance sets in. Could the diabetic enjoy a free diet rather than the inconvenience of a controlled one? In order to answer these important questions, the Equitable Life Assurance Society [8] in 1951 embarked upon a prospective study of all diabetics who applied for insurance regardless of whether a policy was in force, lapsed, not taken or declined.

This mortality study covered 15 years: it included all diabetics who applied for life insurance with the company from 1951 through 1961, observed up to the anniversary of their application in 1966. This study was laborious and tedious, but we were able to trace all except 215 individuals out of a total of 4974 for the entire period of the study; of those with policies declined, not taken out, or lapsed 95.7% were successfully traced. All deaths were verified by copies of death certificates. The expected deaths were computed from the Equitable's select mortality table covering the period 1953 through 1958.

Table 2. Underwriting criteria for the insurability of diabetics

1. Age limits at time of application — 15 to 60 years.
2. Age at onset of diabetes — Not less than 10 years of age or more than 60 years of age.
3. Build — Must qualify for standard insurance on the basis of build alone.
4. Weight — Must be stable unless diagnosis of diabetes has been made within the past year.
5. Observation — Should have been under adequate and competent observation since date of diagnosis.
6. History of blood pressure — Not more than a debit of +15 mortality points.
7. Blood sugar — The fasting blood sugar within 6 months of application should not have exceeded 200 mg per 100 ml.
8. Diabetic coma — No history of coma after initial period of observation unless adequately explained.
9. Insulin dosage — Daily dosage not to exceed 100 units (all types).
10. Pregnancy — Not pregnant at time of application.
11. Urine — Should not contain albumin in amounts of 20 mg per 100 ml or more.
12. Family history — Should not have more than two cases of cardiovascular-renal disease under age 60 in the immediate family (parents, brothers or sisters).
13. Physical condition or history — No history of any impairment, or any impairment on examination, with the exception of diabetes, which would make the applicant a substandard risk.

The underwriting criteria for the insurability of diabetics (Table 2) stated that insurance applicants should be 15 years of age or older, aged not less than 10 years at diagnosis of diabetes, of standard build, under adequate and competent supervision, and with blood pressure within standard limits for age, fasting blood sugar not exceeding 200 mg per 100 ml within 6 months of making application and urine containing not more than 20 mg of albumin per 100 ml, and should not have history of any impairment or any impairment on examination (with the exception of diabetes) which in itself would make the applicant a substandard risk. Any of the following provided grounds for refusal: 1. history or present condition of any impairment (with the exception of diabetes) that would require a substandard rate; 2. 2-hour postprandial blood sugar of 250 mg per 100 ml, or glycosuria exceeding 4%; 3. history of severe insulin shock or coma occurring after the initial period of observation and 4. poor control or supervision of diabetes.

Besides the standard insurance examination, medical requirements for qualified applicants consisted of an applicant's diabetes questionnaire, a special attending physician's statement, an electrocardiogram if applicant was aged 40 or over and \$ 10,000 or more was applied for, and a 2-hour postprandial blood and urine specimen which was sent by the examiner to the Home Office for analysis.

All diabetics who applied for insurance with the Equitable Life from 1951 through 1961 were observed until the anniversary of their application in 1966. As these cases were not homogeneous from an underwriting point of view, they were divided into 3 classes:

Group A: applicants who met the underwriting criteria and who were issued policies regardless of whether they paid for them, did not accept the offer, or subsequently allowed their policies to lapse.

Group B: applicants refused for non-medical reasons or because they failed to comply with the underwriting requirements.

Group C: applicants refused because they failed to meet the medical underwriting criteria.

In investigating the factors thought to be important in determining the mortality of the diabetic, it was found necessary to combine Groups A, B and C when the number of deaths in Group A was not large enough to be statistically significant. Similarly Groups B and C were combined when the number of deaths in Group B was insufficient or when the variation between the mortality ratios was not significant.

Table 3 shows the general characteristics of the study. The total years of exposure covered by the study was 40,143 with an average exposure of 8.1 years. The average age was 39.8 years and the median age 37.3 years. Ninety-two

Table 3. Diabetes mortality study, 1951—1961
General characteristics of the study

		Number	Percent
Applications traced to the 1966 anniversary of application		4,759	95.7
Contact lost one year before the 1966 anniversary		55	1.1
Contact lost two years before the 1966 anniversary		36	.7
Contact lost three or more years before the 1966 anniversary		124	2.5
All cases		4,974	100.0
	Issued	Declined	All
Entrants	1,342	3,632	4,974
Lives	1,151	3,330	4,481
Total exposure years	11,267	28,876	40,143
Average exposure years	8.4	7.9	8.1
Actual deaths	77	645	722
Tabular deaths [a]	41.43	126.48	167.91
Relative mortality	186%	510%	430%
Proportion of males	96%	90%	92%
Average age at application	39.4	40.0	39.8
Median age at application	36.5	37.7	37.3

[a] Tabular deaths were computed using the Equitable standard select mortality table 1953—1958.

percent of the entrants were males. There were 722 actual deaths compared to 167.91 expected deaths, giving a mortality ratio of 430% for the entire study. Among the 1342 entrants in Group A who were issued policies, there were 77 actual deaths giving a mortality ratio of 186% — almost twice that of normal. Among 3632 applicants declined for both medical and non-medical reasons (Groups B and C) there were 645 deaths, giving a mortality ratio of 510%. Group B had a mortality ratio of 540% and Group C 429%.

Mortality of issued applicants by rating classification (Table 4) showed a standard mortality for the best diabetics (Classes B and C with 135–195% predicted

Table 4. Diabetic mortality study, 1951—1961
Observed through 1966 anniversary of application, expected deaths based on the Equitable's select mortality table 1953—1958
All issued cases by rating

		Entrants	Actual deaths	Expected deaths	Ratio actual to expected		Ratio actual to expected premium basis	
Standard	Up to 130%	25	1	.93	a	122% (Standard–C)	a	73% (Standard–C)
B	(135–145%)	59	5	2.70	185%		132%	
C	(150–195%)	398	17	15.23	112		64	
D	(200–245%)	381	15	9.62	156		69	
E	(250–295%)	225	14	6.07	231		84	
F	(300–395%)	183	21	5.44	386	368% (F–G)	110	100% (F–G)
G	(400–500%)	69	4	1.35	a		66	
Combinations		2	—	.09	—		—	
All		1342	77	41.43	186%		81%	

a A/E ratios not shown for less than 5 deaths.

mortality). However, the number of deaths was too small to be statistically significant. In Class D with predicted 200–245% mortality, actual experience was 156% with only 15 deaths. Class C (250–295% mortality) showed a mortality ratio of 231%, and the 300–395% mortality class had a mortality ratio of 386%. Although it appears that the criteria were too conservative, the number of deaths is too small to ensure confidence in these mortality ratios. In addition, one must wait for a longer average duration before coming to definite conclusions. The current mortality study of 20 years, which should be completed by the end of this year, may enable this debatable point to be answered with more confidence in the reliability of the data.

Mortality by age at application (Table 5) showed decreasing mortality ratios with increasing age at time of application. In the issued applicants (Group A) mortality ratios were highest in the 20–29 age group (333%) and lowest in the 40–49 age group (118%) with the mortality at all ages 186%, based upon 77 deaths. For the declined applicants (Groups B and C) the highest mortality ratio was 1741% for age groups 20–29 and progressively declined to a low of 298% for ages 60 and over.

Mortality by duration of diabetes at time of application (Table 6) showed a progressive increase in mortality ratios with increasing duration of the disease.

Table 5. Diabetic mortality study, 1951—1961
Observed through 1966 anniversary of application, expected deaths based on the Equitable's select mortality table 1953—1958
Mortality by age at application

Age at application	Issued				Declined				All			
	Entrants	Actual deaths	Expected deaths	A/E ratio	Entrants	Actual deaths	Expected deaths	A/E ratio	Entrants	Actual deaths	Expected deaths	A/E ratio
10–19	23	—	.14	—	172	8	1.04	769%	195	8	1.18	678%
20–29	213	6	1.80	333%	735	101	5.80	1741	948	107	7.60	1408
30–39	457	18	6.43	280	846	112	11.82	948	1303	130	18.25	712
40–49	407	18	15.31	118	915	160	32.58	491	1322	178	47.89	372
50–59	221	32	15.30	209	720	187	49.38	379	941	219	64.68	339
60 and over	21	3	2.45	[a]	244	77	25.86	298	265	80	28.31	283
All ages	1342	77	41.43	186%	3632	645	126.48	510%	4974	722	167.91	430%

[a] A/E ratios not shown for less than 5 deaths.

Table 6. Diabetic mortality study, 1951—1961
Observed through 1966 anniversary of application, expected deaths based on the Equitable's select mortality table 1953—1958
By duration of diabetes at time of application
All ages combined

Duration in years	Issued				Declined				All			
	Entrants	Actual deaths	Expected deaths	A/E ratio	Entrants	Actual deaths	Expected deaths	A/E ratio	Entrants	Actual deaths	Expected deaths	A/E ratio
0– 5	752	32	23.78	135%	1669	241	67.80	355%	2421	273	91.58	298%
6–10	272	20	9.46	211	819	139	27.91	498	1091	159	37.37	425
11–14	140	9	3.28	274	443	92	11.59	794	583	101	14.87	679
15–19	107	9	3.09	291	355	87	10.27	847	462	96	13.36	719
20 and over	71	7	1.82	385	346	86	8.91	965	417	93	10.73	867
All	1342	77	41.43	186%	3632	645	126.48	510%	4974	722	167.91	430%

Table 7. Diabetic mortality study, 1951—1961
Observed through 1966 anniversary of application, expected deaths based on the Equitable's select mortality table 1953—1958
By age and duration of diabetes at time of application
Issued and declined

Duration of diabetes at time of application in years	Entrants	Actual deaths	A/E ratio	Entrants	Actual deaths	A/E ratio
	Ages 10–19			Ages 40–49		
0– 5	110	7	[a]	687	85	336%
6–10	48	—	—	291	40	375
11–14	29	1	[a]	122	12	282
15–19	8	—	—	110	19	488
20 and over	—	—	—	112	22	587
All	195	8	678%	1322	178	372%
	Ages 20–29			Ages 50–59		
0– 5	345	19	686%	567	95	240%
6–10	246	22	1146	182	57	427
11–14	177	31	2153	79	29	642
15–19	109	19	2159	62	21	504
20 and over	71	16	2712	51	17	572
All	948	107	1408%	941	219	339%
	Ages 30–39			Ages 60 and over		
0– 5	567	32	411%	145	35	227%
6–10	258	18	465	66	22	302
11–14	160	22	944	16	6	288
15–19	155	28	1315	21	9	396
20 and over	163	30	1408	17	8	620
All	1303	130	712%	265	80	283%

[a] A/E ratios not shown for less than 5 deaths.

The mortality ratio was most favorable for a duration of 5 years or less; there was a marked increase in mortality with a duration of 11 to 19 years and even more in the class with a duration of 20 years or more.

Mortality by age and duration of diabetes at time of application (Table 7) shows increasing mortality ratios with increasing duration of the disease at all ages but particularly in the age groups below 40 years. It should be noted that in the age group 20–29, which largely represents juvenile growth-onset diabetes, the mortality ratios are markedly higher for the same duration of the disease than in the adult maturity-onset type of diabetes.

Mortality by age at diagnosis of diabetes (Table 8) reflects the severity of diabetes at earlier ages of onset. It indicates that the juvenile diabetic is a severe diabetic and a poor mortality risk while the adult or maturity-onset diabetic is a relatively mild diabetic with a better survival pattern.

Table 8. Diabetic mortality study, 1951—1961
Observed through 1966 anniversary of application, expected deaths based on the Equitable's select mortality table 1953—1958
Mortality by age at diagnosis of diabetes

Age	Issued				Declined				All			
	Entrants	Actual deaths	Expected deaths	A/E ratio	Entrants	Actual deaths	Expected deaths	A/E ratio	Entrants	Actual deaths	Expected deaths	A/E ratio
Under 15	111	8	1.40	571%	598	97	5.38	1803%	709	105	6.78	1549%
15–19	121	8	1.37	584	359	60	3.92	1531	480	68	5.29	1285
20–29	324	7	5.10	137	678	80	11.68	685	1002	87	16.78	518
30–39	357	12	8.50	141	721	104	20.94	497	1078	116	29.44	394
40–49	300	28	14.72	190	723	180	37.75	477	1023	208	52.47	396
50–59	124	14	9.89	142	452	96	35.92	267	576	110	45.81	240
60 and over	5	—	.45	[a]	101	28	10.89	257	106	28	11.34	247
All ages	1342	77	41.43	186%	3632	645	126.48	510%	4974	722	167.91	430%

[a] A/E ratios not shown for less than 5 deaths.

The expectation of life among all diabetic applicants compared with standard lives by age of onset (Table 9) showed that diabetics who contracted the disease below the age of 15 had another 32 years of life compared to 59 years for standard lives, and that the difference in life expectancy between standard lives and the diabetic decreased as the age of onset increased, being least in diabetics whose age of onset was between 60 and 70 years. Their life expectancy was 11 more years compared to 16 more years of standard lives.

Table 9. Diabetic mortality study, 1951—1963
Observed through 1966 anniversary of application, expected deaths based on the Equitable's select mortality table
Expectation of life among all diabetic applicants compared with standard lives (1958—1963)
By age of onset

	Mortality ratios		Expectation of life in years	
Age of onset	Diabetics	Standard lives	Diabetics	Standard lives
Under 15	1549%	100%	32	59
15–19	1285%	100%	28	54
20–29	518%	100%	33	49
30–39	394%	100%	27	39
40–49	396%	100%	19	30
50–59	240%	100%	17	23
60–70	247%	100%	11	16

Mortality by control of diabetes (Table 10) is difficult to evaluate as it is composed of many variable factors: postprandial sugar determinations, urinary sugar determinations, degree and frequency of supervision, history of insulin shock or coma, and the type of management given by diverse schools of treatment. For the purpose of the study only a certain percentage of the declined cases were considered as showing poor control. Any applicant who was issued a policy was deemed by the underwriter to be fairly well controlled. Among persons not issued policies, only those refused for the following reasons were considered to have poor control: 1. excessive glycosuria (over 4%) or 2-hour postprandial blood sugar of over 250 mg per 100 ml; 2. history of recent high blood sugar; 3. history of severe insulin shock or onset of coma after the initial period of observation. The mortality ratio of the poorly controlled cases was approximately 2½ times that of well-controlled cases, i. e. 468% as against 191%.

Mortality by type of medication (Table 11) confirmed the clinical experience that diabetics who are controlled by diet alone (mortality ratio 241%) or by diet and oral medication alone (mortality ratio 328%) are milder diabetics than those controlled by insulin and diet (mortality ratio 530%).

Mortality by units of insulin (Table 12) increased with increasing number of units of insulin taken daily. This increase appears to be due to the increasing proportion of juvenile diabetics at the higher insulin dosages and is more a reflection of age at diagnosis than of the amount of insulin taken. In diabetics who developed the disease between 10 and 20 years of age there is no appreciable difference in the very high mortality ratios with increasing number of units of insulin

Table 10. Diabetic mortality study, 1951—1961
Observed through 1966 anniversary of application, expected deaths based on the Equitable's select mortality table 1953—1958
Mortality by control of diabetes

Type of Control	Controlled (a)				Poor control (b)			
	Entrants	Actual deaths	Expected deaths	A/E ratio	Entrants	Actual deaths	Expected deaths	A/E ratio
Insulin, less than 50 units	560	35	17.84	196%	292	34	7.87	432%
50 to 74 units	192	13	3.64	357	155	20	2.41	830
75 or more units	44	1	1.12	[a]	55	6	1.14	526
Amount unknown	8	1	.35	[a]	14	—	.17	—
All with insulin	804	50	22.95	218	516	60	11.59	518
No insulin, oral medication or diet only	460	24	25.83	152	140	22	5.93	371
All cases	1264	74	38.78	191%	656	82	17.52	468%

a) Issued cases.
b) Cases declined for the following reasons:
1. Excessive glycosuria or poor blood sugar tests on examination only;
2. History of recent high blood sugar;
3. History of coma or insulin shock only.
[a] A/E ratios not shown for less than 5 deaths.

taken daily. The same holds true of the older age groups where the mortality ratios are markedly lower.

Mortality by reason for declination (Table 13) yielded some surprising results. Hypertension alone showed a mortality ratio of 541%. Unfavorable ECG showed a mortality ratio of 436% but the deaths were too few to be significant. Other circulatory impairments alone or in combination showed a mortality of 734%. Albumin, casts or other urinary findings other than glycosuria showed a very high mortality ratio of 1197%. High postprandial blood sugar or excessive glycosuria on examination showed a mortality ratio of 425%. Applicants who were declined for a history of recent high blood sugar showed a mortality ratio

Table 11. Diabetic mortality study, 1951—1961
Observed through 1966 anniversary of application, expected deaths based on the Equitable's select mortality table 1953—1958
Mortality by medication

	Issued				Declined				All			
Type of medication	Entrants	Actual deaths	Expected deaths	A/E ratio	Entrants	Actual deaths	Expected deaths	A/E ratio	Entrants	Actual deaths	Expected deaths	A/E ratio
Diet only no medication	277	10	11.08	90%	480	79	25.82	306%	757	89	36.90	241%
Insulin	804	50	22.95	218	2324	438	69.07	634	3128	488	92.02	530
Oral medication	183	14	4.75	295	330	40	11.73	341	513	54	16.48	328
Unknown	78	3	2.65	[a]	498	88	19.86	443	576	91	22.51	404
All	1342	77	41.43	186%	3632	645	126.48	510%	4974	722	167.91	430%

[a] A/E ratios not shown for less than 5 deaths.

Table 12. Diabetic mortality study, 1951—1961
Observed through 1966 anniversary of application, expected deaths based on the Equitable's select mortality table 1953—1958

a. Mortality by units of insulin

Units of insulin	Issued Entrants	Actual deaths	Expected deaths	A/E ratio	Declined Entrants	Actual deaths	Expected deaths	A/E ratio	All Entrants	Actual deaths	Expected deaths	A/E ratio
Less than 10	6	1	.13	[a]	28	7	1.72	407%	34	8	1.85	432%
10– 24	181	13	8.02	162%	398	76	19.56	389	579	89	27.58	323
25– 49	373	21	9.69	217	949	188	27.15	692	1322	209	36.84	567
50– 74	192	13	3.64	357	591	102	11.03	925	783	115	14.67	784
75–100	40	1	1.04	[a]	204	33	3.53	935	244	34	4.57	744
Over 100	4	—	.08	[a]	41	6	.80	750	45	6	.88	682
Unknown	8	1	.35	[a]	113	26	5.28	492	121	27	5.63	480
All	804	50	22.95	218%	2324	438	69.07	634%	3128	488	92.02	530%

b. Mortality by units of insulin and age at diagnosis
Units of insulin

Age at diagnosis	10–24 Entrants	Actual deaths	A/E ratio	25–49 Entrants	Actual deaths	A/E ratio	50–74 Entrants	Actual deaths	A/E ratio	75–100 Entrants	Actual deaths	A/E ratio
10–19	60	5	811%	403	63	1514%	387	62	1610%	146	19	1450%
20–29	97	6	338	391	40	591	238	19	470	62	6	455
30–39	170	19	373	289	37	416	111	21	519	19	1	[a]
40–49	164	38	384	172	45	403	39	9	398	14	6	526
50–59	79	19	207	62	20	396	10	4	656	3	2	[a]
60–over	9	2	[a]	9	4	[a]	2	—	—	—	—	—
All ages	579	89	323%	1326	209	567%	787	115	784%	244	34	744%
Ages 20 and over	519	83	309%	923	146	447%	400	53	490%	98	15	460%

[a] A/E ratios not shown for less than 5 deaths.

Table 13. Diabetic mortality study, 1951—1961
Observed through 1966 anniversary of application
Mortality by reason for declination

Reason	Number of entrants	Actual deaths	Expected deaths	A/E ratio
Hypertension only	268	68	12.56	541%
Hypertension combined with non-circulatory impairments	181	57	8.36	682
Unfavorable ECG only	52	12	2.75	436
Other circulatory impairments alone or in combination	195	55	7.49	734
Albumin, casts or other urinary findings other than glycosuria only	115	34	2.84	1197
Albuminuria, in combination with impairments other than hypertension	56	17	1.67	1018
Excessive glycosuria or poor blood sugar tests on examination only	513	59	13.88	425
Not under good supervision	377	64	14.50	441
History of recent high blood sugar	64	13	2.00	650
History of coma or insulin shock only	87	12	1.77	678
Not standard build only	66	6	2.40	250
Combination of impairments excluding hypertension or albuminuria only	167	38	7.81	487
Miscellaneous single impairments not listed above	191	34	6.05	562
Age of applicant only	89	18	8.74	206
Age at onset of diabetes only	158	23	1.33	1729
Other non-medical reasons	218	35	7.57	462
Incomplete data	835	100	24.76	404
All declined	3632	645	126.48	510%

of 650%. The group with a history of coma or insulin shock only had a mortality ratio of 678%. Diagnosis of diabetes below the age of 10 showed one of the highest mortality ratios of the entire study — 1729%. Miscellaneous impairments had a mortality ratio of 562%. Poor supervision (441%) does not appear to render the applicant uninsurable but it is doubtful whether it is wise to insure a diabetic individual who has had insufficient exposure to a trained medical observer.

Causes of death (Table 14) showed an increased incidence of arteriosclerotic heart disease in diabetics at all ages, but most marked in the younger age groups. Out of 633 deaths 392 individuals, or 59.1%, were due to cardiovascular disease and 61, or 9.2%, to renal disease. 6.3% of deaths were due to malignant neoplasm, 4.4% to diabetes (coma and unspecified cause other than diabetes), 1.7% to diseases of the digestive system, 4.1% to accidents and 15.2% to other diseases.

We have accumulated a body of data that is unique in insurance and clinical medicine in that it pertains to a population which may be considered a cross section of the diabetic population of the United States. It is the first prospective mortality study in the Life Insurance Industry in which both the issued and declined cases were traced to determine the mortality for both groups.

In summary, we believe that this mortality study has shown that certain conclusions may be drawn concerning diabetics who apply for life insurance:

Table 14. Diabetic mortality study, 1951—1961
Observed through 1966 anniversary of application
Classification of causes of death

Causes of death	Number of deaths	Percent distribution	Number of individuals	Percent distribution
Malignant neoplasms	48	6.6	42	6.3
Diseases of the cardiovascular system	424	58.7	392	59.1
Renal diseases	65	9.0	61	9.2
Diabetes (coma and unspecified)	31	4.3	29	4.4
Diseases of digestive system	13	1.8	11	1.7
Other diseases including unknown	113	15.7	101	15.2
Accidents and suicides	28	3.9	27	4.1
All causes	722	100.0%	663	100.0%

Cardio-vascular-renal diseases

Diseases of cardiovascular system	Number of deaths	Percent distribution	Number of individuals	Percent distribution
Arteriosclerotic heart disease with or without angina	33	6.7	30	6.6
Acute coronary occlusion	264	54.0	244	53.8
Other diseases of the heart	80	16.4	75	16.6
Vascular lesions affecting the central nervous system	44	9.0	40	8.8
Other vascular diseases	3	.6	3	.7
Total cardiovascular disease	424	86.7%	392	86.5%
Renal diseases				
Kimmelstiel-Wilson disease	57	11.7	53	11.7
Nephritis	8	1.6	8	1.8
Total renal disease	65	13.3%	61	13.5%
Total cardiovascular-renal disease	489	100.0%	153	100.0%

1. Mortality declines progressively with increasing age at time of application.
2. Mortality increases with increasing duration of the disease, particularly in the age groups below 40 years. The mortality ratios are markedly higher for the same duration of the disease in the juvenile growth-onset diabetic than in the adult maturity-onset diabetic.
3. Age at diagnosis of diabetes is the most significant factor in mortality and showed the highest mortality ratio of the study at age 14 and under. The juvenile insulin-dependent diabetic is a poor insurance risk.
4. Poor control shows 2½ times the mortality of the well controlled group.
5. Diabetics on diet alone, or on diet and oral medication, show lower mortality ratios than insulin-dependent diabetics.
6. The presence of albuminuria on examination was an extremely unfavorable prognostic factor with a mortality ratio of 1197%.
7. 68.3% of the deaths were due to cardiovascular-renal disease, with almost 60% due to cardiovascular disease alone.

Summary

Diabetes is a widespread disease affecting 50,000,000 people in the world and 2 million in the United States with its highest incidence in the Pima Indians and its lowest in the Alaskan Eskimos. The natural history of diabetes is divided into 4 stages of development 1. prediabetes, 2. subclinical diabetes, 3. chemical or latent diabetes and 4. overt diabetes, the last three being reversible. It is debatable whether the increased incidence of glucose intolerance in the aged is due to the physiological effects of aging or due to prediabetics developing diabetes but the evidence to-date favors the latter.

The duration of life after diagnosis of diabetes among individuals who died of the disease rose from 4.9 years in the Naunyn Era to 18.2 years in the Charles H. Best Era.

A 15-year mortality study of diabetic applicants who applied for insurance between the years 1951—1961 to the Equitable Life Assurance Society was completed in 1966. There were 4974 applicants with a total of 40,143 exposure years and an average exposure of 8.1 years. There were 722 actual deaths, giving a mortality ratio of 430% for the entire study. Issued cases showed a mortality ratio of 186% while declined cases showed a mortality of 510%. Mortality decreased with increasing age at time of application, and with increasing age at diagnosis of diabetes. Mortality increased with increasing duration of the disease and with increasing severity of diabetes. Mortality was lowest in the cases treated by diet only and highest in cases treated by insulin and diet. Mortality in cases with poor control was two and a half times that of cases with good control. Albuminuria on examination was an extremely unfavorable prognostic factor. Out of 633 deaths by number of individuals, almost 60% were due to cardiovascular disease and almost 10% to renal disease.

References

1. Wilkerson, H. L., Krall, L. P.: Diabetes in a New England Town. J. Amer. med. Ass. **135,** 209—216 (1947).
2. U.S. National Center for Health Statistics: Glucose tolerance of adults. United States 1960 to 1962, U.S.P.H.S. Pub. No. 1000 Series II, No. 2, 1964.
3. Ellenberg, M., Rifkin, H.: Diabetes mellitus: Theory and practice, 1970, pp. 450—454.
4. Butterfield, W. J. H.: Summary of results of the Bedford diabetes survey. Proc. roy. Soc. Med. **57,** 196 (1962).
5. Jackson, W. P., Vinik, A. I.: In: Ellenberg and Rifkin: Diabetes mellitus: Theory and practice, 1970, pp. 528—529.
6. Cochran, H., Buck, N.: A mortality study for insured diabetic population. Medical Section, American Life Convention, 1961.
7. Breithaupt, D. J.: Discussion — A mortality study of insured diabetics. Medical Section, American Life Convention, 1961.
8. Goodkin, G., Wolloch, L. B.: Trans. Ass. Life Insur. med. Dir. Amer. **52,** 211—236 (1968).

VI Sesión

Tema: Narcomanías

Presidente: Dr. Jorge Rendón, México

Social Mechanisms in the Inception of Drug Abuse and Addiction

NILS BEJEROT, M.D.

Drug abuse and drug addiction have increased very rapidly in many countries especially during the last decade. In some countries drug abuse has increased like an avalanche and has been accompanied by an intensive and often contradictory debate. The failure to agree on suitable countermeasures has, in my opinion, been due to lack of an adequate analysis of the mechanisms of inception and of a systematic classification of the main groups of addiction.

To date, types of addiction have been classified along pharmacological lines, being divided into morphinism, heroinism, cocainism, amphetaminism, barbiturism, alcoholism, etc. A classification of this type, however, covers only one dimension of the problem. For prevention in particular, but also for therapy, it is also necessary to classify addictions according to the mode of inception. From this viewpoint three main groups may be distinguished: addictions of therapeutic, epidemic, and endemic type. These three types of addiction affect different risk groups.

A. Addiction of the Therapeutic Type

This type of addiction will have arisen without the influence of other addicts. We can distinguish three subtypes:

1. *Addiction Resulting from a Calculated Risk During Medical Treatment.* This is mainly a matter of the relief of pain in incurable and dying patients, and a complicating addiction in these cases has to be accepted. Generally there is no great problem in regard to this type of addiction.

2. *Addiction Inadvertently Caused by Medical Treatment.* Last century morphinism was a common therapeutic complication, but today we see only isolated cases that have arisen in this way. The risk of addiction is small in correct medical treatment of pain. On the other hand, it is not unusual for nervous and anxious patients to become addicted through slowly increasing doses of sedatives and hypnotics. The risk is particularly great if the patients apply to many different physicians and receive drugs from several without any coordination of medication.

3. *The Third Form of Therapeutic Addiction is Due to Self-Medication by Medical Staff* in Conditions of Pain, Depression, or Stress. Most addicted physicians are careless in their prescribing of dangerous drugs, and some of them also draw their wives into abuse. With this exception, addicts of therapeutic type do not tend to initiate others into abuse. Iatrogenic addictions are thus not contagious.

Addicts of therapeutic type are mainly responsible, middle-aged persons in their most active years, and women and men develop this form of addiction about equally often. The social mechanisms operating in the inception of therapeutic addiction in women are usually disturbances in their private lives: problems of love, marriage, family and children, or loneliness and isolation. With men, it is more often stress and difficulties in the occupational sphere which form the background.

People who develop addiction of the therapeutic type often have above-average ambition but are highly sensitive to criticism and reverses. Various types of neurosis and distress due to inability to live up to these ambitions increase the risk of becoming dependent on psychotropic drugs prescribed by physicians in the usual way. Therapeutic addicts experience their dependence as a great tragedy and feel shame at being unable to resist their craving. They try to hide their drug problem, even from friends and relatives. Character disorders and criminal behavior preceding addiction are rare in this group.

Therapeutic addiction is evenly distributed in time and place, but may be correlated with the density of physicians. The drugs are legally obtained, anyway in the beginning, and usually only one type of drug is abused.

B. Addiction of the Epidemic Type

Many people think that some kind of microbes must be present before we can talk of epidemics. Psychological contagion also occurs, however. There were, for instance, hysterical mass phenomena during the Middle Ages, such as epidemics of dancing. Outbreaks of suicide and arson also occur now and then.

Epidemic types of addiction have a number of qualities in common in which they differ from therapeutic types. I will mention ten such characteristics.

1. *Contagion.* The type of epidemic addiction which currently afflicts most Western industrial countries depends upon direct personal contact between an established abuser and a beginner. No-one can learn to inject drugs into the veins unless he has been taught by an experienced person. It is perhaps less widely recognized that you cannot even learn to smoke hashish properly without being taught the technique.

Contagion in epidemic addictions spreads almost exclusively via close personal contact. It is a common misconception that pushers initiate people into abuse of this type. Pushers come into the picture later, when they play a pernicious role as suppliers and reinforcers.

2. *Rapid Spread.* As long as the population at risk is large enough and the social situation and drug policy remain unchanged, epidemic addiction tends to spread by geometric progression. In Britain the incidence of heroinism doubled every 16 months between 1959 and 1968, and the Swedish epidemic of intravenous abuse of central stimulants doubled every 30 months between 1949 and 1968. The number of therapeutic addicts on the other hand is usually fairly constant within society.

3. *Historical Boundaries.* Epidemics of addiction always start suddenly as when a spark sets off a forest fire; on the other hand, the fire may smoulder in the undergrowth for a long while before the flames break out in full force.

Drug epidemics may be brought to an end, like the great amphetamine epidemic in Japan after the second World War, or the Chinese opium smoking, which was checked by drastic action after the revolution of 1949. The cocaine epidemics in England and Germany in the 'twenties were also checked by law-enforcement methods.

4. *Geographic Boundaries.* A drug epidemic may be limited to a school, a district in a city, a region, or a country. Epidemic addiction is usually checked for long periods by political and geographical boundaries, even if communications accross the borders are lively.

5. *Ethnic Boundaries.* This kind of addiction is usually also contained within ethnic groups for long periods. Once a drug epidemic breaks through into another ethnic group it develops rapidly by personal contact within the new group. Up to 1965 the large Finnish population in Stockholm was untouched by the amphetamine epidemic, which affected thousands of Swedes in the capital. In that year the first cases appeared among the Finns, and since then they have become quite frequent in this population. A daughter epidemic was established in Finland in 1965, closely followed by the same phenomenon in Denmark and Norway.

6. *Sex Ratios.* In early stages of drug epidemics there is always a large male preponderance — up to eight males to every female. As the epidemic spreads, the male excess is reduced, often to four or three males per female, as in the heroin epidemic in the United States and the amphetamine epidemic in Sweden.

7. *Age Boundaries.* Drug epidemics first affect narrow age groups. Glue sniffing usually occurs in the lower 'teens, hashish smoking in the upper 'teens and early twenties; intravenous drug abuse originally spread among 25 to 30-year-olds.

The more a drug epidemic spreads, the broader the age distribution becomes. Among persons arrested in Stockholm in the spring of 1965 there were very few persons under 20 or over 40 who took drugs intravenously; yet at that time every fourth arrestee aged between 20 and 40 was injecting drugs. The rate for this advanced form of abuse in the youngest and oldest age groups among those arrested (those aged 15–20 and 40—45) increased *tenfold* between 1965 and 1967, from 3 to 30 percent, parallel to an experiment with a more liberal drug policy.

8. *Sensitivity to Fashion in Choice of Drugs and Methods of Administration.* Abuse of central stimulants began in Sweden at the end of the 'forties with amphetamine. In 1957—1958 the new slimming drug Preludin (phenmetrazine) came into the picture and took the place of amphetamine. When Preludin was taken off the legal market, illegally manufactured central stimulants came into fashion. Now the main importer to Sweden of illegally produced drugs of this type is in prison, there has been a rapid changeover to abuse of morphine-base in addict circles in Sweden. In general, multiple addiction is common among epidemic addicts. On the other hand therapeutic addicts, when unable to obtain their favorite drug, rarely switch to preparations that have a different pharmacological action.

For a long while tablets were taken orally in addict circles. Around 1950 addicts in Sweden began to inject drugs into their veins. By the end of the sixties there were few addicts who were content to take the drugs by mouth.

9. *Group Boundaries.* Cannabis smoking was brought to Europe by American jazz musicians in the late 'forties and for a long while hashish was confined to these circles both in England and Sweden. In 1965 there were about 200 hashish smokers in Sweden, nearly all in Stockholm. Four years later there were tens of thousands of schoolchildren and students all over the country who had tried hashish, and it is now difficult to estimate how many are severely addicted.

Intravenous drug abuse, on the other hand, has quite another background and affects quite different groups, mainly criminals. The more widely an epidemic of this type spreads, the more the original group boundaries disappear as more and more "ordinary" people are drawn into the risk zone.

10. *Massivity.* Drug abuse, as opposed to addiction, is often a symptom of maladjustment of various kinds. This is particularly the case when the drugs cannot be obtained legally. It is often deviant individuals who are prepared to engage in criminal activity in order to obtain drugs for which, in the beginning, they have no craving. Maladjusted youths always form the core of new drug epidemics. It should be remembered, however, that many youths start on drugs during a critical phase in what might otherwise have been a normal course of development. When addicts are asked why they took the first dose, the reason most commonly given is that it was out of curiosity or from the desire to belong to an "in-group".

The more widespread abuse becomes, the less are predisposing personality disorders and social difficulties required for an individual to be drawn in. This corresponds to the massivity phenomenon in epidemics spread by microbes. This mechanism has been exemplified very clearly in the present cannabis epidemic where, after a time, large groups of ordinary youths have been drawn in because of the massive abuse taking place in their environment.

In comparison with therapeutic addiction, epidemic addiction constitutes a completely different form of illness, even when the addicts are dependent upon the same drug. The most alarming factor is that all addicts of epidemic type are potentially contagious. After alcoholism, the epidemic types of addiction today constitute the greatest health risk to young persons in many industrial countries.

Those drawn into drug epidemics differ statistically in almost every respect from therapeutic addicts. They are generally young, unstable, adventurous, insecure and easily led individuals. Those who are unsuccessful in life in some way run a greater risk of being drawn in. Another high-risk group consists of those who have difficulty in finding acceptance in the ordinary groups and therefore experiment with drugs in order to be accepted at least by deviant groups — a solidarity of outcasts.

Unsatisfactory childhood conditions are far more common among epidemic addicts than among ordinary youths or among therapeutic addicts, but many come from very good homes.

All epidemic addicts have in common that they have not taken the drugs in order to reduce pain, anxiety or sleeplessness but in the pursuit of pleasure, euphoria, and "kicks". It follows from this that the epidemic addicts, even before the first contact with drugs, statistically showed an above-average tendency to seek other forms of immediate satisfaction of desires; they have also experienced greater difficulty in tolerating frustration and in following long-term goals. This has been demonstrated in a higher frequency of truancy from school, absence from work, change of job, etc. Experimentation with drugs in this group is part of a way of life expressed in the search for immediate satisfaction of desires. Many of these addicts have shown signs of character disorders before the inception of drug abuse. Far from being ashamed of taking drugs, they often boast of it among their friends, and they can talk about drugs ad infinitum with other addicts just as normal boys talk of girls and sex.

Therapeutic addiction and epidemic addiction are in fact two quite different diseases, even if the same drug is abused. Different types of individual are affected by the two conditions, and the mode of inception is completely different. Particularly in regard to prevention, confusion has been caused by regarding these two diseases as a single entity.

C. Addiction of Endemic Type

Some types of addiction are constantly present in a country and have arisen because it is more or less socially accepted that certain addicting substances may be used for enjoyment, relaxation or stimulation.

Among endemic addictions we can include opium smoking in pre-revolution China, hashish smoking in North Africa, and coca chewing among South American Indians. In principle, of course, alcoholism is an endemic addiction also. It exists mainly in the Christian parts of the world, while Buddhist and Muhammadan countries up to now have been spared alcoholism thanks to their religious precepts. It is possible that we are today witnessing the conversion of a marijuana epidemic into an endemic in the United States.

Since endemic forms of addiction arise on the basis of a drug being more or less socially tolerated within the country, endemic addiction affects a more average and "normal" selection of the population than does epidemic addiction.

Prognosis is poor in all types of addiction and, as with cancer, a five-year observation period is necessary before we can judge the outcome. Also the mortality risks are very high — about one per cent per annum among young addicts; this is ten times the normal rate for these age groups.

When a disease has a severe effect on the individual, and when the outcome is uncertain whatever the treatment, prevention is of overriding importance. In regard to therapeutic addiction stricter indications and better control of over-prescribing of psychotropic drugs are the most important measures. Experience in many countries shows that endemic addictions like alcoholism are best prevented by a general reduction in the consumption of these socially accepted drugs in society. Finally, in regard to drug epidemics there seems to be no exception in history to the rule that a more permissive drug policy increases drug abuse, while a more restrictive drug policy decreases the acceleration of epidemics, reduces them, and may even stop them. To be successful, a drug policy must have broad public support and this is mainly formed by the mass media. The responsibility of the mass media in this matter is therefore enormous. The education of politicians and journalists in this complicated field may be the best way of protecting a society against that plague of modern society — drug epidemics.

Author Index

Figures in *italics* are references to the literature. Figures in square brackets [ ] are the numbers under which the literature references are cited

Åkerlünd, A. [13], 169, *177*
Aguirre, A. F. 86
Aguirre Garcia, J., see González Montesinos, F. [5], 141, *144*
Albert, B. L., Sellers, T. F. [1], 149, *150*
Albores Saavedra, J. [3], 140, *144*
Allen 181
Allison, P. R. [14], 170, *177*
Alvarez Alva, R., De la Loza Salvídar, A. [2], 140, *144*
Amdur, M. O. [1], 37, *47*
Anderson, D. O., see Ferris, B. G., Jr. [15, 16], 42, *48*
Anderson, F., see Cobb, S. 98, *113*
Ansell, B. 120, 121
Ansell, B. M., Bywaters, E. G. *113*
Appleman, R. et al. [1], 166, *176*
Arianoff, A. A. et al. [2], 167, *176*
Arner, E. C., Rhoades, R. A. [2], 37, *47*
Arriaga, J. 86
Asch, M. J., Markowitz, A. M. [22], 173, *177*
Aubanel, M., see Landa, L. [6], 143, *144*
Auerbach, O., Cuylerhammond, E., Garfinkel, H., Carmine, B. [3], 40, *47*
Austin, J. H. M., see Nadel, J. A. 40, *49*, [53]
Aviado, D. M., Sadavongvivad, C., Carillo, L. R. [4], 40, *47*
Aviado, D. M., see Inoh, T. [37], *49*
Azen, S. P., see Sherwin, R. P. 40, *50*, [62]

Bach, F. 116
Baehr, G., Klemperer, P. *113*
Baggenstoss, A. H., see Rosenberg, E. F. *115*
Banting 181
Baragar, F. D., see Duthie, J. J. R. 99, *113*
Barceló, J. E. *77*
Baretta, E. D., see Stewart, R. D. 37, *50*, [65]
Barkin 101
Barnes 107
Battermann, R. C., see Steinbrocker, O. [2], 124, *128*
Bauer, W., see Cobb, S. 98, *113*
Bauer, W., see Short, C. L. 104, 106, *115*
Beall, G., Cobb, S. *113*
Beard, O. W., Hipp, H. R., Robins, M., Verzolini, V. R. [5], 158, *163*
Beck, D. 108, 109, *113*
Behrend, H., see Behrend, T. *113*
Behrend, T., Lawrence, I. S., Behrend, H., Koch, R. 97, *113*
Bejerot, N. 199
Belart 99
Bell, M. F., see Bolt, W. R. [4], 158, *163*
Bennett, A. E., see Holland, W. W. [35], 43, *49*
Bennett, P. H., see Lawrence, J. S. *114*
Benoist, M., see Pouget, G. 109, *114*
Berson, S. A., Yalow, R. S., Saito, T., Selikoff, I. J. [5], *47*
Best 181
Bignon, J., Bonnaud, G., Jaurand, M. C., Goni, J., Dufour, G. 39, *51*, [86]
Bignon, J., Depierre, A., Bonnaud, G., Goni, J., Brouet, G., De Dufour, G., Jaurand, M. G., Leturcq, E., Monchaux, G., Saint-Étienne, L. 39, *51*, [85]
Bignon, J., see Brouet, G. 39, *51*, [87]
Bignon, J., see Goni, J. 39, *51*, [88]
Binzus, G., see Josenhans, G. 106, *114*
Björkmann, S. A. 98, *113*
Blade, E., see Hart, F. C. [33, 34], 42, *48*, *49*
Boerma, F. W., see Otten, H. A. *114*
Boisvert, P. L., see De Forest, G. K. *113*
Boles, J., Jordan, J. M. [23], 174, 175, *177*
Boles, S. et al. 173
Bolt, W. R., Bell, M. F., Harnes, J. R. [4], 158, *163*
Bonnaud, G., see Bignon, J. 39, *51*, [85, 86]
Bonnaud, G., see Brouet, G. 39, *51*, [87]
Bonnaud, G., see Goni, J. 39, *51*, [88]

Bouhuys, A. [6], 40, *47*
Bouhuys, A., Peters, J. M. [7], *47*
Bouley, G., see Stupfel, M. 43, *50*, [66]
Bove, J. L., Siedenberg, S. [8], 37, 39, *47*
Boye-Nielsen, J. 124
Bradley, H. W., see McCaroll, J. R. 42, [47], 49
Brandt, H., Pérez Tamayo, R. [4], 140, *144*
Breithaupt, D. J. [7], 196
Brenes, P. C., see Medrano, G. A. [4], *85*
Brewer, E. J. 101, *113*
Brille, D., see Kourilsky, R. [41], 42, 43, *49*
Brochner-Mortensen, K. 124
Brouet, G., Bignon, J., Bonnaud, G., Goni, J. 39, *51*, [87]
Brouet, G., see Bignon, J. 39, *51*, [85]
Brouet, G., see Goni, J. 39, *51*, [88]
Brown, E., see Russel, M. A. 40, *49*, [59]
Brown, P. E., see Duthie, J. J. R. 99, *113*
Brunet, M., see Garbe, E. [23], 42, *48*
Bruno, M. S., see De Pascuale, N. P. [6], 83, *85*
Buck, N., see Cochran, H. [6], 182, *196*
Bureau, G., see Kochmann, S. 39, 40, [40], *49*
Burgess, W., see Speizer, F. E. 43, *50*, [64]
Burry, H. 121
Butterfield, W. J. H. [4], 180, *196*
Bywaters, E. G. L. 94, 95, *113*, 120
Bywaters, E. G. L., Curwen, M., Dresner, E., Dixon, A. St. J. *113*
Bywaters, E. G. L., Dresner, E. *113*
Bywaters, E. G., see Ansell, B. M. 95, *113*

Cabezas, G. A., see Nadel, J. A. 40, *49*, [53]
Calabro 101
Calkins, E., see Sharp, J. T. *115*
Calnau, J. S., see Nicolle, F. W. 109, *114*
Camacho, R. M. 71
Camner, P., Helstrom, P. A., Philipson, K. [9], 40, *48*
Campbell, K. J., see Lewis, T. R. 37, [45], *49*
Cantú, G. R., see Fernández, L. D. [4], 145, *150*
Cárdenas Loaeza, M. 74
Carillo, L. R., see Aviado, D. M. [4], 40, *47*
Carmine, B., see Auerbach, O. [3], 40, *47*
Carton, J., see Kourilsky, R. [41], 42, 43, *49*
Casarella, W. J. et al. [24], 174, *177*
Cauchoi, C. J., see Pouget, G. 109, *114*
Chahinian, Ph., Chretien, J. [10], 35, *48*
Chapa, G. R., see Fernández, L. D. [4], 145, *150*
Chapin, C. V. [1], 25, 26, *34*
Charreire, J., see Desplaces, A. [12], 40, *48*
Chretien, J. [11], 39, *48*
Chretien, J., see Chahinian, P. H. [10], 35, *48*
Cobb, S. 96, 97, 98, *113*
Cobb, S., Anderson, F., Bauer, W. 98, *113*
Cobb, S., see Beall, G. *113*
Cobb, S., see Lincoln, T. A. 97, *114*
Cochran, H., Buck, N. [6], 182, *196*
Coffin, D. L., see Freemann, G. [22], 38, *48*
Cohen, A. S., see Sharp, J. T. *115*
Cohen, S., Harris [15], 170, *177*
Cole, P. V., see Russel, M. A. 40, *49*, [59]
Comroe, J. H., see Nadel, J. A. 40, *49*, [54]
Contreras, C. J., see Madrid, S. G. [12], 145, *150*
Coombs, R. A., see Gell, P. G. [24], 40, *48*
Cork *65*
Cortés, L. L. 145
Cortés, L. L., see Fernández, L. D. [4], 145, *150*
Cosh 117, 121
Cosh, J. A., see Jacoby, R. K. 106, *114*
Costilla, S. A., see Fernández, L. D. [4], 145, *150*
Cotta, H., Schulitz, K. P., Städler, J. *113*
Crane, S. C., see Freemann, G. [17, 19, 20, 21], 37, *48*
Cremerius 108
Curwen, M., see Bywaters, E. G. L. *113*
Cutler, S. J., see Griswold, M. H. [7], 159, *163*
Cuylerhammond, E., see Auerbach, O. [3], 40, *47*

Deane, M., see Ipsen, J. 35, [38, 39], 42, *49*
Deburge, A., see Pouget, G. 109, *114*
Decroix, G., Feldmann, A. 39, *51*, [89]
Denoux *65*
Depierre, A., see Bignon, J. 39, *51*, [85]
Desplaces, A., Charreire, J., Izard, C. [12], 40, *48*
Devulder, B., see Tacquet, A. 39, 42, *50*, [72]
Diamond, H., see Sztejnbok, K. 112, *115*
Diaz Barroso, G., see Landa, L. [6], 143, *144*
Diberardinis, L., see Speizer, F. E. 43, *50*, [64]
Dickson, E. C., Gifford, M. A. [2], 146, *150*
Dilley, R. B., Nadel, J. A. [13], 39, *48*
Dixon, A. St. J., see Bywaters, E. G. L. *113*
Dodd, H. C., see Stewart, R. D. 37, *50*, [65]
Dohan 42
Domm, B. M., see Vassalo, C. *50*, [74]
Donadio, J. V., Holley, K. E., Wagoner, R. D., Ferguson, R. H., McDuffie, F. C. 112, *113*
Dresner, E., see Bywaters, E. G. L. *113*
Drivsholm, A. 124

Dubinska, A., see Jakubowski, S. 109, *114*
Dubois de Montrenaud, J. M., see Kochmann, S. 39, 40, [40], *49*
Dufour, G., see Bignon, J. 39, *51*, [86]
Duncombe, M., see Vassalo, C. *50*, [74]
Duthie, J. J. R. 120
Duthie, J. J. R., Brown, P. E., Truelove, C. H., Baragar, F. D., Lawrin, A. J. 98, 99, 104, 105, 106, *113*

Eagle, M. C., see Golstein, E. [28], *48*
Easton, R. E., Murphey, S. D. [14], 40, *48*
Edwards, P. Q., Palmer, C. E. [3], 145, *150*
Ehrich 133
Elizari, M. V., see Rosenbaum, M. B. [2], 77, *85*
Ellenberg, M., Rifkin, H. [3], 180, *196*
Elsdon-Dew, R. [1], 139, *144*
Epstein, W. V., Tan, M. 111, *113*
Ernstene, A. C., see Rourke, M. D. *115*

Fajans 179
Farrington, E., see Ragan, C. *114*
Fauvreau, see Laurin 101
Feldmann, A., see Decroix, G. 39, *51*, [89]
Ferguson, R. H., see Donadio, J. V. 112, *113*
Fernández, L. D., Cortés, L. L., Guadalajara, M. J., Costilla, S. A., Chapa, G. R., Salinas, V. R., Pacheco, P. L., Cantú, G. R., Iglesias, O. T., Posadas, M. R. [4], 145, *150*
Ferrand, F., see Hart, F. C. [33, 34], 42, *48*, *49*
Ferris, B. G., Jr., Anderson, D. O. [15, 16], 42, *48*
Ferris, B. G., Jr., see Speizer, F. E. 43, *50*, [64]
Fiese, M. J. [5], 149, *150*
Fischer 136
Fisher, T. N., see Stewart, R. D. 37, *50*, [65]
Flament, R., see Lasserre, O. 42, [44], *49*
De Forest, G. K., Mucei, M. B., Boisvert, P. L. *113*
Foster, J. J., Knutson, D. L. [3], 164, *176*
Freeman, G., Crane, S. C., Furiosi, N. J. [17], 37, *48*
Freeman, G., Crane, S. C., Stephens, R. J., Furiosi, N. J. [19, 20], 37, *48*
Freeman, G., Furiosi, N. J., Haydon, G. B. [18], 37, *48*
Freeman, G., Stephens, R. J., Coffin, D. L., Stara, J. P., [22], 38, 40, *48*
Freeman, G., Stephens, R. J., Crane, S. C., Furiosi, N. J. [21], 37, *48*
Freyberg, R. H. 107, *113*
Furiosi, N. J., see Freeman, G. [17, 18, 19, 20, 21], 37, *48*

Garbe, E., Brunet, M. [23], 42, *48*
Garbe, E., see Lasserre, O. 42, [44], *49*
Garcia, F., see González-Ochoa, A. [6], 145, *150*
Garcia, S. R., see Verduzco, E. [13], 145, *150*
Garfinkel, H., see Auerbach, O. [3], 40, *47*
De la Garza, S. 145
Gee, J., see Vassalo, C. *50*, [74]
Gell, P. G., Goombs, R. A. [24], 40, *48*
Gernez-Rieux, C., Voisin, C., Wallarert, C., Roussel, P. A. [25], 39, *48*
Gilson, J. C. [26], 39, *48*
Godin, G., Wright, G., Shepard, R. [27], 37, *48*
Goel, K. M., Shanks, R. A. *114*
Goetz, E. J., see Steinberg, A. D. 112, *115*
Golstein, E., Eagle, M. C., Hoeprich [28], *48*
Goni, J., Remond, G., Jaurand, M. C., Bignon, J., Bonnaud, G., Brouet, G. 39, *51*, [88]
Goni, J., see Bignon, J. 39, *51*, [85]
Goni, J., see Bignon, J. 39, *51*, [86]
Goni, J., see Brouet, G. 39, *51*, [87]
González, J. E. 146
González Montesinos, F. [5], 141, *144*
González Montesinos, F., Lee Ramos, F., Aguirre Garcia, J. [5], 141, *144*
González-Ochoa, A. [7, 8], 146, *150*
González-Ochoa, A., Garcia, F. [6], 145, *150*
Goodkin, G. 178
Goodkin, G., Wolloch, L. B. [8], 183, *196*
Gordon, T., see Kannel, W. B. [6], 158, *163*
Greenbury, C. C., see Hill, A. *114*
Griswold, M. H., Wilder, C. S., Cutler, S. J., Pollack, E. S. [7], 159, *163*
Gross, P., Harvey, R. A., Treville, R. T. P., de [29], *48*
Guadalajara, M. J., Fernández, L. D., Costilla, S. A., Chapa, G. R., Villarreal, R., Chávez, S. A. [9], 150, [150]
Guadalajara, M. J., see Fernández, L. D. [4], 145, *150*
Gütgemann, A. et al. [25], 174, *177*
Gwon, N., see Siegel, M. 111, *115*

Hagedorn, H. C. 181
Hagstrom, R. M., see Zeidberg, L. D. 42, *50*, [78]
Halit, T., see Holland, W. W. [35], 43, *49*
Halliday, J. L. 109, *114*
Hammond, E. C. [30], 35, *48*
Hammond, E. C., Selikoff, I. J. [31, 32], 35, 39, 42, *48*
Harnes, J. R., see Bolt, W. R. [4], 158, *163*
Harris 116
Harris, see Cohen, S. [15], 170, *177*
Hart, F. C., Ferrand, F., Blade, E. [33, 34], 42, *48*, *49*
Hartmann, F. 93

Harvey, R. A., see Gross, P. [29], *48*
Hatte, J., see Kourilsky, R. [41], 42, 43, *49*
Haydorn, G. B., see Freeman, G. [18], 37, *48*
Hefti, M. L. 164
Helstrom, P. A., see Camner, P. [9], 40, *48*
Hench, P., see Rosenberg, E. F. *115*
Hench, P. S., Kendall, E. C., Uloocumb, C. H., Polley, H. F. [1], 124, *128*
Hendry 39
Herrmann, A. A., see Stewart, R. D. 37, *50*, [65]
Hill, A., Greenbury, C. C. *114*
Hill, A. G. S. 101, 102, *114*
Hinglais, J. C., see Kourilsky, R. [41], 42, 43, *49*
Hipp, H. R., see Beard, O. W. [5], 158, *163*
Hoeprich [28], *48*
Hofmann, A. F., see Thistle, J. L. [10], 165, *177*
Holland, W. W., Halit, T., Bennett, A. E. [35], 43, *49*
Holley, K. E., see Donadio, J. V. 112, *113*
Holt, P. J. L., see Nicolle, F. W. 109, *114*
Holtz, G., see Schubert, J. C. F. *115*
Horner, J. L. [26], 172, 173, *177*
Horton, R. J. M., see Zeidberg, L. D. 42, *50*, [78]
Hosko, M. J., see Stewart, R. D. 37, *50*, [65]

Iglesias, O. T., see Fernández, L. D. [4], 145, *150*
Imbus, H. R., Sum, M. W. [36], 39, *49*
Ingenito, F. E., see Ipsen, J. 35, [38, 39], 42, *49*
Inoh, T., Aviado, D. M. [37], *49*
Ipsen, J., Deane, M., Ingenito, F. E. 35, [39], 42, *49*
Ipsen, J., Ingenito, F. E., Deane, M. 35, [38], 42, *49*
Ishizaki, A. 22, 23
Izard, C., see Desplaces, A. [12], 40, *48*

Jackson, W. P., Vink, A. I. [5], 180, *196*
Jacoby, R. K., Cosh, J. A., Jayson, M. J. V. 106, *114*
Jakubowski, S., Ruszczynska, J., Dubinska, A. 109, *114*
Jammet, R. *65*
Janssen, G., see Schreiber, A. *115*
Jasso, J. *77*
Jaurand, M. C., see Bignon, J. 39, *51*, [85, 86]
Jaurand, M. C., see Goni, J. 39, *51*, [88]
Jayson, M. J. V., see Jacoby, R. K. 106, *114*
Jenner *27*
Jesty, B. 27
Jinich, H., Schmaas, F. [7], 143, *144*
Jonsson, E. *114*
Jordan, J. M., see Boles, J. [23], 174, 175, *177*
Josenhans, G. 107, *114*
Josenhans, G., Binzus, G. *114*

Kaltreider, H. B., see Steinberg, A. D. 112, *115*
Kannel, W. B., Gordon, T., Offutt, D. [6], 158, *163*
Kaplan, D., see Sztejnbok, K. 112, *115*
Kark, R. M., see Muehrke, R. C. 111, *114*
Kay, A. 120
Kellgren, J. H. 118
Kellgren, J. H., O'Brien, W. M. *114*
Kendall, E. C., see Hench, P. S. [1], 124, *128*
Killech 43
Kitamura, S. 17
Kjevekjarto, M. v. *114*
Klemperer, P., see Baehr, G. *113*
Knutson, D. L., see Foster, J. J. [3], 164, 165, *176*
Knutson, D. L., see Según Foster, J. J. 164
Koch, R., see Behrend, T. *113*
Kochmann, S., Martin, J. C., Bureau, G., Dubois de Montrenaud, J. M. 39, 40, [40], *49*
Kourilsky, R., Brille, D., Hatte, J., Carton, J., Hinglais, J. C. [41], 42, 43, *49*

Kozoll, D. D. et al. [4], 165, 166, 168, *176*
Krall, L. P., see Wilkerson, H. L. [1], 178, 182, *196*

Laaksonen, A. L. 101, *114*
Landa, L., Segovia, E., Diaz Barroso, G., Aubanel, M., Sepúlveda [6], 143, *144*
Landau, E., see Zeidberg, L. D. 42, *50*, [76, 77, 78]
Langer, A. M., Rubin, I. B., Selikoff, I. J. 39, [42], *49*
Langer, A. M., Rubin, I. B., Selikoff, I. J., Pooley, F. D. 39, [43], *49*
Langer, A. M., see Selikoff, I. J. 39, *50*, [61]
Lasserre, O., Garbe, E., Flament, R. 42, [44], *49*
Laurin, Fauvreau 101
Lawrence, I. S. 99, *114*
Lawrence, J. S., Bennet, P. H. *114*
Lawrence, I. S., see Behrend, T. *113*
Lawrin, A. J., see Duthie, J. J. R. 99, *113*
Lawther 42
Lazzari, I., see Rosenbaum, M. B. [2], *77*, *85*
Lebouffan, L., see Tacquet, A. 39, 42, *50*, [72]
Lee, S. L., see Siegel, M. 111, *115*
Lee Ramos, F., see González Montesinos, F. [5], 141, *144*
Lepeschkin, E., see Rosenbaum, M. B. [3], *77*, *85*
Leturcq, E., see Bignon, J. 39, *51*, [85]
Levin, D. L., see Schenidermann, M. A. 41, *50*, [60]
Lewis, T. R., Moormann, W. J., Ludmann, M. F., Campbell, K. J. 37, [45], *49*
Li, C. C. [46], *49*
Lilienthal 43
Lincoln, T. A., Cobb, S. 97, *114*
Lindbjerg 101
Lindenberg 43
Lira, D. F. 145
Localio, S. A., Stahl, W. M. [27], 175, *177*
Lockie, see Norcross 101

Lorenzo, J. A. 86
De la Loza Saldivar, A., see Alvarez Alva, R. [2], 140, 143, *144*
Ludmann, M. F., see Lewis, T. R. 37, [45], *49*

Mackler, A. D., Nicholson, W. J., Rohl, A. N., Selikoff, I. J. 39, [49], *49*
MacLeod, see Norcross 101
Macquet, V., see Voisin, C. 39, 42, *50*, [75]
Maddy, K. T. [10], 146, *150*
Maddy, K. T., Coccozza, J. [11], *150*
Madrid, S. G., Contreras, C. J. [12], 145, *150*
Maegraith 137
Magnier, M., see Stupfel, M. 43, *50*, [69]
Mahonny 42
Malo Camacho, R. 71, 75
Malorny 43
Manousos, O. N. et al. [28], 170, 173, *177*
Margolick, J. B., see Sherwin, R. P. 40, *50*, [62]
Marín, R. 3
Marique, J.-V. 52, *65*
Markowitz, A. M., see Asch, M. J. [22], 173, *177*
Martin, H., see Schubert, J. C. F. 112, *115*
Martin, J. C., see Kochmann, S. 39, 40, [40], *49*
Martin, J. C., see Tacquet, A. 39, 42, *50*, [72]
McCaroll, J. 42, [48], *49*
McCaroll, J. R., Bradley, H. W. 42, [47], *49*
McDuffie, F. C., see Donadio, J. V. 112, *113*
McLeod 101
Medina Mora, O. 69, 86
Medrano, G. A., Brenes, P. C., De Michelli, A., Sodi Pallares, D. [4], *85*
Medrano, G. A. et al. [5], 78, 79, *85*
Meeus-Bith, L. 35
Méndez, A. *77*
Merrel, M., Schulmann, L. E. *114*
Metz, G., see Röckl, H. 111, *115*
De Meyer, M. J. V. *65*
De Michelli, A., see Medrano, G. A. [4], *85*
Miescher, P. *114*
Mobley, J. E. et al. [16], 170, *177*
Mohanny 42
Mohing, W. *114*
Mohr, W. 131, 137
Molina, C. 39, *49*, [50]
Monchaux, G., see Bignon, J. 39, *51*, [85]
Monjardin, S., see Verduzco, E. [13], 145, *150*
Mooney, T. F., Jr., see Roy-Chondhury, A. K. 39, *49*, [58]
Moormann, W. J., see Lewis, T. R. 37, [45], *49*
Morson, B. C. [29], 172, *177*
Mucci, M. B., see De Forest, G. K. *113*
Muehrke, R. C., Kark, R. M., Pirani, C. L., Pollak, V. E. 111, *114*
Müller, C. J. B. [6], 164, *176*
M̃unguia, C. 86
Murphy, S. D. *49*, [51]
Murphy, S. D., Ulrich, C. E. *49*, [52]
Murphy, S. D., see Easton, R. E. [14], 40, *48*
Musselmann 43

Nadel, J. A., Cabezas, G. A., Austin, J. H. M. 40, *49*, [53]
Nadel, J. A., Comroe, J. H. 40, *49*, [54]
Nadel, J. A., Salem, H., Tamplin, B., Tokiwe, Y. *49*, [55]
Nicholson, W. J., see Mackler, A. D. 39, [49], *49*
Nicholson, W. J., see Selikoff, I. J. 39, *50*, [61]
Nicolle, F. W., Holt, P. J. L., Calnau, J. S. 109, *114*
Norcross, Lockie, MacLeod 101

O'Brien, W. M., see Kellgren, J. H. *114*
Offutt, D., see Kannel, W. B. [6], 158, *163*
Olascoaga, A. 164
Otten, H. A., Boerma, F. W. *114*
Den Oudsten, S. A., Planten, O., Posthuma, E. P. S. 102, *113*
Pacheco, P. L., see Fernández, L. D. [4], 145, *150*
Palmer, E. D. [17], 170, *177*
De Pascuale, N. P., Bruno, M. S. [6], 83, *85*
Pavia, D., see Thomson, M. L. 40, *50*, [73]
Peña, J. *77*
Pepys, J. 39, 40, *49*, [56]
Pérez Tamayo, R., see Brandt, H. [4], 140, *144*
Peters, J. M., see Bouhuys, A. [7], *47*
Peterson, J. E., see Stewart, R. D. 37, *50*, [65]
Philipson, K., see Camner, P. [9], 40, *48*
Pickard 101
Pirani, C. L., see Muehrke, R. C. 111, *114*
Planten, O., see Den Oudsten, S. A. 102, *113*
Plügge, H. *114*
Poe, R., see Vassalo, C. *50*, [74]
Polianski, J., see Stupfel, M. 43, *50*, [69]
Pollack, E. S., see Griswold, M. H. [7], 159, *163*
Pollak, V. E., Priani, C. L., Schwartz, F. D. 111, *114*
Pollak, V. E., see Muehrke, R. C. 111, *114*
Polley, H. F., see Hench, P. S. [1], 124, *128*
Pooley, F. D., see Langer, A. M. 39, [43], *49*
Portales, A., see Verduzco, E. [13], 145, *150*
Posadas, M. R., see Fernández, L. D. [4], 145, *150*
Posthuma, E. P. S., see Den Oudsten, S. A. 102, *113*
Pouget, G., Benoist, M., Deburge, A., Cauchoi, C. J. 109, *114*
Priani, C. L., see Pollak, V. E. 111, *114*
Pridie, R. B. [18], 170, *177*
Prindle, R. A., see Zeidberg, L. D. 42, *50*, [76, 77]

Quinn, W. C. [30], *177*

Ragan, C. 105, *114*
Ragan, C., Farrington, E. *114*
Reah, T. G. 99, *114*

Reeves, A. L., see Roy-Chondhury, A. 39, *49*, [58]
Remond, G., see Goni, J. 39, *51*, [88]
Rendón, J. 1
Reynolds, W. E., see Short, C. L. 104, 106, *115*
Rhoades, R. A., see Arner, E. C. [2], 37, *47*
Rifkin, H., see Ellenberg, M. [3], 180, *196*
Rimon, R. 109, *115*
Rivero, J., see Siegel, M. 111, *115*
Rivolier, J., Rivolier, C. 39, *49*, [57]
Robins, M., see Beard, O. W. [5], 158, *163*
Rodier 65
Röckl, H., Metz, G. 111, *115*
Rösch, J. et al. [31], *177*
Rohl, A. N., see Mackler, A. D. 39, [49], *49*
Romary, F., see Stupfel, M. 43, *50*, [69]
Romero Reverón, G. *77*
Rosenbaum, M. B. [1], *77*, *85*
Rosenbaum, M. B., Elizari, M. V., Lazzari, I. [2], 77, *85*
Rosenbaum, M. B., Lepeschkin, E. [3], 77, 79, *85*
Rosenbaum, M. B., Medrano, G. A. 78, 79
Rosenberg, E. F., Baggenstoss, A. H., Hench, P. 98, *115*
Rosenberg, I. K., Rosenberg, B. F. [32], 173, *177*
Rourke, M. D., Ernstene, A. C. *115*
Roussel, A., see Stupfel, M. 43, *50*, [71]
Roussel, P. A., see Gernez-Rieux, C. [25], 39, *48*
Roy-Chondhury, A. K., Mooney, T. F., Jr., Reeves, A. L. 39, *49*, [58]
Rubin, I. B., see Langer, A. M. 39, [42, 43], *49*
Russel, M. A., Cole, P. V., Brown, E. 40, *49*, [59]
Ruszczynska, J., see Jakubowski, S. 109, *114*
Rutstein, D. D. [2], 25, 34, *34*
Sadavongvivad, C., see Aviado, D. M. [4], 40, *47*
Sadoul 42, 43
Saint-Etienne, L., see Bignon, J. 39, *51*, [85]
Saito, T., see Berson, S. A. [5], *47*
De la Loza Saldivar, A., see Alvarez Alva, R. [2], 140, 143, *144*
Salem, H., see Nadel, J. A. *49*, [55]
Salinas, V. R., see Fernández, L. D. [4], 145, *150*
Schenidermann, M. A., Levin, D. L. 41, *50*, [60]
Schmidt, H. W. [19], 171, *177*
Schnaas, F., see Jinich, H. [7], 143, *144*
Schreiber, A., Janssen, G. *115*
Schubert, H., see Schubert, J. C. F. 112, *115*
Schubert, J. C. F., Schubert, H., Holtz, G., Martin, H. 112, *115*
Schulhof, O. *115*
Schulitz, K. P., see Cotta, H. *113*
Schulmann, L. E., see Merrel, M. *114*
Schwartz, F. D., see Pollak, V. E. 111, *114*
Segovia, E., see Landa, L. [6], 143, *144*
Segun Foster, J. J. 164
Selikoff, I. J., see Berson, S. A. [5], *47*
Selikoff, I. J., see Hammond, E. C. [31, 32], 35, 39, *48*
Selikoff, I. J., see Langer, A. M. 39, [42, 43], *49*
Selikoff, I. J., see Mackler, A. D. 39, [49], *49*
Selikoff, I. J., Nicholson, W. J., Langer, A. M. 39, *50*, [61]
Sepulveda, B. 139
Sepulveda, B., see Landa, L. [6], 143, *144*
Shanks, R. A., see Goel, K. M. *114*
Sharp, J. T., Calkins, E., Cohen, A. S. et al. *115*
Shepard, R., see Godin, G. [27], 37, *48*
Sherwin, R. P., Margolik, J. B., Azen, S. P. 40, *50*, [62]
Shigematsu, J. 9, 21
Shimizu 11
Shinya, see Wolff, W. J. [34], 175, *177*
Short, C. L. 99, 105, *115*
Short, C. L., Bauer, W., Reynolds, W. E. 104, 106, *115*
Shubik, Ph. 41, *50*, [63]
Shurtleff, D. [3], 158, *163*
Siedenberg, S., see Bove, J. L. [8], 37, 39, *47*
Siegel, M., Gwon, N., Lee, S. L., Rivero, I., Wong, W. 111, *115*
Sievers, K. *115*
Sim, G. P. G. [20], 169, *177*
Simon, S. *65*
Singer, R. B. 155
Small, D. M. [7], 165, *176*
Sodi Pallares, D., see Medrano, G. A. [4], *85*
Speizer, F. E., Ferris, B. G., Jr., Burgess, W., Diberardinis, L. 43, *50*, [64]
Sprague, H. A., see Zeidberg, L. D. 42, *50*, [78]
Spratka, J. L. et al. [21], *177*
Städler, J., see Cotta, H. *113*
Stahl, W. M., see Localio, S. A. [27], 175, *177*
Staples, P. J., see Steinberg, A. D. 112, *115*
Stara, J. F., see Freeman, G. [22], 38, *48*
Steinberg, A. D., Kaltreider, H. B., Staples, P. J., Goetz, E. J., Talal, N. 112, *115*
Steinbrocker, O. 107
Steinbrocker, O., Traeger, C. H., Battermann, R. C. [2], 124, *128*
Stephens, R. J., see Freeman, G. [19, 20, 21, 22], 37, 38, *48*
Steward, A., see Sztejnbok, K. 112, *115*
Stewart, R. D., Peterson, J. E., Fisher, T. N., Hosko, M. J., Baretta, E. D., Dodd, H. C., Herrmann, A. A. 37, *50*, [65]
Stupfel, M. 35, 43, *50*, [68, 70]
Stupfel, M., Bouley, G. 43, *50*, [66]
Stupfel, M., Magnier, M., Romary, F., Tran, M. H., Moutet, J. P. 43, *50*, [67]
Stupfel, M., Romary, F.,

Magnier, M., Polianski, J. 43, *50*, [69]
Stupfel, M., Roussel, A. 43, *50*, [71]
Sturdevant, R. A. L. et al. [8], 165, *176*
Sum, M. W., see Imbus, H. R. [36], 39, *49*
Sury 101
Sutor, D. J. et al. [9], 165, *176*
Sze, T. S. *115*
Sztejnbok, K., Steward, A., Diamond, H., Kaplan, D. 112, *115*

Tacquet, A. 43
Tacquet, A., Devulder, B., Martin, J. C., Lebouffan, L. 39, 42, *50*, [72]
Takizawa, Y. 19
Talal, N., see Steinberg, A. D. 112, *115*
Tamplin, B., see Nadel, J. A. *49*, [55]
Tan, M., see Epstein, W. V. 111, *113*
Taylor, D. 116
Thistle, J. L., Hofmann, A. F. [10], 165, *177*
Thomson, M. L., Pavia, D. 40, *50*, [73]
Tokiwe, Y., see Nadel, J. A. *49*, [55]
Torvik, A. et al. [11], 165, 166, 168, *177*
Traeger, C. H., see Steinbrocker, O. [2], 124, *128*
Treville, R. T. P., de, see Gross, P. [29], *48*
Truelove, C. H., see Duthie, J. J. R. 99, *113*
Truesdell, E. D. [12], 167, *177*
Turcolle, M. [33], *177*

Ulocumb, C. H., see Hench, P. S. [1], 124, *128*
Ulrich, C. E., see Murphy, S. D. *49*, [52]

Valkenburg, H. A. 97, *115*
Vassalo, C., Domm, B. M., Poe, R., Duncombe, M., Gee, J. *50*, [74]
Verduzco, E., Portales, A., Monjardin, S., Garcia, S. R. [13], 145, *150*
Verzolini, V. R., see Beard, O. W. [5], 158, *163*
Vider, P. V. 11
Vinik, A. I., see Jackson, W. P. [5], 180, *196*
Voisin, C., Macquet, V. 39, 42, *50*, [75]
Voisin, C., see Gernez-Rieux, C. [25], 39, *48*
Volkmer 134
Voller 133

Wagoner, R. D., see Donadio, J. V. 112, *113*
Waich T, S. *77*
Wallarert, C., see Gernez-Rieux, C. [25], 39, *48*
Wilder, C. S., see Griswold, M. H. [7], 159, *163*
Wilkerson, H. L., Krall, L. P. [1], 178, 182, *196*
Winn, W. A. [14], 147, *150*
Wolff, W. J., Shinya [34], 175, *177*
Wolloch, L. B., see Goodkin, G. [8], 183, *196*
Wong, W., see Siegel, M. 111, *115*
Woodruff 137
Wright, G., see Godin, G. [27], 37, *48*

Yalow, R. S., see Berson, S. A. [5], *47*

Zeidberg, L. D., Horton, R. J. M., Landau, E., Hagstrom, R. M., Sprague, H. A. 42, *50*, [78]
Zeidberg, L. D., Prindle, R. A., Landau, E. 42, *50*, [76, 77]

MIX
Papier aus verantwortungsvollen Quellen
Paper from responsible sources
FSC® C105338

If you have any concerns about our products,
you can contact us on
ProductSafety@springernature.com

In case Publisher is established outside the EU,
the EU authorized representative is:
Springer Nature Customer Service Center GmbH
Europaplatz 3, 69115 Heidelberg, Germany

Printed by Libri Plureos GmbH
in Hamburg, Germany